MW01155945

Italian and Italian American Studies

Stanislao G. Pugliese
Hofstra University
Series Editor

This publishing initiative seeks to bring the latest scholarship in Italian and Italian American history, literature, cinema, and cultural studies to a large audience of specialists, general readers, and students. I&IAS will feature works on modern Italy (Renaissance to the present) and Italian American culture and society by established scholars as well as new voices in the academy. This endeavor will help to shape the evolving fields of Italian and Italian American Studies by re-emphasizing the connection between the two. The following editorial board consists of esteemed senior scholars who act as advisors to the series editor.

Queer Italia: Same-Sex Desire in Italian Literature and Film
edited by Gary P. Cestaro, July 2004
Frank Sinatra: History, Identity, and Italian American Culture
edited by Stanislao G. Pugliese, October 2004
The Legacy of Primo Levi
edited by Stanislao G. Pugliese, December 2004
Italian Colonialism
edited by Ruth Ben-Ghiat and Mia Fuller, July 2005
Mussolini's Rome: Rebuilding the Eternal City
Borden W. Painter Jr., July 2005
Representing Sacco and Vanzetti
edited by Jerome H. Delamater and Mary Anne Trasciatti, September 2005
Carlo Tresca: Portrait of a Rebel
Nunzio Pernicone, October 2005
Italy in the Age of Pinocchio: Children and Danger in the Liberal Era
Carl Ipsen, April 2006
The Empire of Stereotypes: Germaine de Staël and the Idea of Italy
Robert Casillo, May 2006
Race and the Nation in Liberal Italy, 1861–1911: Meridionalism, Empire, and Diaspora
Aliza S. Wong, October 2006
Women in Italy, 1945–1960: An Interdisciplinary Study
edited by Penelope Morris, October 2006
Debating Divorce in Italy: Marriage and the Making of Modern Italians, 1860–1974
Mark Seymour, December 2006
A New Guide to Italian Cinema
Carlo Celli and Marga Cottino-Jones, January 2007
Human Nature in Rural Tuscany: An Early Modern History
Gregory Hanlon, March 2007

The Missing Italian Nuremberg: Cultural Amnesia and Postwar Politics
    Michele Battini, September 2007
Assassinations and Murder in Modern Italy: Transformations in Society and Culture
    edited by Stephen Gundle and Lucia Rinaldi, October 2007
Piero Gobetti and the Politics of Liberal Revolution
    James Martin, December 2008
Primo Levi and Humanism after Auschwitz: Posthumanist Reflections
    Jonathan Druker, June 2009
Oral History, Oral Culture, and Italian Americans
    Edited by Luisa Del Giudice, November 2009
Italy's Divided Memory
    John Foot, January 2010
Women, Desire, and Power in Italian Cinema
    Marga Cottino-Jones, March 2010
The Failure of Italian Nationhood: The Geopolitics of a Troubled Identity
    Manlio Graziano, September 2010
Women and the Great War: Femininity under Fire in Italy
    Allison Scardino Belzer, October 2010
Italian Jews from Emancipation to the Racial Laws
    Cristina M. Bettin, November 2010
Murder and Media in the New Rome: The Fadda Affair
    Thomas Simpson, December 2010
Anti-Italianism: Essays on a Prejudice
    edited by William J. Connell and Fred Gardaphé, December 2010

Anti-Italianism

Essays on a Prejudice

Edited by William J. Connell and Fred Gardaphé

February 4, 2011

Dear Harold,

thank you for all you do to promote Italian americans and Italians in psychology.

Warmest respect.
Elizabeth

palgrave
macmillan

ALBERTO
Italian Studies Institute

Research supported by the Charles and Joan Alberto Italian Studies Institute, Seton Hall University.

First published in 2010 by PALGRAVE MACMILLAN® in the United States—a division of St. Martin's Press LLC, 175 Fifth Avenue, New York, NY 10010.

Where this book is distributed in the UK, Europe and the rest of the world, this is by Palgrave Macmillan, a division of Macmillan Publishers Limited, registered in England, company number 785998, of Houndmills, Basingstoke, Hampshire RG21 6XS.

Palgrave Macmillan is the global academic imprint of the above companies and has companies and representatives throughout the world.

Palgrave® and Macmillan® are registered trademarks in the United States, the United Kingdom, Europe and other countries.

ISBN (hardcover): 978–0–230–10829–5
ISBN (paperback): 978–0–230–10830–1

Library of Congress Cataloging-in-Publication Data

Anti-Italianism : essays on a prejudice / edited by William J. Connell, Fred Gardaphé.
   p. cm. — (Italian and Italian American studies)
   Includes bibliographical references.
   ISBN 978-0-230-10829-5 (hardback : alk. paper) — ISBN 978-0-230-10830-1 (pbk. : alk. paper)
   1. Italian Americans—Ethnic identity. 2. Italian Americans—Cultural assimilation. 3. Italian Americans—Social conditions. 4. Italian Americans—Public opinion. 5. Discrimination—United States—History. 6. Stereotypes (Social psychology)—United States—History. 7. Prejudices—United States—History. 8. United States—Ethnic relations. 9. Italian Americans in mass media—History. 10. Popular culture—United States—History. I. Connell, William J. II. Gardaphé, Fred L.

E184.I8A55 2010
973'.0451—dc22   2010022019

A catalogue record of the book is available from the British Library.

Design by Scribe Inc.

First edition: December 2010

10 9 8 7 6 5 4 3 2 1

Printed in the United States of America.

To the memory of Peter R. D'Agostino

Contents

Contributors   ix

Preface   xi
    William J. Connell

Introduction
    Invisible People: Shadows and Light in Italian American Writing   1
    Fred Gardaphé

1   Darker Aspects of Italian American Prehistory   11
    William J. Connell

2   "Between White Men and Negroes": The Perception of Southern
    Italian Immigrants Through the Lens of Italian Lynchings   23
    Peter Vellon

3   "Utterly Faithless Specimens":
    Italians in the Catholic Church in America   33
    Peter R. D'Agostino

4   Perversions of Knowledge: Confronting Racist
    Ideologies behind Intelligence Testing   41
    Elizabeth G. Messina

5   Frank Sinatra and Notions of Tolerance: *The House I Live In*   67
    Anthony Julian Tamburri

6   What Luigi Basco Taught America about Italian Americans   77
    Dominic L. Candeloro

7   Affirmative Action for Italian Americans:
    The City University of New York Story   87
    Joseph V. Scelsa

8   The Changing Roles of Italian American Women:
    Reality vs. Myth   95
    Susanna Tardi

9   Prejudice and Discrimination:
    The Italian American Experience Yesterday and Today   107
    Salvatore J. LaGumina

10   "Good Enough": An Italian American Memoir   117
    Joanne Detore-Nakamura

11   Stereotypes Sell, But We're Not for Sale   131
       Gina Valle

12   *Shark Tale*—*"Puzza da cap'"*: An Attempt at Ethnic Activism   137
       Jerome Krase

13   If Defamation Is Serious, Why Don't Italian American
       Organizations Take It Seriously?   151
       LindaAnn Loschiavo

14   Narrating Guido: Contested Meanings of an
       Italian American Youth Subculture   163
       Donald Tricarico

Index   201

Contributors

Dominic L. Candeloro is the former executive director of the American Italian Historical Association and the author of three books on Italians in Chicago. He serves as curator of the Casa Italia Library in the Chicago area. In 2005 he organized an exhibition on Italian American immigration at the Archivio Centrale dello Stato in Rome.

William J. Connell, professor of history, holds the Joseph M. and Geraldine C. La Motta Chair in Italian Studies and was founding director of the Charles and Joan Alberto Italian Studies Institute at Seton Hall University. His recent books include *Sacrilege and Redemption in Renaissance Florence*, 2nd rev. ed. (with G. Constable) and a new translation of Machiavelli's *Prince*.

Peter R. D'Agostino (†) was associate professor of history and Catholic Studies at the University of Illinois, Chicago. His book, *Rome in America: Transnational Catholic Ideology from the Risorgimento to Fascism*, won the Frank S. and Elizabeth D. Brewer Prize of the American Society of Church History.

Joanne Detore-Nakamura is associate professor of humanities and communication at Embry-Riddle Aeronautical University in Daytona Beach, Florida. Her creative and scholarly work has appeared in over 20 publications including *Italian Americana*. She has made over 40 scholarly presentations and has appeared on national television. She is finishing a collection of poetry and a scholarly study of women's friendship in literature, under contract with Mellen Press.

Fred Gardaphé is the City University of New York Distinguished Professor in Italian American Studies in Queens College, CUNY. He is the author of *From Wiseguys to Wise Men: The Gangster and Italian American Masculinities* and *Italian Signs, American Streets: The Evolution of Italian American Narrative*.

Jerome Krase is Murray Koppelman Professor emeritus at Brooklyn College, CUNY. His books include *The Review of Italian American Studies, Race and Ethnicity in New York City, Ethnic Landscapes in an Urban World, Italian Americans Before Mass Migration, The Staten Island Italian American Experience, Italian American Politics: Local, Global/Cultural, Personal* and *Italian Americans in a Multicultural Society*.

Salvatore J. LaGumina is professor emeritus and director of the Center for Italian American Studies at Nassau Community College. Editor of *The Italian American Experience: An Encyclopedia*, his many books include *Wop! A Documentary History of Anti-Italian Discrimination; The Humble and the Heroic: Wartime Italian Americans;* and

The Great Earthquake: America Comes to Messina's Rescue. He has served as national president of the American Italian Historical Association.

LindaAnn Loschiavo is a writer and dramatist whose latest play is *Courting Mae West: A Comedy About Sex, Censorship and Secrets.* She was a featured poet for *Italian Americana.* Her column on Italian culture and Italian American issues has been published in the magazine *L'IDEA* since 1995.

Elizabeth G. Messina is a psychologist in private practice in Manhattan, faculty member in the Department of Psychiatry at Lenox Hill Hospital and cofounder in 2005 of the Italian American Psychology Assembly. She is the author of numerous articles and chapters that focus on Italian American culture and behavior and the editor of the book *In Our Own Voices: Multidisciplinary Perspectives on Italian and Italian American Women.*

Joseph V. Scelsa was the first dean of the John D. Calandra Italian American Institute. He is professor emeritus at Queens College, CUNY and founder and president of the Italian American Museum in New York City. In 2000 he organized the exhibition *The Italians of New York: Five Centuries of Struggle and Achievement* at the New-York Historical Society.

Anthony Julian Tamburri is dean of the John D. Calandra Italian American Institute and professor of Italian and Italian American Studies at Queens College, CUNY. He was president of the American Association of Teachers of Italian. He is author or editor of more than one hundred books and articles on Italian and Italian American literature and culture.

Susanna Tardi is professor of sociology at William Paterson University of New Jersey. She is an international scholar whose publications include "The Traditional Italian American Family Is Alive and Well and Living in New Jersey" (*Italian American Review*). She received widespread media attention for her lecture "Desperately Seeking Real Italians: An Antidote to *The Sopranos.*"

Donald Tricarico is professor of sociology at Queensborough Community College, CUNY. He is author of *The Italians of Greenwich Village* and numerous publications in urban and ethnic sociology and on youth culture.

Gina Valle has a PhD in multicultural studies and teacher education. She is the author of *Our Grandmothers, Ourselves: Reflections of Canadian Women* and the director and producer of the documentary *The Last Rite.* She lives in Toronto.

Peter Vellon is assistant professor of history at Queens College, CUNY. His publications include "The Delta Italians" (*Journal of Southern History*) and "Immigrant Son: Mario Procaccino and the Rise of Conservative Politics" (*Italian American Review*).

Preface

William J. Connell

This volume attempts something new. Nowadays, discussions of prejudice involving Italian Americans take place mostly on television, and they are centered around the stereotyping found in portrayals of Italian Americans in contemporary films and television shows. As our news outlets have discovered, these discussions, which pit celebrity actors and directors against Italian American activists, have a certain entertainment value. In an irony all too typical of our media-driven age, the resultant publicity contributes both to the success of the movies and shows that are being denounced and to the furthering of the very stereotypes that were at issue.

Meanwhile, the long history of discrimination against ordinary Italian Americans, and the slights or slurs they still encounter occasionally today, remain largely ignored by the American public—apart from their consideration as the subject of humor. The phenomenon finds a mirror in the academic world, notwithstanding the impressive growth of programs in Italian and Italian American Studies at American colleges and universities. The only academic, book-length treatment of American anti-Italian prejudice, a documentary sampling of a century of newspaper and magazine articles showing instances of discrimination, was published in 1973.[1] A recent history of American lynching mentioned only one instance of the lynching of Italians, and in an aside, although Italians were a target of lynching in the American South.[2] There exist splendid studies of immigration from Italy, Hollywood representations of Italian Americans, Italian American novel-writing, Italian American religious practices, Italian American radicalism, Italian Americans in organized crime, the Italian American family, the speech and linguistic practices of Italian American immigrants, and of how Italians feel about their own ethnicity.[3] Yet the story of the largely hostile reception that Italian immigrants found upon arriving in the United States, and of the subsequent, nuanced evolution of the image of the Italian in American culture, awaits its historian.[4]

None of the contributors to this volume would consider discrimination against Italian Americans to be among the most pressing social issues of twenty-first century America, even though all believe strongly that Italian Americans have every right to be concerned to set the historical record straight and to combat misrepresentation and prejudice. As a problem, however, anti-Italianism is on the wane—so much so that one could call this a history of social progress. Indeed, some Italian Americans argue that to investigate a problem that has been resolved mostly to their satisfaction is only to stir up trouble. Complainers are penalized in traditional Italian society. Bringing up the topic, even in a historical context, induces feelings of unease.

There is, moreover, an air of embarrassment hovering about the issue of discrimination that most Italian Americans freely acknowledge. It has not helped that so many of the directors and stars of the movies and television shows that Italian American organizations have accused of stereotyping have been Italian American—and that they have often received honors and awards from those same organizations. Nor did it help that in the 1960s and early 1970s, when two national organizations (soon defunct) were established specifically to defend Italian Americans against discrimination, several of the founders were involved in organized crime. Joseph Colombo's leadership of the Italian-American Civil Rights League, which culminated in his being shot at a League rally in 1971, probably set back Italian American antidefamation efforts by at least two decades.[5]

Contrary to popular belief, Italian Americans have never had an organization dedicated to pursuing legal action on their behalf in discrimination cases in the manner of the Anti-Defamation League or the NAACP Legal Defense Fund. Outsiders often read current efforts by Italian American groups to protest instances of stereotyping as coming from what they mistakenly label an antidefamation "industry," but it is worth noting that none of the three organizations that represent Italian American interests on a national scale—the Order Sons of Italy in America (OSIA, founded in 1905), UNICO National (founded in 1922), and the National Italian American Foundation (NIAF, founded in 1975)—is particularly focused on antidiscrimination activity, which sometimes encounters resistance even among their members. These organizations, which are splendidly democratic, devote most of their time and energy to raising funds for educational and medical causes, which they consider their principal mission. In 1979 OSIA decided to delegate matters involving discrimination to a Commission for Social Justice, and the handling of the same issues was delegated by UNICO to an Anti-Bias Committee in the early 1980s. Although these subgroups project a more focused message, the funding they receive from their national organizations is remarkably small. To give one example, UNICO National's Anti-Bias Committee, which in 2009–2010 spearheaded protests against the MTV reality series *Jersey Shore*, operated with an annual budget of five thousand dollars.[6] An emphasis on stereotyping in the media, which dates back to a campaign of 1960 against fictional portrayals of gangsters as Italian Americans in ABC's series *The Untouchables*, is encouraged by the free publicity surrounding a new film or television series, which these organizations are able to leverage.[7] Whether this achieves the desired results is open to question, but it certainly does not cost very much.

When thinking about anti-Italian discrimination, many Italian Americans prefer a narrative according to which "everyone" (a somewhat elastic term) suffered when they first got to America. Then, so goes the preferred narrative, World War II offered an opportunity for Italians to enter the American mainstream, and this they did with remarkable success. The idea that American culture has had a specific image of Italians (as distinguished from other groups), that this specific image has had negative aspects (as well as positive ones), that it had historical roots, that it evolved over time even as Italians blended with American society, and that Italian Americans have been agents in shaping and manipulating their image, is a proposition that to many Italian Americans sounds faintly ominous. It challenges a belief in their basic *americanità* or *'mericanezza*—the "American-ness" with which they grew up, that they share with their neighbors.

Suggesting that Italian Americans have tried in various ways to manage their own image can be misconstrued as accusing them of self-dealing. As for the discrimination suffered by their ancestors, all that remains are those annoying stereotypes. Best to shrug one's shoulders and ignore them . . .

The essays in this volume were written instead with the idea of looking very hard at the experiences Italian Americans have had with issues of discrimination and stereotyping. The chapters are arranged more or less chronologically, beginning with an essay on American perceptions of Italy before the age of mass immigration and ending with a study of the interaction of "Guido" youth culture with mainstream American and Italian American culture. The goal is to offer the reader access to a set of authentic perspectives removed from media hype and grounded in historical understanding. This is a series of reflections: some are historical, some sociological, and some quite personal. Many of the authors disagree with one another, both on specific points and in their broader beliefs concerning Italian Americans and their relationship with American society. Most importantly, all of the voices are genuine, reflecting serious positions and professional and personal commitments.

Anti-Italianism: Essays on a Prejudice had its origins in a conference that was held by the Charles and Joan Alberto Italian Studies Institute at Seton Hall University in 2004, shortly after a campaign by a united front of Italian American organizations to condemn ethnic stereotyping in the cartoon characters of the animated film *Shark Tale*. The campaign was seen by some as successful, by others as a failure, but it had brought much publicity to the question of the stereotyping of Italian Americans in the media, while at the same time exposing numerous sore spots within the Italian American community. The Seton Hall conference brought together in an academic setting a group of scholars, politicians, actors, writers, community organizers, and Italian American activists and representatives of the Italian government for a serious, considered discussion of the history of anti-Italian discrimination. The proceedings were filmed and became the basis of a 30-minute documentary, *Anti-Italianism*, produced by Paul Budline, that has sold more than 3,000 copies on DVD and continues to be shown regularly in college classes in Italian American Studies.

The academic participants in the conference were asked to draft papers on problems associated with anti-Italian discrimination, and these, after reflection and revision, have become the essays published in the present volume. William Connell organized the conference and invited the contributions to the volume, while Fred Gardaphé assisted throughout and consented to the publication of his essay as the volume's Introduction. External support for the conference was provided by UNICO National, the National Italian American Foundation, the Columbus Citizens Foundation, the Commission for Social Justice of the Order Sons of Italy in America, the New Jersey Italian American Heritage Commission, and many individual donors. Connell's work at Seton Hall University is generously supported by the Joseph M. and Geraldine C. La Motta Chair in Italian Studies.

For help on a series of fronts the editors are especially grateful to Gabriella Romani (the current Director of the Alberto Italian Studies Institute), Barbara Ritchie, Manny Alfano, Dona De Sanctis, Manny Alfano, Daniel Leab, Tom DeGenaro, John Marino, Frank Cannata, Steve Aiello, Bill Dal Cerro, John Alati, Joe Piscopo, Tony Lo Bianco, the Hon. Bill Pascrell, Joseph and Elda Coccia, the late Martin Picillo, Paul DiGaetano, Nazario Paragano, Sr., Joseph Sciame, Salvatore Valente, Marlie Wasserman, the American Italian Historical Association, the Dante Alighieri Society of Massachusetts, the

Italic Institute, the Congrès National des Italo-Canadiens, the International Association for Media and History, Antonio Bandini (Italian Consul General in New York) and Paolo Toschi (Italian Vice-Consul in Newark). At Palgrave Macmillan we would like especially to thank our series editor, Stanislao Pugliese, along with Lee Norton and Brigitte Shull of the editorial staff, and the volume's anonymous readers. Roger Schillerstrom, who draws magnificent cartoons for *Fra Noi*, provided our cover illustration. Maria Mazziotti Gillan gave permission to quote from her poem, "Public School No. 18: Paterson, New Jersey."

This volume is dedicated to Peter D'Agostino, a fine historian and a good man who died tragically, shortly after writing the essay published here. He is missed.

Notes

1. Salvatore J. LaGumina, *Wop! A Documentary History of Anti-Italian Discrimination*, 2nd ed. (San Francisco: Straight Arrow Books, 1973; Toronto: Guernica, 1999).
2. Christopher Waldrep, ed., *Lynching in America: A History in Documents* (New York: New York University Press, 2006). Compare Clive Webb, "The Lynching of Sicilian Immigrants in the American South, 1886–1910," *American Nineteenth Century History* 3 (Spring 2002): 45–76.
3. Donna Gabaccia, *Italy's Many Diasporas* (London: Routledge, 2000); Peter Bondanella, *Hollywood Italians: Dagos, Palookas, Romeos, Wise Guys, and Sopranos* (New York: Continuum, 2004); Fred L. Gardaphé, *Italian Signs, American Streets: The Evolution of Italian American Narrative* (Durham, NC: Duke University Press, 1996); Robert Orsi, *The Madonna of 115th Street: Faith and Community in Italian Harlem*, 2nd ed. (1985; New Haven: Yale University Press, 2002); Philip V. Cannistraro and Gerald Meyer, eds., *The Lost World of Italian American Radicalism* (Westport, CT: Praeger, 2003); Gay Talese, *Honor Thy Father*, updated ed. (1971; New York: Harper, 2009); Virginia Yans-McLaughlin, *Family and Community: Italian Immigrants in Buffalo, 1880–1930* (Ithaca, NY: Cornell University Press, 1977); Nancy C. Carnevale, *A New Language, A New World: Italian Immigrants in the United States, 1890–1945* (Champaign: University of Illinois Press, 2009); Thomas J. Ferraro, *Feeling Italian: The Art of Ethnicity in America* (New York: New York University Press, 2005).
4. As a field, Italian American Studies has yet to produce a work to compare with Winthrop D. Jordan, *Black over White: American Attitudes toward the Negro, 1550–1812* (Chapel Hill: University of North Carolina Press, 1968); or George M. Fredrickson, *The Black Image in the White Mind: The Debate on Afro-American Character and Destiny, 1817–1914*, 2nd ed. (1971; Middletown, CT: Wesleyan University Press, 1987). John Higham's *Strangers in the Land: Patterns of American Nativism, 1860–1925*, 2nd ed. (1955; New Brunswick, NJ: Rutgers University Press, 2004) suggests the depth of the available material.
5. The American Italian Anti-Defamation League was founded by Judge Ross DiLorenzo in early 1966, and in 1967 Frank Sinatra became its national chairman. In 1968, it changed its name to Americans of Italian Descent (AID) and Sinatra stepped down as chairman, with the result that it rapidly lost credibility and membership. The Italian-American Civil Rights League was founded by Joseph Colombo, Sr., in 1970, and it fell apart after his shooting.
6. According to Manny Alfano, chairman of UNICO National's Anti-Bias Committee, the appropriation from the national organization for fiscal year 2009–2010 was $2,000. Annual donations from local chapters amount to about $3,000 annually. (Email message to author, April 20, 2010).
7. Laura Cook Kenna, "Exemplary Consumer-Citizens and Protective State-Stewards: How Reformers Shaped Censorship Outcomes Regarding *The Untouchables*," *The Velvet Light Trap* 63 (2009): 34–44, treats the 1960 *Untouchables* campaign as an instance in which citizen action succeeded in reforming mass media programming content.

Introduction

Invisible People

Shadows and Light in Italian American Culture

Fred Gardaphé

"I am invisible, understand, simply because people refuse to see me."

—Ralph Ellison, *Invisible Man*

Italian Americans are invisible people. Not because people refuse to see them, but because, for the most part, they refuse to be seen. Italian Americans became invisible the moment they could pass themselves off as being white. And since then they have gone to great extremes to avoid being identified as anything but white, they have even hidden the history of being people of color.

Whether they like it or not, Italian Americans cannot escape the fact that they weren't always white. They were lynched, burned out of homes, chased, captured and killed by vigilantes and the Ku Klux Klan. At the direction of politicians and businessmen, they were herded into ghettos and then redlined and relocated into acceptable neighborhoods. They were discriminated against by political, social, economic, and religious institutions. And in spite of sharing the experiences of other minorities, many of them have adopted the attitudes and stances of the dominant culture of racism, a culture that maintains control by dividing by difference and uniting by illusion of similarity. By becoming white, they have paid a price, and that price is the extinction of their culture. It is that near extinction of Italian American culture that has enabled them to remain invisible. However, in spite of the efforts of many, Italian Americans are not always invisible, nor can they always control when and how we are seen when they do become visible. What does appear in the mainstream media are stereotypical images that have been created by others and used to control the presentation of what is Italian in the United States.

Against these images are those created by Italian American writers and filmmakers that counter those stereotypes.

The 1989 murder of Yusef Hawkins in Bensonhurst, New York, is a perfect example of what it takes to make Italian Americans visible. As long as African Americans stayed out of Bensonhurst, Bensonhurst remained invisible, a small, provincial island of Italian American culture. When Yusef Hawkins walked into Bensonhurst, he unfortunately was not invisible; when a dead Yusef Hawkins was carried out of Bensonhurst, the neighborhood became a visible representation of the worst of Italian America.

In *Do the Right Thing* (1989), a film by Spike Lee, African American culture is pitted against racist American culture represented by an Italian American pizzeria owner and his sons. There are many statements made in this film, but the most powerful is that racism is as American as pizza. To become white is to buy into a racist insurance fraud. The message is "Become like us, and then you too can be better than those others who cannot become like us. We'll stop racism against your people, if you help us keep it alive against others."

Now, of all the ethnic groups in America, why did Spike Lee choose Italians to represent American racism? That is a question that only Lee can answer for certain. Yet I would like to suggest several reasons. That he chose Italian Americans because he knew them as whites from his experience growing up in Brooklyn seems clear. But because he knew them, he also knew they would not gather in numbers to protest the portrayal. But finally, and most importantly, Lee chose Italian Americans because they represented the absurdity of divisions among minority groups. Initial responses by Italian Americans to both the Bensonhurst murder and the Spike Lee film were primarily defensive and reactionary. Why portray us like that? Why use Italian Americans to demonstrate America's racist philosophy? It's a short ride from here to the latest distorted representation of Italian American Guido culture on MTV's *Jersey Shore*.

Is it right? Is it fair? Is it true? These, I feel are the wrong questions to be asking. Like it or not there are Italian Americans who are racist, who in buying into the American dream also swallowed the American illusion that white America is better than colored America. The right questions to ask are "How can the very victims of racism adopt racist ideas?" and "Why don't Italian Americans present alternative views of relationships between Italian and African Americans?"

A little reading of Italian American history and literature by Italian Americans will demonstrate that in spite of the shades of difference in skin color, Italian Americans share much in common with other minority cultures; those commonalities have been hidden from consciousness by selective portrayals of American history. This ignorance of alternative histories is responsible for the Italian American lawyers who work to destroy labor unions for which their grandparents fought and died to create and preserve. Ignorance of Italian American history invites us to regenerate a racist mentality that insures that white will dominate.

We Weren't Always White

"No one was white before he/she came to America."

—James Baldwin, "On Being 'White' . . . and Other Lies"

I'm tired of being overlooked and then
categorized as colorless,
as though I've never had
a good spaghetti fight in my life.
I'm tired of being told to
shut up and assimilate.

—Rose Romano, "Vendetta"

After the Yusef Hawkins murder, a number of Italian American intellectuals, including Robert Viscusi, Jerome Krase and Marianna DeMarco Torgovnick, wrote essays and editorials that attempted to demonstrate that not all Italian Americans were racists. These essays, accompanied by the actions of New York radical activists like the Italian Americans for a Multicultural United States (IAMUS), marked the beginning of a culturally critical interaction that led to the creation of larger public forums such as the 1997 American Italian Historical Association's national conference "Shades of Black and White: Conflict and Collaboration between Two Communities." In a contribution to the volume, *Are Italians White?*, Joseph Sciorra's essay, "Italians against Racism" (which won an award from the Italian American Writers Association), presents one of the strongest autobiographical accounts of the experience of taking part in a march protesting racism in Bensonhurst.[1] You could not appreciate these shining moments of clarity in Italian American consciousness unless you were aware of some of the shadows cast upon Italian America by racist acts.

References to blacks in Mario Puzo's *The Godfather*, as "the dark people" and "animals" who "have no respect for their wives or their families or themselves,"[2] are uncomfortably close to the gist of Richard Gambino's attempts to explain the differences between Italian and African Americans in his 1973 *Blood of My Blood: The Dilemma of the Italian-Americans*. Gambino, one of the first to make observations of the interaction of the two communities, sees them as having "diametrically opposed value systems." "It is difficult to think of two groups of Americans," he writes, "whose ways of life differ more. The two cultures are at odds with each other in superficial styles and in critical values. The groups clash more and more as ghetto blacks confront lower-middle-class whites in inner cities over efforts to integrate schools and housing and in competition for jobs and political power."[3] Confrontation is inevitable, he suggests, because the two groups often inhabit adjacent urban spaces. As evidence, Gambino presents examples of how music, body language, and notions of family differ between blacks and Italians.

A more hopeful possibility was advanced by Patrick Gallo in his 1974 study, *Ethnic Alienation: The Italian-Americans*. Gallo saw enough similarities between Italian and African Americans to suggest the creation of an alliance of, in his words, "whites and Blacks, white-collar and blue-collar workers, based on mutual need and interdependence . . . Italian-Americans may prove to be a vital ingredient in not only forging that alliance but in serving as the cement that will hold urban centers together."[4]

That Gambino's contrasting approach has gone unchallenged, and Gallo's suggested bridge building has been mostly ignored until only recently, is the result of the very slow development of an Italian American intelligentsia, one that the reader will find has matured through the essays in this volume. This intelligentsia is also producing a great number of poems, stories, essays, and book-length studies that challenge Gambino's weak explanations and attempt to fulfill Gallo's prophecy. Thirteen years before either Gambino's or Gallo's analyses appeared, Daniela Gioseffi put her body and soul on the line in the early 1960s struggle for civil rights. She documented her experiences in a short story, "The Bleeding Mimosa," which recounts the terror of a night spent in a Selma, Alabama jail during which she was raped by a southern sheriff.[5] An essay by Frank Lentricchia in *Lingua Franca* reminds us that the cultural interactions between Italian and African Americans did not begin in response to Bensonhurst. In "Confessions of an Ex-Literary Critic," Lentricchia points to Willard Motley's *Knock on Any Door* as a signal text in his early development as a reader and writer.[6] Lentricchia is only one of an increasing number of American writers of Italian descent who have explored the interaction of Italian and African Americans, and in the process have created light by which we can see both the discrimination against Italian Americans and the activities they have participated in to achieve justice for all.

For Italian Americans, "making it" has come with a high price. It has cost them the language of their ancestors—the main means by which history is preserved and heritage passed on from one generation to the next. They have had to trade in or hide any customs that have been depicted as quaint, but labeled as alien, in order to prove equality to those above them on the ladder of success. In this way, Italian Americans have become white, but a different kind of white than those of the dominant Anglo-Saxon culture. Italian Americans have become whites on a leash. And as long as they behave themselves (act white), as long as they accept the images of themselves as presented in the media (don't cry defamation) and as long as they stay within corporate and cultural boundaries (don't identify with other minorities) they will be allowed to remain white. This behavior has led to Italian Americans being left out of most discussions of multiculturalism. In *A Different Mirror*, Ronald Takaki's revision of American history, the European immigrants and their descendants are either lumped in the falsely monolithic category of whites or overlooked entirely.[7] The fact is that each of these groups has its own unique history of subjugation that aligns it more closely with Takaki's oppressed minorities than with the Anglo majority. We all need to come to grips with the fact that there is a great diversity and much oppression within white America. Until then, we are doomed to repeat the mistakes of the earlier histories that we are trying to correct.

For too long, the U.S. media were all too ready to help restrict Italians' attempts to assimilate as white Americans. The vast majority of Italian Americans are law-abiding citizens, but you wouldn't know it by watching television, listening to the radio, or reading books. We have been viciously framed by the constant repetition of negative portrayals. Most histories of mafia in America begin with the 1891 murder of the corrupt New Orleans Police Chief Hennessy. The aftermath of his murder lead to one of the largest recorded mass lynchings in this country's history. America's obsession with the mafia has overshadowed the real history of Italians in America that includes indentured servitude, mass lynchings, Ku Klux Klan terrorism against Italians, and strong participation in civil rights struggles. For Italian Americans, overt oppression has given way to more covert techniques of discrimination. Italians have replaced Indians and blacks as the accepted "bad guys" in films, and this image was regularly reinforced and perpetuated through contemporary remakes of *The Untouchables* and the establishment of museums such as the old "Capone's Chicago."

These portrayals have become the building blocks of an American cultural imagination that has petrified a stereotype. This never ending reproduction of negative stereotypes has so impoverished American minds that anything Italian is immediately connected to gangsterism and ignorance. To become American, Italians would have to do everything in their power to show how they were unlike the gangsters and buffoons who dominated public representation of their culture. As the first and second generation achieved material success, they were able to direct energies toward defending Italians from defamatory attacks. A number of social and civic organizations such as the Commission for Social Justice of the Order Sons of Italy in America, UNICO National, and Chicago's Joint Civic Committee of Italian Americans were strong in their battle against defamation and their efforts to change America's myopic perception of Italian American culture. But their approaches, by necessity, were restricted to taking defensive stands, severely limiting their ability to mount any type of counteroffense.

While their efforts in the past have made overt discrimination a fading memory, Italian Americans are still plagued by covert manipulation of their image in American culture. This manipulation is fostered by what critic Robert Viscusi calls a lack of "discursive power." In an essay written in response to the Yusef Hawkins murder in Italian American Bensonhurst, Viscusi pointed to the ease with which the Italian American community, both local and national, slipped into public silence in the aftermath of the event. Viscusi ascribes this silence to the inability of Italian Americans to develop power over their language. "Persons who lack discursive power," he writes, "are often reduced to servile responses—to violence or to dumb-show—when confronted with serious personal, social, or political problems."[8] The three components toward gaining discursive power, according to Viscusi, are mastery over language (both English and Italian), the development of historical narratives, and a return to the tradition of dialectic that fostered internal critiques and oppositional voices. Viscusi's essay tells Italian Americans that they can no longer afford to wait for attitudes toward their heritage to change; they must change the the attitudes themselves. While the earlier generations' battles were fought and won on the economic and sociological front, the battle for the grandchildren of the immigrants has moved to the cultural front. Financial resources, the rewards for having "made it," would need to be invested in promoting representations that Italian Americans can live with. This is the only chance Italian Americans have to effectively change the image of Italians in America.

Sociologist Jerry Krase, in a search for the reasons why Italian Americans are "perceived as being so much more [biased] than other ethnic groups," looks to geographical proximity for an explanation: "Given that working class Italian-American populations occupy residential territories which are directly in the path of minority group expansion, they are the most likely to experience inter-racial and inter-ethnic conflict on a local level."[9] In another study, Krase points to the ignorance of their own history as one reason why Italians might lash out against blacks. "Parallels between the African American and Italian American experiences are numerous," he writes, "and should be the source of cooperation rather than conflict."[10]

Robert Orsi, in what is perhaps the best examination of relationships between an African American and an Italian American community, put forth the idea that how Italian American identity was created can be directly tied to the interaction between these two groups. Orsi noted as Italian immigration occurred at the same times as migration of southern African Americans and African Caribbeans, Italians became part of "the first wave of dark-skinned immigrants" which lead to what he calls their "inbetweenness": "The immigrants' inbetweenness and the consequent effort to establish the border against the dark-skinned other required an intimate struggle, a context against the initial uncertainty over which side of the racial dichotomy the swarthy immigrants were on and against the facts of history and geography that inscribed this ambiguity on the urban landscape."[11] Orsi's conclusion is that Italian immigrants became Italian Americans as soon as they learned how to become white.

There are many examples of Italian Americans who have both broken the silence and created the historical narratives that will challenge long established notions of ethnic whiteness. In his keynote address to the 1994 American Italian Historical Association's national conference, Rudolph Vecoli challenged the notion of Italian Americans being white. Using numerous examples from history in which Italian Americans were not always considered white, he argued that "Our experience has taught us the fallacy of the very idea of race and the mischief of racial labels. It has taught us that both total assimilation and total separatism are will-o'-the-wisps, unachievable—and undesirable if they were. It has taught us that a healthy ethnicity is compatible with, indeed essential to, a healthy America. For these reasons, we, Italian Americans, have something important to contribute to the national dialogue." Vecoli concludes his speech with the idea that the key to Italian American participation is the creation of the ability to define themes, "distinguished by our unique experience" that is not "white, nor black, nor brown, nor red, nor yellow."[12] But regardless of how well Vecoli substantiates the historical racism against Italians, no matter how well he argues the point that Italian Americans have been categorically excluded from the recent benefits of attention given to a multicultural United States, there remains the fact that at some point, Italian Americans became white. This is a point made by the writing on whiteness, in which David Roediger's work has been seminal.

In an early paper presented at a 1996 Newberry Library summer seminar, Roediger and James R. Barrett wrote that "Italians, involved in a spectacular international Diaspora in the early twentieth century, were racialized as the 'Chinese of Europe' in many lands. But in the U.S. their racialization was pronounced, as *guinea*'s evolution suggests, more likely to connect Italians with Africans."[13] But the whiteness of Italian Americans was more delayed than totally denied, and thus the danger, according to Roediger, is not only swallowing the myth of white superiority, but "being swallowed by the lie of whiteness."[14] This danger is very real as today's Italian Americans grow up ignorant of their history and firm in their belief of being white. As poet Diane di Prima noted in a response to Vecoli's keynote address: "In most ways, my brothers and I were pushed into being white, as my parents understood that term,"[15] which included being forbidden to speak Italian. Di Prima argued that "We need to admit that this pseudo 'white' identity with its present non-convenience was not something that just fell on us out of the blue, but something that many Italian Americans grabbed at with both hands. Many felt that their culture, language, food, songs, music, identity, was a small price to pay for entering American mainstream. Or they thought, like my parents probably did, that they could keep these good Italian things in private and become 'white' in public."[16]

That Italian Americans could have it both ways might be seen as an advantage, but according to Noel Ignatiev, choosing whiteness means clinging to "the most serious barrier to becoming fully American."[17] Ignatiev, who, with John Garvey, edits the journal *Race Traitor*, presents the most radical alternative to Italian Americans, that of aiding in the abolishment of whiteness altogether. "Normally the discussion of immigrant assimilation is framed by efforts to estimate how much of the immigrants' traditional culture they lose in becoming American. Far more significant, however, than the choice between the old and the new is the choice between two identities which are both new to them: white and American."[18]

Although racial discrimination against Italians was more prevalent in the past, it has not disappeared. Today, Italian American youth suffer from association with a different stereotype; the image of the organ-grinding immigrant has been replaced by the mafioso and the dumb street kid à la Rocky Balboa. These images do not come from family interaction, but from the larger society. So that when Italian Americans look into the cultural mirror, they receive a distorted view, as though it was one of those funny mirrors found in an amusement park. Consciously or unconsciously, those distorted images affect their identity, and they must face the reality that the dominant culture is comfortable with Italians as seriocomic figures, caricatures made up of the most distorted aspects of their culture. The question all Italian Americans must confront these days is, "Who controls the image-making process and why are their social images so distorted?" Reinforcement of a positive cultural identity that was created in the home is necessary for the maintenance of and a willingness to continue that identification outside the home. If children get the idea that to be Italian is to be what the media and white histories say Italian is, then they will either avoid it, if it shames them, or embrace it if it gets them attention. Philosopher Raymond Belliotti, in *Seeking Identity*, writes, "Italian Americans have been submerged in the cruel, overly broad category of 'White Europeans,' a category which eviscerates their particularity and renders their special grievances invisible. Italian Americans are given the shroud, but not the substance of privilege."[19] But in some instances the "particularity" of Italian Americans has been recognized.

Conclusion

When it comes to Italian America, presentation of our image is, more often than not, out of our control, especially when we choose not to tell our story. In choosing to be silent, we have given up control of our culture; in choosing to remain invisible, we have chosen to leave our fate in the hands of others. As long as difference remains invisible, it is impossible to see any similarities. It is unfortunate that when difference becomes visible, it overshadows similarity.

In terms of processes, the stories of our past, especially when told by our elders, have been the major means by which our heritage is transmitted from generation to generation. This process became endangered when Italians migrated to the United States. Loss of shared primary languages, lack of shared environments (as children leave not only the homes, but the neighborhoods and often the states of their upbringing), contributed to the distortion of our heritage. When our families relinquished the task of storytelling to radio, television and film, the inside stories remained locked away and only the outside stories were accessible. Those outside stories are the shadows that haunt us in stereotypes. Shadows are caused whenever an object is illuminated. The purpose of throwing light on a subject is to get a better look at it. Unfortunately, it seems that whenever the light is thrown on Italian Americans, the only things that people see are the shadows. If you think of media exposure as the light and Italian Americans as the subject, then you might wonder why all the beauty (and most of the reality) of our heritage ends up in the shadows. I believe the answer lies not in what our heritage is, but how it is perceived. To determine appropriate perceptions means controlling the light. Whether it is writing, sculpting, dancing, or singing, Italian Americans in the arts are often practicing their talents in the shadows of their community. I know of many actors who must resort to playing Italian stereotypes in order to survive in the business; to feed their families they must often play the parts that producers and directors have designed for them. And how many of us know and read our Italian American writers?

Occasionally, we control the aim of the light—for example, at organizational gatherings, conferences, exhibitions, and performances—but for the most part, the number of viewers at these events is minimal compared with the number who see such media presentations as *The Untouchables*, *Saturday Night Fever*, *Moonstruck*, *Goodfellas*, and *The Sopranos*.

Many regions that have Italian cultural centers are able to create and promote alternatives to these Hollywood visions. But, in comparison to Hollywood, the light is of low wattage. Often there are events as such as *Feste Italiane*—Italian festivals that can provide a regular forum for the experiencing of Italian American life, but even then the light only lasts a few short days. For many years, Italian American artists have learned the process of creating and projecting light onto Italian American heritage, but it is not enough to provide a means for Italian Americans artists to reach the public (through educational opportunities); the public must reach their art. The future of our heritage will be insured only if we take control of the light.

The transmission of anyone's heritage is more and more being controlled by institutions; artistic, educational, economic, political, and religious institutions have replaced the family as the means of conveying cultural values. When we have learned this, and moved to insure that such institutions are sensitive to our Italian American identities and heritage, then we will begin to concentrate on the light that illuminates and not the shadows that distort.

Notes

The first epigraph comes from Ralph Ellison, *Invisible Man* (New York: Vintage Books, 1972), 3; the second comes from James Baldwin, "On Being 'White' . . . And Other Lies," *Essence* (April 1984), 90–92; the third from Rose Romano, "Vendetta," *La bella figura: a choice* (San Francisco: Malafemmina Press, 1993), 35–42.

1. Joseph Sciorra, "Italians against Racism," in *Are Italians White?: How Race is Made in America*, ed. Jennifer Guglielmo and Salvatore Salerno (New York: Routledge, 2003), 192–209.
2. Mario Puzo, *The Godfather* (New York: G. P. Putnam, 1969), 290.
3. Richard Gambino, *Blood of My Blood: The Dilemma of the Italian-Americans.* (1973; New York: Anchor, 1975), 329.
4. Patrick J. Gallo, *Ethnic Alienation: The Italian-Americans* (Rutherford, NJ: Fairleigh Dickinson University Press, 1974), 209.
5. Daniela Gioseffi, "The Bleeding Mimosa," *Voices in Italian Americana* 2, no.1 (1991): 59–65.
6. Frank Lentricchia, "Confessions of an Ex-Literary Critic," *Lingua Franca* (September–October 1996), 59–67.
7. Ronald Takaki, *A Different Mirror: A History of Multicultural America* (New York: Little, Brown, 1993).
8. Robert Viscusi, "Breaking the Silence: Strategic Imperatives for Italian American Culture," *Voices in Italian Americana* 1, no. 2 (1990), 1–14: 3.
9. Jerome Krase, "Bensonhurst, Brooklyn: Italian-American Victimizers and Victims," *Voices in Italian Americana* 5, no. 2 (1994), 43–53; quote from page 44.
10. Krase, "Bensonhurst," 51.
11. Robert Anthony Orsi, "The Religious Boundaries of an Inbetween People: Street *Feste* and the Problem of the Dark-Skinned Other in Italian Harlem, 1920–1990," *American Quarterly* 44, no. 3 (September 1992), 313–347; see especially 316, 318.
12. Rudolph J. Vecoli, "'Are Italian Americans Just White Folks?'" In *Through the Looking Glass: Italian and Italian/American Images in the Media*, ed. Mary Jo Bona and Anthony Julian Tamburri (Staten Island, NY: American Italian Historical Association, 1996), 3–17; quote from page 17.
13. James R. Barrett and David Roediger, "Inbetween Peoples: Race, Nationality and the 'New Immigrant' Working Class," unpublished paper presented at the Newberry Library, summer 1996, 7.
14. David W. Stowe, "Uncolored People: The Rise of Whiteness Studies," *Lingua Franca* (September–October 1996), 68–77: 74.
15. Diane di Prima, "'Don't Solidify the Adversary!' A Response to Rudolph Vecoli," in *Through the Looking Glass,* 24–29; quote from page 25.
16. Di Prima, "'Don't Solidify,'" 27.

17. Noel Ignatiev, "Immigrants and Whites," in *Race Traitor*, ed. Noel Ignatiev and John Garvey, (New York: Routledge, 1996), 15–23; quote from page 18.
18. Ignatiev, "Immigrants," 23.
19. Raymond A. Belliotti, *Seeing Identity: Individualism Versus Community in an Ethnic Context* (Lawrence: University Press of Kansas, 1995), 163.

1

Darker Aspects of Italian American Prehistory

William J. Connell

The period from the 1870s onward has rightly been the focus of Italian American historical studies. In earlier decades, the number of Americans of Italian ancestry was miniscule compared with the numbers in the great wave of immigration that started in the 1870s and peaked in the period before World War I. Three generations of historians have told us a great deal about who the Italians in this massive movement of human beings were. We know how many people came, where they came from, how they were received in this country, and we also know about the various ways in which they have assimilated, contributed to, and resisted mainstream American culture and how they sometimes succeeded in creating new cultures and subcultures of their own.[1] For important reasons, almost all of this work has attempted to see American culture from the point of view of Italian immigrants. As a result, there is still much interesting work to be done to look at the arriving Italians from the point of view of the Americans who were already here.

During what might called the "prehistory" of Italian Americans, in the period before 1870, a set of beliefs and prejudices was formed that in large part shaped the way Italian immigrants were received by American society at large. This was not a history whose subjects created it for themselves. It was confected well in advance of the coming of most Italians to the United States, and a large share of it was imported from the Old World in the first centuries of American colonization and growth. It was this prehistory that conditioned the terms on which Italians were first accepted into American society. In subtle ways, it still affects perceptions of Italian Americans in American culture.

Treatments of the earliest periods of Italian American history have usually overlooked tendencies in the larger culture while emphasizing the contributions of exemplary individuals of Italian ancestry. Beginning with the important study of Giovanni Schiavo, the focus has been on identifying particular Italians who, starting with Columbus, achieved things that were noteworthy in the project of settling North America and building the United States.[2] Since before the Civil War there were so few Italians in the United States—the Census of 1860 reports that in the state of New Jersey there were only 106 residents born in Italy—that the work has been hard going.[3] Often all that survives are a few names. Interestingly, because written records of military service were preserved more systematically than other kinds of records, there is a decidedly martial cast to most lists of early Italian Americans, who are recorded as serving in the republic's early wars.

All the same, fine research continues to fill out our knowledge of these first Italian Americans.[4] Historians have studied and admired (properly so) the contributions of Italian Americans like William Paca, who signed the Declaration of Independence,[5] and especially Filippo Mazzei, who was a close friend of Thomas Jefferson, and who seems to have provided the literary inspiration for Jefferson's assertion in the declaration that "all men are created equal."[6] Recently there has been interest in the interaction of Italian and American theories concerning the republican form of government, both at the time of the American Revolution, as seen in studies of the friendship between Gaetano Filangieri and Benjamin Franklin,[7] and in the 1830s and 1840s, as in an excellent study of the early Italian American writer Joseph Rocchietti.[8] Much has been made of Garibaldi's stay in New York in the early 1850s and of the mystique that continued to surround the "Hero of the Two Worlds" throughout the Civil War period, when Abraham Lincoln offered him a generalship in the Union Army.[9]

There is something naturally satisfying about reconstructing the past lives of people one might wish to identify with. But once we move beyond the edifying accounts of these few individuals and their political, cultural, and intellectual contributions and begin to look at the broader perception of Italy and Italians in early American culture, Italian American prehistory starts to assume a character quite different from the one these honor rolls of early Italian Americans might seem to indicate. Knowledge of the lives and careers of a few noteworthy individuals should not stand in the way of the unpleasant fact that the prevailing views in early America concerning Italy and Italians were not favorable. At the same time, it is not sufficient to attribute these negative opinions to the broader phenomenon of American nativism. To be sure, there was much sentiment against immigrants, and against Catholic immigrants in particular, that impacted Italians along with other ethnic groups.[10] But a survey of early American interactions with and perceptions of Italians reveals that early Americans were more knowledgeable about Italy than is generally supposed. There was an existing reservoir of cultural attitudes that helped to shape and direct the nativist response to immigrants from Italy.

We know that many early Americans were knowledgeable about Italy first of all from the books they read. Among educated Americans in the 1600s and 1700s it was not uncommon to find persons who read the books of important Italian authors. This was particularly true in Massachusetts. Governor Bradford of the Plymouth Colony owned a copy of Francesco Guicciardini's *History of Italy* in English translation; and Plymouth elder William Brewster owned Machiavelli's *The Prince*, Paolo Sarpi's *History of the Interdict*, and Stefano Guazzo's *Civil Conversation*. Whether these books were actually brought over on the Mayflower or imported later hardly matters. (We cannot know, since the information comes from estate inventories—Brewster died in 1643, Bradford in 1657.)[11] What is important is that the owners thought they were valuable enough to bring them across the Atlantic. But it is possible. Later the Puritan divine Cotton Mather read and owned many books printed in Italian.[12] That a tradition of Italian learning persisted in New England is evidenced by the extensive collection of Italian books left to the Boston Public Library by John Adams.[13]

History, philosophy, law, agronomy, economics, and theology were all areas in which Italian books were read and commented on by early Americans. Americans also learned about Italy from books by non-Italian Europeans—above all from travelers' accounts of the Grand Tour, and from novels that were set in Italy.[14] Most importantly, some knowledge of Italy came to America along with Europe's musical culture, most notably the opera. Mozart's librettist, Lorenzo da Ponte, wrote extensively and revealingly about his last decades in America (1805–1838), but today his *Memoirs* are read chiefly for what they tell us about Vienna in the time of Mozart and Salieri.[15] Da Ponte had a hard time in America, and he sometimes found himself having to defend Italy and Italians against what he perceived as slanderous statements. His own efforts to establish an opera failed, but from the 1830s opera enjoyed a remarkable success, becoming the principal way in which Americans experienced Italy and Italians.[16] The need to sing in Italian, particularly to piano accompaniment at home, was one of the reasons Italian was considered a language, along with French, that respectable American women should learn, although, as Joseph Rocchietti tells us, American men avoided it.[17]

Americans, therefore, possessed a considerable body of views and impressions concerning Italy, even though there were very few Italians actually here. It should be stressed that all of this learning concerning things Italian did not mean that most early Americans viewed Italy favorably. Van Wyck Brooks and Helen Barolini have written richly detailed books that explain the lure of Italy to the oddball American writers, artists, and art collectors who traveled there in the nineteenth century and early twentieth centuries.[18] Yet the fact that the spirited, eccentric geniuses of the time were smitten with Italy stands as a reminder that most Americans were of a different opinion.

The causes of early America's largely unfavorable opinion of Italy are most certainly complex and deep-rooted. In the interest of clarity, however, and in order to more effectively challenge a number of received interpretations, they will be sketched here as stemming from three chief causes, the first having to do with Italian economic history, the second with religious controversies, and the third with the ambitious republican theories of America's Founding Fathers.

A Later Italian Economic Collapse

Let's begin with a small lesson in Italian economic history. Many of us learned in school that after the great voyages of discovery created new trade routes around Africa and to the New World, the Italian economy went into a centuries-long tailspin, caused above all by Italy's loss of control over Europe's spice trade with the East. Challenges to this chronology have appeared from time to time, however, and in that last four decades it has become clear that overall prosperity throughout Italy continued for more than one hundred years after the discoveries of the 1490s and probably well into the first decades of the 1600s.[19] For tourists who have seen the great churches (like St. Peter's), the public buildings, and the private palaces that were built in Venice, Genoa, Florence, Rome, Naples, Lecce, and Messina in the sixteenth and early seventeenth centuries, this should really come as no surprise, since building projects like these hardly seem evidence of an economy that was on the ropes.

What is even more interesting than the revised chronology is that recent research shows that when economic collapse finally did arrive, after 1620, it was more severe and lasted longer than was previously realized.[20] From the mid–1600s through the 1700s—at precisely the time the American colonies were being established—the great Italian cities experienced waves of beggars and the homeless. Orphanages expanded and multiplied. Famine and disease were rampant. The Italian collapse of the mid–1600s coincided with the rise of Britain and France as economic powerhouses. By the mid-seventeenth century the British had even taken control from Venice of Mediterranean shipping.[21] It was this seventeenth-century crisis that plunged Italy into that economically backward state from which she only began to emerge in areas like Piedmont and Lombardy in the second half of the 1800s. Confirmation of this new chronology, of a prosperity that lasted into the 1600s and then came to a crashing and catastrophic halt can be found in the accounts of Northern European travelers. When the Frenchman Michel de Montaigne traveled to Italy in the 1560s, he found a place that was prosperous and generally well-ordered, and he was quite proud when he reached Rome that he was made an honorary citizen.[22] But when the Englishman Tobias Smollett traveled in Italy in the 1760s, he complained incessantly that the country was poor, dirty, and, above all, unsafe.[23]

To be sure, not many early Americans traveled in Italy and saw these conditions firsthand. But it is important to realize that the accounts of travelers like Smollett were widely read in America and that Americans learned about the circumstances of Italy the way Europeans did, via newspaper accounts and published travel diaries. Throughout the formative years of the American Republic, long before Italians began arriving in the United States, the Italian peninsula was widely understood as a receptacle of human misery.

Calvinist and English Anti-Italianism

A second important reason for the negative image of Italy and Italians in early America had to do with Old World religion. It was not simply the Catholicism of most Italians and the presence of the papacy in Rome that encouraged anti-Italian prejudice among Protestant Americans. After all, Catholics, too, had settled in the United States, especially in Maryland, and religious toleration became a hallmark of the culture of early America in the course of the eighteenth century.[24] A contributing factor, certainly, was a medieval tradition of anti-Italianism in England that had economic roots.[25] In the Middle Ages, Italian merchants made considerable profits in the English wool trade, establishing a wealthy quarter for themselves in London that became the focus of the famous Evil May Day riot of 1517. But a mix of much stronger anti-Italian feelings became predominant in English culture in the second half of the sixteenth century, particularly among Calvinists, and it was this prejudice that was brought to New England with the Puritans.

There was a strong belief in Protestant circles that Italians were hypocritical in matters of religion. Although Catholicism itself was objectionable, what was even worse was that the Italians as a nation were given over to cowardly and deceptive religious practices. The origins of this belief can be traced back to John Calvin. Few people today realize how angry John Calvin was with the Italians of his day and how virulent were the treatises he wrote against them. His earlier contemporary in Germany, Martin Luther, wrote attacks on the papacy and Rome, but his attacks were focused on the outright corrupt he saw in Italy, not on the deceptive inner moral character that Calvin criticized. During the time in which Calvin established himself as preacher and principal religious authority in the Swiss city of Geneva in 1541, a small number of Italians reformers had established themselves in Geneva, where they lived as exiles for their religious beliefs. These Italian exiles encouraged Calvin to believe that there were more people like them back in Italy, Italians who would one day rise up against the church and establish the reformed faith in their homeland. Unfortunately—from Calvin's point of view— this did not happen, and the Italian peninsula remained Catholic territory. Yet to his great irritation, Calvin continued to hear reports of Italians who believed in the Protestant reform movement, but who publicly continued to live and go to Mass as Catholics. Meanwhile, in his native France, where Calvin's followers were persecuted as heretics, Protestants proved increasingly willing to confess their faith in public, even if it meant martyrdom.[26] The unwillingness of Italians to admit in public to following the Reformed faith became for Calvin a circumstance that was intolerable. Calvin had "misgivings" about the moral stability of Italians.[27] In his treatises and his sermons he denounced the Italians as hypocrites and lazy religionists who put themselves and their families ahead of both the communal good and of God's truth. When thousands of French Huguenots were killed by Catholics in the St. Bartholomew's Day Massacre, with the connivance of a Queen Regent, Catherine de' Medici, who happened to be Italian, fuel was added to the flames. Anti-Italianism was rampant in the Calvinist movement, and it resulted in repeated condemnations of Italians as villainous, deceitful, and concerned only with family and self—qualities that can still be found in many of the stereotypes pinned to today's Italian Americans.[28]

It may seem a great leap to connect John Calvin's treatises with representations of Italians in the American mass media of the late nineteenth and early twenty-first centuries. But it is not so difficult to show that Calvin's diatribes had a profound impact on the representation of Italians in English drama at the time of Shakespeare and throughout the seventeenth century.[29] That Shakespeare remained fundamental to American popular culture has been one of the fascinating conclusions of historians of the American nineteenth century.[30]

Romeo and Juliet and *Othello* were big hits with middle and lower class audiences in American both before and during the decades of mass immigration in

Italy. The image of Italy and of Italians these plays convey is far from flattering.[31] *Romeo and Juliet* portrays a feuding Italian city in which family honor destroys civic peace. *Othello* is a drama in which Iago—a type associated especially with Italians that has its original in Machiavelli—uses particularly "Italian" modes of deception to tragic purpose in a case that again involves the use of violence in a matter where personal honor takes precedence over other values.

It would impoverish our culture if we were to be deprived of such master-pieces by politically correct modern censors for the reason that they offer images of Italians that later stereotypes have drawn upon. In the wake of the Holocaust, a number of Jewish organizations campaigned against various productions of *The Merchant of Venice* for reasons one can understand without condoning. As recently as 1981 the Anti-Defamation League (ADL) tried to prevent the broadcast on PBS of a BBC production of *The Merchant of Venice*. Times change, and today the ADL instead uses the *Merchant of Venice* to teach about anti-Semitism. To my knowl-edge no Italian American organization has ever tried to block a production of *Romeo and Juliet*. But if we acknowledge that at least some of the modern stereo-types concerning Italian Americans have roots in literary archetypes, we can begin to see why some of the stereotypes concerning Italian Americans have proved enduring and difficult to combat.

The Italian Republics and American Republicanism

A third reason why Italy and Italians were seen in a negative light in early America has to do with the ambitious political project undertaken by America's Founding Fathers. In casting off the British monarchy, the American founding generation set about and succeeded in the difficult task of establishing a republic—a government in which the citizens are subject to no sovereign dynasty and instead rule them-selves. Italy had had a long history of experiments in republicanism, dating back to the ancient Romans, and in recent decades several historians have tried to argue that the American project was inspired in crucial ways by Italian examples. Some have said that the Florentine civic humanism of Leonardo Bruni, the democratic republicanism espoused by Niccolò Machiavelli, or the well-balanced constitu-tion of the Republic of Venice provided models for America's early leaders.[32] But a rereading of some of the key texts of the American founding quickly shows that what impressed the Founding Fathers the most about Italy's many experiments with republicanism was that they had all failed.[33]

The *Federalist Papers* are eloquent on the differences between the small repub-lics of ancient Greece and medieval Italy and the large one that the American founders proposed to create.[34] But perhaps the most illuminating work concern-ing early American attitudes toward the Italian republics is John Adams's *Defence of the Constitutions of Government of the United States of America*, a three-volume work that includes nearly two entire volumes dedicated to the history of the Ital-ian republics of the Middle Ages.[35] Why did the Italian republics fail? Adams uses the real history of Italy to tell the story of Shakespeare's Italian tragedies all over again. As in Shakespeare, family honor, selfishness, corruption, and the absence of a sense of community interest undermine the public trust, leading to tyrannies either of princes or of a small circle of aristocrats. To understand how to avoid the fate of the Italian republics, Adams urged young Americans to learn to read Italian. As he put it, in a passage that addresses an imagined young reader,

> There were in Italy, in the middle age, an hundred or two of cities, all independent republics, and all constituted nearly in the same manner. The history of one is the history of the all: and all had the same destiny, excepting two or three that are still decided aristocracies, an exit into monarchy. There are extant a multitude of particular histories of these cities, full of excellent warning for the people of America. Let me recommend it to you, my young friend, who have time enough before you, to make yourself master of the Italian language, and avail your country of all the instruction contained in them.[36]

Adams was rare in recommending the learning of Italian, but his arguments concerning the Italian city-states were typical of the time, and they remained influential for later generations of American writers on republics, who continually sought to distance American republicanism from the failed republics of the Old World.

Venice in particular became the subject of treatments that emphasized the moral corruption that proceeded from rule by a tyrannical oligarchy.[37] This is the thrust, for instance, of James Fenimore Cooper's underappreciated but quite engaging novel, *The Bravo*, which was published in 1831 but set in seventeenth-century Venice.[38] Three convergent plot lines emphasize the corruption, deceit, and violence that Cooper—along with most educated Americans—thought typical of the Italian republics.[39] In the plot that occupies the novel's foreground, the aristocratic families that control Venice interfere with the love of Violetta, an orphaned heiress of aristocratic birth, for a Calabrian nobleman, Don Camillo, whom she secretly marries and who, at novel's end, rescues her from their clutches. In the meantime, Antonio, an aged fisherman and a veteran of Venice's wars with the Turks, seeks to have his grandson spared from mandatory service on the galleys, where his father had died. It is a matter about which Antonio becomes vocal, leading the families in charge of the state to arrange his assassination. To cover their traces, the same patricians falsely charge one of their own agents, Jacopo, with Antonio's murder, and the novel ends with his beheading. The noble rhetoric of republicanism, which speaks of virtue, justice, and self-reliance, was consciously manipulated, according to Cooper, to serve the selfish interests of a few Venetian oligarchs while winning the adherence of the people. As Cooper's hero, Jacopo, says, "'A system like this of Venice leaves none of us masters of our own acts. The wiles of such a combination are stronger than the will. It cloaks its offenses against right in a thousand specious forms, and it enlists the support of every man, under the pretence of a sacrifice for the common good.'"[40] The fact that the Southern Kingdom, which was under Spanish control in the seventeenth century, is actually described in bright tones when compared with Venice is indicative of Cooper's dim view of the Republic at the head of the Adriatic. (It may also reflect that fairly brief period in the early nineteenth century when the Bourbon monarchy was perceived as progressive.) Cooper's message in *The Bravo* was that Americans needed to carefully construct a republicanism fundamentally different from the republicanism that had existed in Italy. It would not be sufficient to rely on the virtue of the citizens. New institutions would be required to protect the republic against the corrupting influences that took over the Italian republics. As in economics and religion, so too in political theory. Italy represented the faults of the Old World in the extreme: a model of what to avoid.

***

Studies of American reactions to Italian immigrants have rightly focused on fears and attitudes that were proper to the late 1800s. There is no question that the harsh reception and outright discrimination that Italian immigrants faced was conditioned by contemporary phenomena, such as neo-Darwinian racialist theories that saw Italians and other Mediterranean and eastern European immigrants as belonging to inferior groups. Italian immigrants also suffered from anti-Catholicism, which survived the eclipse of the Know-Nothing movement. And they were certainly affected by the resentments and jealousies of other immigrant groups that arrived in America before them. Clearly these were the immediate reasons for the poor reception that Italians found when they arrived in the United States.

But if instead we ask the question why, more than a century later, pejorative portrayals of Italian Americans remained widespread in the media, at a time when negative stereotypes were fading with respect to many other ethnic groups, it is hard to turn to the same explanations. Darwinian racialism still surfaces from time to time in American academic and political discourse, but it almost never concerns Italian Americans, and when it crops up it is quickly denounced by the culture at large. Anti-Catholicism persists in American society in some quarters, and unflattering images of the Roman church and its clergy are often paired with negative images of Italian Americans in the movies and on television. But it would be hard to argue that anti-Catholicism is the major reason for the stereotyping of Italian Americans in the mass media.

Perhaps there is something deeper and more traditional at work in the perpetuation of stereotypes concerning Italian Americans. Long before Italians began to arrive in the United States in large numbers, Italians were already imagined here as a people who represented values opposite to those the American republic claimed to stand for. Perhaps if it is more generally recognized that throughout so much of America's intellectual and cultural history Italians were imagined as moral foils to virtuous Americans, we will be better able to move beyond the stereotypes concerning Italian Americans that abound in our popular culture.

Notes

1. Samuel L. Baily, *Immigrants in the Lands of Promise: Italians in Buenos Aires and New York City, 1870–1914* (Ithaca: Cornell University Press, 1999); Stefano Luconi, *From Paesani to White Ethnics: The Italian Experience in Philadelphia* (Albany: SUNY Press, 2001). On new directions in immigration history see Donna R. Gabaccia and C. Wayne Leach, eds., *Immigrant Life in the U.S.: Multidisciplinary Perspectives* (London: Routledge, 2004); and Donna R. Gabaccia and Vicki L. Ruiz, eds., *American Dreaming, Global Realities: Rethinking U.S. Immigration History* (Urbana: University of Illinois Press, 2006).

2. Giovanni Ermenegildo Schiavo, *The Italians in America Before the Civil War* (New York: Vigo Press, 1934).

3. Dennis Starr, *The Italians of New Jersey: A Historical Introduction and Bibliography* (Newark: New Jersey Historical Society, 1985), xx.

4. See, for instance, the collection *Italian Americans Before Mass Migration: We've Always Been Here*, ed. Jerome Krase, Frank B. Pesci, Sr., and Frank Alduino (New York: American Italian Historical Association, 2007).

5. Gregory A. Stiverson and Phebe R. Jacobsen, *William Paca: A Biography* (Annapolis: Maryland Historical Society, 1976). On Paca's connections to classical culture, but with not even a mention of Italian culture, see Joseph Manca, "Cicero in America: Civic Duty and Private Happiness in Charles Willson Peale's Portrait of William Paca," *American Art* 17, no. 1 (2003): 68–89. Paca's marital life was as exciting as that of a number of Founding Fathers, and also some recent politicians, although it did not diminish his historical role.

6. Mazzei is known to Americans through the work of Margherita Marchione. See Philip Mazzei, *Jefferson's "Zealous Whig,"* ed. Margherita Marchione (New York: American Institute of Italian Studies, 1975); *Philip Mazzei: Selected Writings and Correspondence*, ed. Margherita Marchione, 3 vols. (Prato, Italy: Cassa di Risparmi e Depositi, 1983); Margherita Marchione, *The Adventurous Life of Philip Mazzei* (Lanham: University Press of America, 1995). Her work should be compared with that of the Italian scholars who underline the radicalism that emerged especially in Mazzei's later years after his return to Europe: *Edoardo Tortarolo, Illuminismo e rivoluzioni. Biografia politica di Filippo Mazzei* (Milan: Franco Angeli, 1985); Mario Montorzi, "I processi contro Filippo Mazzei ed i liberali pisani nel 1799," in his *Giustizia in contado. Studi sull'esercizio della giurisdizione nel territorio pontederese e pisano in età moderna* (Pisa: Pacini, 1997), 289–300.

7. Filangieri figures importantly in Antonio Pace, *Benjamin Franklin and Italy,* Memoirs of the American Philosophical Association 47 (Philadelphia: American Philosophical Association, 1958). See also Marcello Maestro, "Benjamin Franklin and the Penal Laws," *Journal of the History of Ideas* 36 (1975): 551–62; Maestro, *Gaetano Filangieri and His "Science of Legislation,"* Transactions of the American Philosophical Society, n.s., 66:6 (Philadelphia, 1976); and Maestro, "Gaetano Filangieri and His Laws of Relative Goodness," *Journal of the History of Ideas* 44 (1983): 687–91, and the important study by Vincenzo Ferrone, *La società giusta ed equa. Repubblicanesimo e diritti dell'uomo in Gaetano Filangieri* (Bari, Italy: Laterza, 2005).

8. Carol Bonomo Albright and Elvira G. Di Fabio, *Republican Ideals in the Selected Literary Works of Italian-American Joseph Rocchietti, 1835–1845* (Lewiston, NY: Mellen, 2004).

9. See the forthcoming acts of several conferences held in 2007 to commemorate the two-hundredth anniversary of Garibaldi's birth. Useful diplomatic correspondence

was published by H. Nelson Gay, "Lincoln's Offer of a Command to Garibaldi: Light on a Disputed Point of History," *Century Magazine* 68 (October 1909): 63–74; and H. Nelson Gay, "Garibaldi's American Contacts and His Claims to American Citizenship," *American Historical Review* 38 (1932): 1–19.

10. Compare John Higham, *Strangers in the Land: Patterns of American Nativism, 1860–1925*, 2nd ed. (1955; New Brunswick, NJ: Rutgers University Press, 2004)

11. Giorgio Spini, "The New England Puritans and Italy," *Storia nordamericana* 3 (1986): 95–105; see especially 95–96. See also the same author's masterly *Autobiografia della giovane America. La storiografia Americana dai Padri Pellegrini all'Independenza* (Turin, Italy: Einaudi, 1968)—a work never translated but still superior to the existing English language treatments of early American historical writing. Spini, who passed away in Florence in 2006, studied with Perry Miller at Harvard and taught at the University of Wisconsin, Madison, before returning to Italy. For his bibliography see Daniele Spini, et al., eds., *Bibliografia degli scritti di Giorgio Spini* (Florence: Olschki, 2007).

12. Spini, "The New England Puritans," 99–103. The Italian learning of Increase and Cotton Mather, which Spini treated as a family intellectual inheritance, did not figure in Robert Middlekauff's *The Mathers: Three Generations of Puritan Intellectuals, 1596–1728*, 2nd ed. (Berkeley: University of California Press, 1999).

13. Alfred Iacuzzi, *John Adams, Scholar* (New York: S. F. Vanni, 1952), 12–16 and passim.

14. Roderick Cavaliero, *Italia Romantica: English Romantics and Italian Freedom* (London: Tauris, 2005), is most informative. See also James Patty, *Salvator Rosa in French Literature: From the Bizarre to the Sublime* (Lexington: University Press of Kentucky, 2005).

15. *Lorenzo Da Ponte, Memoirs*, trans. Elisabeth Abbot, ed. Arthur Livingston (New York: NYRB, 2000). See also Sheila Hodges, *Lorenzo Da Ponte: The Life and Times of Mozart's Librettist* (Madison: University of Wisconsin Press, 2002). The American years of Da Ponte remain to be fully investigated.

16. Hodges, *Lorenzo Da Ponte*, 217–18; Lawrence W. Levine, *Highbrow/Lowbrow: The Emergence of Cultural Hierarchy in America* (Cambridge, MA: Harvard University Press, 1988), 85–104.

17. See Joseph Rocchietti, *Why a National Literature Cannot Flourish in the United States of North America*, reprinted in Albright and Di Fabio, eds., *Republican Ideals*, especially 180–84, on the "learned lady."

18. Van Wyck Brooks, *The Dream of Arcadia: American Writers and Italy, 1760–1915* (New York: Dutton, 1958); Helen Barolini, *Their Other Side: Six American Women and the Lure of Italy* (New York: Fordham University Press, 2006). While looking at earlier periods, both writers reflect the glow of the American encounter with Italy after World War II. Other contributions to an extensive body of literature, still enjoyable to read but in need of a good historical overhaul include Paul R. Baker, *Fortunate Pilgrims: Americans in Italy, 1800–1860* (Cambridge, MA: Harvard University Press, 1964); George Wynne, *Early Americans in Rome* (Rome: Dapco, 1966); Erik Amfiteatrof, *The Enchanted Ground: Americans in Italy, 1760–1980* (Boston: Little, Brown, 1980); Leonardo Buonomo, *Backward Glances: Exploring Italy, Reinterpreting America (1831–1866)* (Madison, NJ: Fairleigh Dickinson University Press, 1996); Robert K. Martin and Leland S. Person, eds., *Roman Holidays: American Writers and Artists in Nineteenth-Century Italy* (Iowa City: University of Iowa Press, 2002).

19. The case for prolonged Italian prosperity was first advanced by the French historian, Fernand Braudel, and further developed by Ruggiero Romano, "L'Italia nella crisi del secolo XVII," in his *Tra due crisi: l'italia del Rinascimento* (Turin, Italy: Einaudi, 1971), 187–206.

20. Gregory Hanlon, *Early Modern Italy, 1550–1800* (New York: St. Martin's Press, 2000), 205–16.

21. Maria Fusaro, *Uva passa: una guerra commerciale tra Venezia e l'Inghilterra (1540–1640)* (Venice: Il Cardo, 1996).

22. Michel de Montaigne, *Journal de voyage*, ed. Fausta Garavini (Paris: Flammarion, 1983).

23. Tobias Smollett, *Travels Through France and Italy*, ed. Osbert Sitwell (London: Lehmann, 1949).

24. On religious toleration, see the polemical but still largely accurate essay of Brooke Allen, *Moral Minority: Our Skeptical Founding Fathers* (Chicago: Ivan R. Dee, 2006).

25. Fernand Braudel, "L'Italia fuori d'Italia. Due secoli e tre Italie," in *Storia d'Italia*, 9 vols., ed. Ruggiero Romano and Alberto Tenenti (Turin, Italy: Einaudi, 1972–76), vol. 2, pt. 2, 2089–2248; David Abulafia, "Gli italiani fuori d'Italia," in Gabriella Airaldi, ed., *Gli orizzonti aperti. Profili del mercante medievale* (Turin, Italy: Paravia, 1997), 175–98; Jacques Le Goff, *L'Italia nello specchio del Medioevo*, trans. Corrado Vivanti (Turin, Italy: Einaudi, 2000).

26. Nikki Shepardson, *Burning Zeal: The Rhetoric of Martyrdom and the Protestant Community in Reformation France, 1520–1570* (Bethlehem, PA: Lehigh University Press, 2007), 108–46.

27. Antonio d'Andrea, "Geneva 1576–78: The Italian Community and the Myth of Italy," in Joseph C. McLelland, ed., *Peter Martyr Vermigli and Italian Reform* (Waterloo, Canada: Wilfred Laurier University Press, 1980), 53–63: 60.

28. Henry Heller, *Anti-Italianism in Sixteenth-Century France* (Toronto: University of Toronto Press, 2003). See also Donald R. Kelley, "Murd'rous Machiavel in France: A Post Mortem," *Political Science Quarterly* 85 (1970): 545–59; and Edmond M. Beame, "The Use and Abuse of Machiavelli: The Sixteenth Century French Adaptation," *Journal of the History of Ideas* 43 (1982): 33–54.

29. Mario Praz, "Machiavelli and the Elizabethans," *Proceedings of the British Academy*, 14 (1928): 1–49 offers good indications.

30. Lawrence W. Levine, "William Shakespeare and the American People: A Study in Cultural Transformation," *American Historical Review* 89 (1984): 34–66.

31. See Michele Marrapodi et al., eds., *Shakespeare's Italy: Functions of Italian Location in Renaissance Drama* (Manchester, England: University of Manchester Press, 1997).

32. J. G. A. Pocock, *The Machiavellian Moment: Florentine Political Thought and the Atlantic Republican Tradition*, rev. ed. (1975; Princeton, NJ: Princeton University Press, 2003).

33. William J. Connell, "The Republican Idea," in James Hankins, ed., *Renaissance Civic Humanism: Reappraisals and Reflections*, (Cambridge: Cambridge University Press, 2000), 14–29.

34. See especially *The Federalist*, no. 10.

35. John Adams, *A Defence of the Constitutions of Government of the United States of America*, 3 vols., 3rd ed. (1797; rpt. Union, NJ: Lawbook Exchange, 2002).

36. Adams, *Defence*, 2: 444–45.

37. Richard MacKenney, "'A Plot Discover'd?': Myth, Legend, and the 'Spanish' Conspiracy against Venice in 1618," in John Jeffries Martin and Dennis Romano, eds., *Venice Reconsidered: The History and Civilization of an Italian City-State* (Baltimore: Johns Hopkins University Press, 2000), 185–216, argues that the view of the Venetian regime as tyrannical dates from the early seventeenth century. On outsiders' understandings of Venetian morals see especially the fascinating study by Roberto Bizzocchi, *Cicisbei. Morale privata e identità nazionale in Italia* (Bari, Italy: Laterza, 2008).

38. James Fenimore Cooper, *The Bravo* (Amsterdam: Fredonia, 2002).

39. John P. Diggins, *The Lost Soul of American Politics: Virtue, Self-Interest, and the Foundations of Liberalism* (New York: Basic Books, 1984), 180–91, offers a perceptive reading.

40. Cooper, *The Bravo*, 231–32.

2

"Between White Men and Negroes"

The Perception of Southern Italian Immigrants through the Lens of Italian Lynchings

Peter Vellon

"You shoot my goat, you better shoot me," an exasperated Francesco DiFatta informed Dr. J. F. Hodge, a well respected coroner in the town of Tallulah, Louisiana. In the summer of 1899, a dispute over a goat sparked a melee that would eventually end in the brutal murder and lynching of five Italian immigrants. The goat, owned by three Italian shopkeepers, Francesco, Carlo, and Giacomo DiFatta, had been the subject of strife due to the goat's penchant for roaming upon Hodge's property. Hodge took the matter into his own hands by firing several shots and killing DiFatta's goat. The resulting argument between the DiFatta brothers and Hodge left Carlo with a gunshot wound and Hodge near death.

Although Hodge would survive, a lynch mob consisting of almost the entire population of the town, as well as several hundred men from the surrounding county, coalesced to find the Italians who killed Hodge. The sheriff stormed to Francesco's store, arresting him and two friends of the family, Rosario Fiducia and John Cirano. All three were taken to jail. At the same, time a mob found Carlo and Giacomo, who were both taken to a nearby slaughter post where butchers skinned and dressed cattle. The post was a simple structure with two posts planted in the ground, a beam across the top, and two pulleys with a rope in each bolted to the crosspiece. With the mob in a frenzy, Carlo and Giacomo were raised to their death. Thirsty for more blood, the mob proceeded to the jail where they seized Francesco, Rosario, and John, and hung them on a nearby cottonwood tree in the jailyard. Ironically, this tree had been utilized three times in the past four years to lynch African Americans. Right before the rope was pulled sending his body into the air, Francesco DiFatta shouted to the crowd, "I liva here sixa years. I knowa you all—you alla my friends."[1]

Riddled with bullets, the bodies of the five Italians would be left hanging all night. In the next few days, residents of Tallulah rationalized the murder by stating the Italians had been troublemakers since they arrived in North Louisiana, and they probably conspired to kill Dr. Hodge. Referencing the 1891 murder of New Orleans chief of police David Hennessy, the *New Orleans Daily States* added, "Every man in that crowd knew all about the mafia and all about the Hennessey [sic] murder. They were determined there should be no repetition of that—they looked on these degenerates as monsters, capable of any infamy and they determined to destroy them root and branch, just as the traveler places his armed heel upon the head of the viper."[2]

The lynching would not be the final act in the Tallulah mob's desire to stamp out the Italian presence in their midst. In addition to the five Italians lynched, there is the story of the DiFattas' brother-in-law, Giuseppe Defina, who lived in nearby Millikens Bend. According to local newspaper reports, the lynch mob had dispersed after it had completed its task, but Giuseppe Defina told a different story to the Italian Consulate. Defina maintained that he had received a warning that he should leave Millikens Bend and Madison Parish or risk the same fate as the other Italians. The local newspaper account claimed that the lynch mob gave Defina three days to leave town; however, Defina waited only three hours to purchase a skiff for six dollars and hire Buck Collins, a black man, to pull his son and him to Vicksburg.[3] A friend named Ward informed Defina that on the night of the lynching, a crowd from Tallulah was headed to Millikens Bend to lynch him as well. Ward pleaded with the crowd to spare Defina's life and was told he should warn Defina that he had 24 hours to leave the area or suffer the consequences. The next day, another friend of Defina, Dr. Ganes, informed the Italian that he learned in Tallulah the deadline had been shortened to two hours. Upon hearing this new information, Defina claimed he immediately fled.[4]

Seeking assistance from the Italian Consulate, Defina brought a list that he had been given by two African American brothers of the 19 persons who had threatened to lynch him. One of the two brothers, Joe Evans, who had worked in Francesco DiFatta's store for two years, witnessed the DiFatta lynchings, and was willing to testify that the people involved in the Millikens Bend affair were the same people who carried out the lynching in Tallulah. The list named a Mr. Rogers, as the "leader who was to go to Millikens Bend to hang Joe Delfino [sic] and his son," a Mr. Coleman, "who was the one that climbed the tree and held the rope," Fred Johnson, "the one that carried the rope," and Anden Severe, the one who "furnished the ropes." Evans mentioned that two other African Americans, the brothers Paul and Bill Bruse, could also testify against the lynchers. Defina was instructed by the Italian Consul to return to Vicksburg in order to obtain a signed affidavit of Evans's testimony, but he discovered that no notary public would take down their statement. Defina's experience with Southern racial mores was deepened when he learned that one of the Evans brothers had been murdered because he had spoken too much about the lynching.[5]

Later, in March 1900, the District Attorney of the 19th Judicial District in Louisiana completed his investigation into the lynching at Tallulah and informed the Governor of Louisiana that "all the witnesses mentioned in your communication, whose attendance could be compelled, were summoned and testified on oath that they knew nothing of the affair." He added, somewhat exasperated, that "this is the third Grand Jury which has thoroughly investigated this matter and each investigation has been thorough and has resulted in failure to implicate anyone."[6] Upon learning the results of the investigation, the Italian Ministry of Foreign Affairs was "disgusted" with what they believed was a "whitewashing of the incident by the U.S. government."[7] In a highly ironic and harsh statement to the U.S. State Department in May, the Italian Ambassador expressed his dismay that a report such as this could be issued by a "state belonging to a great and highly civilized republic . . . It cannot but provoke shock and discouragement on the part of friendly nations like Italy, who have had constant and cordial relations with the United States."[8]

Although on January 29, 1901 President William McKinley recommended that Congress provide indemnities to the Italian government for the crimes committed against Italian subjects, Italy was not satisfied.[9] The Italian government had maintained throughout the ordeal that its fervency in seeking justice had nothing to do with pecuniary motives. As the foreign minister stated in April 1900, the government's involvement "is not for economic gain but for the heinous crime committed not only against Italian subjects, but against the interests and laws of civilization."[10] Although this payment officially brought closure to the investigation of the Tallulah lynching of 1899, it did not serve to ameliorate conditions for Italians in the South.

Lynch mobs would continue to victimize southern Italians as many white Americans called into question not only their racial character and suitability for citizenship but frequently their color status as well.[11] Aside from the most notorious lynching, that of 11 Italian immigrants in New Orleans in 1891, there was a long pattern of violence against Italians. In the 1890s alone, five other lynchings of Italian immigrants occurred in various states. Including 1891, there were three in Louisiana, one in West Virginia and two in Colorado; in Mississippi there were lynchings in 1886 and 1901; one in Arkansas in 1901; one in Florida in 1910; and two in Illinois in 1914 and 1915. In total, 46 Italians were murdered at the hands of lynch mobs. It cannot be stressed enough that the number of Italians lynched never came close to the number of African Americans victimized.[12] Nevertheless, the brutal reality and symbolic nature of lynching served as a powerful reminder to all of the entrenched racial hierarchies in the South.[13]

The perceived racial characteristics of southern Italian immigrants would play the primary role in the sort of racial violence they would experience in the American South at the hands of white mobs. The Tallulah lynching was rumored to have occurred due to the facile manner in which the Italian shopkeepers mingled with the African American community. "Leading citizens" of Tallulah defended the lynching by stating "they were obliged to take the step they did . . . and that to insure white supremacy no other course was possible than the course pursued."[14] One report stated that the people of Tallulah "believe they were justified in the action they took and there is no way of convincing them otherwise. It is the same old story which is ever recurrent . . . the story of the 'maintenance of white supremacy at any cost.'"[15] A contemporary newspaper offered its interpretation of the Tallulah lynching by arguing that in the South "the average man will classify the population as whites, dagoes, and negroes. This is the explanation of the lynching of Italians in Louisiana . . . The unwritten law of the South is that a white man shall not be lynched . . . The only exception is the Italian, who in this respect has been placed on terms of equality with the Negro."[16]

White or Black?

Southern Italian racial characteristics were clearly intertwined with assumptions about whether these immigrants were "white" or "inbetween" white and black.[17] Robert Orsi points out that over the last two centuries the skin color of immigrants to the United States had been darkening as the points of embarkation shifted from northern Europe to southern and eastern Europe, the Caribbean, East Asia, and Mexico, and then again most recently to South Asia and South and Central America. Because the immigration from southern Italy coincided with the great migration northward of southern African Americans, African Caribbeans, and a little later Puerto Ricans and Mexicans, Italians belonged to the first wave of dark-skinned, or "non-white" immigrants.[18] In 1886, Frederick Douglass noted on his European tour that, as one moves southward from Paris to Rome, "he will observe an increase of black hair, black eyes, full lips, and dark complexions."[19] The complexion of these "new immigrants" was raised in Ralph Waldo Emerson's observation regarding his preference for the "old" immigrant. Emerson waxed nostalgically about the immigration that brought the "light complexion, the blue eyes of Europe," rather than "the black eyes, the black drop, the Europe of Europe."[20]

The Federal Government commented in 1907 when the Dillingham Commission on Immigration was appointed by President Theodore Roosevelt to offer Congress a plan to solve the immigration *problem*. The commission consisted of three senators, three representatives, and presidential appointees; it was chaired by Senator William P. Dillingham, who favored immigration restriction, and took more than 3 years and issued 41 volumes of findings. In 1911, the U.S. Immigration Bureau published their purportedly "objective and scientific" study, concluding that the "new" immigrants were harder to assimilate, prone to crime and disease, less literate, and were decidedly less desirable than northern Europeans. In essence, the commission had concluded what they had already assumed to be true before their investigation began and reinforced the conventional negative racial view of the "new" immigrants. In particular, the commission argued that racially the "new" immigrants" from southern and eastern Europe were "unlike the British, German, and other peoples who came during the period prior to 1880."[21] The findings aligned the many nationalities of these immigrants into two major groups and proceeded to fit the evidence into a preset conclusion. In the end, they claimed to have "demonstrated" the divergent nature, or race, of the old and new immigrants.[22]

Volume Five of the Dillingham Commission's findings, titled a *Dictionary of Races or Peoples*, maintained that humanity was divided among the "white, black, yellow, brown, and red races." This categorization would enable the commission to establish that there was a scientifically sanctioned hierarchy of races rooted in the specific skin color of the various peoples. What the commission said about Italians served to reinforce and shape the contours and parameters of racial nativism by separating southern Italians from northern Europeans and linking them with perceived darker races. "It must be remembered," stated the commission, "that the Hamites are not Negrotic or true African, although there may be some traces of an infusion of African blood in this stock in certain communities of Sicily and Sardinia, as well as in northern Africa."[23] However, the *Dictionary of Races or Peoples* noted that members of the Hamitic stock "would be taken by travelers to be Negroes."[24]

The commission had followed the guidelines set forth by the Bureau of Immigration in 1899, which classified arriving immigrants by races or peoples. This list identified some 45 different "races," of which Italians were divided into two parts, northern Italian and southern Italian.[25] This demarcation was crucial in the Commission's findings because it illuminated stark racial differences between the two, noting that, unlike their northern opposites, southern Italian were characterized as a "long-headed, dark, 'Mediterranean' race of short stature." Therefore, a "new" immigrant's ability to assimilate and become a worthy citizen of the republic was questioned, as well as feared. The open door policy that the United States had long advocated was now under scrutiny and liberty was perceived as an ideal only "white" Americans could aspire to and enhance. Indeed, in Thomas Bailey Aldrich's nativist poem, "Unguarded Gates," which appeared in the *Atlantic Monthly* in 1892, he lamented that the United States would one day become the "cesspool of Europe." Aldrich wrote,

> In the street and alley what strange tongues are these
> Accents of menace alien to our air,
> Voices that once the tower of Babel knew!
> O, Liberty, white goddess, is it well
> To leave the gate unguarded?

Liberty wears a white face in Aldrich's vision of an America whose greatness was being sapped by "swarthy" undesirables. The poem, although published in 1892, was later used by Henry Cabot Lodge in his Congressional statement in support of the Literacy Test Bill, which he sponsored in 1896, and it was even entered as testimony into the Dillingham Commission Report's volume on immigration and its restriction.[26]

Although recent scholars have grown accustomed to using the phrase "inbetween" to describe Italian racial status in America, the concept was already being used in the contemporary press of the 1890s. An 1899 headline in a New York newspaper read: "Italians in Louisiana: Lynch Law Applied to Italians Alone Among White Men Because They Are Classed Somewhere Between White Men and Negroes." The newspaper theorized that the southern Italian, "is as it were a link connecting the white and black races. Swarthy in color the Sicilians are darker than the griffes and quadroons, the Negro half-breeds of southern Louisiana."[27]

Ironically, what David Roediger has called the "confusion of inbetweeness" carried over to the southern African American press. In many instances, southern Italians were referred to simply as "white men," while at other times Italians were grouped together with Mexicans and referred to as "darky."[28] The confusion over southern Italian racial identity is most vividly illustrated in a chart in an African American newspaper, *The Richmond Planet*. Listing the number of persons lynched in 1899, the paper printed the "names," "race-or color," "charges made," and "place" where the lynching occurred. Out of a total of 364 lynchings that year, the overwhelming majority came under the racial heading "colored." Ten or so came under the heading "white." The five Italian immigrants who were lynched in Tallulah, Louisiana in 1899 were labeled neither "colored" nor "white" but "Italian."[29] Even through the eyes of American blacks, the southern Italian appeared lost in the confusion of indeterminate racial status.

Although recruited by white planters to replace what were considered "lazy" African American workers, the perception by white Americans that southern Italians immigrants were racially "between" white and black, or in fact a third race, caused concern.[30] Prescott F. Hall, who cofounded the Immigration Restriction League in 1893, believed that the biological fact that southern Italians possessed a "Negro strain," coupled with their indifference to intermarriage with black races, could upend the South's social and political order. According to Hall,

> What would happen if a large Mediterranean population should be colonized in our Southern States and should interbreed with the negro population it finds there? This is not an imaginary possibility, for the dark-skinned races are more likely to settle in the southern part of this country . . . Will the descendants of the emotional, fiery Italians submit to the social judgment that a man with a sixteenth or a thirty-second part of negro blood is a colored man who must occupy a position socially, if not politically, inferior? Assuredly not, and thoughtful Southerners are already alarmed by this prospect.[31]

This "between" status ascribed to Sicilians was partially due to their association with traditional "black labor." Many Sicilian immigrants worked during the "*zuccarata*," or sugar harvest, in the parishes of Louisiana in the same system of farm labor and tenant farming that blacks had traditionally worked. According to the work of Jean Scarpaci, in Louisiana the occupation of landless agricultural laborer bore a double stigma of low status. First, dirty and low paying work remained at the bottom of the occupational scale in a social system that equated job prestige with "clean" and high paying positions. Second, since blacks predominated in this position, the prejudices expressed against them influenced the way in which Sicilians were regarded.[32]

An article in *The New York Sun* in 1899 contended that southern Italians "are willing to live in the same quarters with the Negroes and work side by side with them, and seem wholly destitute of that anti-negro prejudice which is one of the distinguishing features of all the white races in the South."[33] This report, an effort to illuminate the reasons behind the lynching of five Italians in Louisiana in 1899, revealed a great deal about the increasing concern by white southerners over the maintenance of racial hierarchies in the South. Even though in certain sections of the Jim Crow South Italians would be considered white enough to be naturalized and to vote, socially they were seen to represent a problem. The phenotypic differences created confusion on the part of white Southerners as to exactly what color or race these immigrants belonged. Southern newspapers described Italian immigrants in racial terms that ranged from being "black as the blackest Negro in existence," to being "white," or simply as "Dagoes."[34] Some plantation time books illustrated this confusion or "betweeness" by separating African Americans, "Dagoes" and whites in the payroll accounts.[35]

Adding to the consternation on the part of white southerners was that Italian immigrants tended to ignore entrenched racial codes in the South. Interviews with the descendants of plantation workers reveal that Italians did not readily acclimate themselves to the racial norms of the South. Sicilians in Louisiana, the most populous Italian immigrant state in the South, appear to have borne no ill will against African Americans, whom they had no reason to dislike.[36] Scarpaci claims that hailing from such a diverse culture as Sicily, these immigrants came with no predisposition to racial prejudice.[37] Rather, the prevailing attitude of Sicilian immigrants toward African American coworkers appeared to be curiosity or indifference.

Further, because an anticipated labor shortage never developed, job competition between these groups did not become a source of conflict. Although altercations inevitably occurred, racial tension does not appear to have been the source. The daughter of a sugar plantation owner in Louisiana observed with tremendous surprise that given the "stiletto agility of the Italians, and the ability of the negro with the quick razor, it was amazing that we had so few troubles."[38] In fact, the *Times-Democrat* noted the mutual sympathy evident at the burial of the three Italians lynched in 1896, when African Americans and Italians mourned together and "went home from the scene almost terror-stricken." Indeed, many whites feared that the Italians would join with the African Americans to seek revenge for the murders.[39]

Adding to this perception of southern Italians was the indiscriminate manner in which Italian shopkeepers, merchants, and peddlers engaged in business transactions with and sold to African American customers. In Louisiana, commercial activity brought Italian fruit peddlers into direct contact with African Americans. To be sure, however, there were practical reasons for the business relationship. Since in many areas of Louisiana, as well as other counties in the South, the native white population dominated the retail trade, Italian merchants saw the African American community as a splendid market for cheap goods. By catering to this market, Italian peddlers established themselves in a competitive situation by taking their products on the road.[40] Selling fruit or owning saloons in African American communities did not carry much "prestige" for Italians with the white population but offered them economic opportunity. Indeed, the fact that an economic, and hence a social relationship, was forged drew the suspicion and ire of the native white community. The Italian peddlers were known to have employed African Americans, especially young boys, to help them with their fruit vending businesses.[41] After a fight between whites and Italians at a baseball game in Independence, Louisiana, an editorial in the *Daily Picayune* warned that these Italians "are able to make money out of the negroes, and the result is a sort of traffic that causes serious disagreements with the balance of the population."[42]

Scarpaci stated, "direct economic competition for jobs obviously provoked hostility against Italians in Louisiana." Further, she argued that "much of the hostility directed against Italians in a period of crime, as had been the case in the . . . Tallulah [episode], appeared to be connected with economic competition." However, although economic competition was certainly a factor influencing white perceptions of Italians, the "serious disagreements" that the "balance of the population" had with Italians did not rest on economics alone.[43]

***

How white southerners perceived Italians as a race, as well as how they interpreted their economic position and social interaction through the prism of the Jim Crow South, served to situate Italian immigrants on a level with African Americans unlike other European immigrants had experienced in the United States. Given the uncertain racial status of Italian immigrants, the manner in which these newcomers violated standing racial norms provoked suspicion and made southern Italian immigrants vulnerable to racial violence. It was this "between" status that would, at times, "license" white southerners to employ the racial tool of lynching to control Italians, as they had so often with African Americans.

Notes

1. *New Orleans Times-Democrat*, July 24, 1899.
2. *New Orleans Daily States*, July 24, 1899.
3. Edward F. Haas, "Guns, Goats, and Italians: The Tallulah Lynching of 1899," *Journal of the North Louisiana Historical Association* 13, no. 2–3 (Spring–Summer 1982): 50.
4. Haas, "Guns, Goats, and Italians," 52.
5. Italian Consul in New Orleans to Ambassador, January 13, 1900, in Archivio Storico Diplomatico del Ministero degli Affari Esteri [hereafter abbreviated as "ASMAE"], Ambasciata di Washington, busta 103, p8, n1866, "Linciaggio di Tallulah: bills Davis e Hitt: 1900–1901" [hereafter abbreviated as "Washington, 'Linciaggio di Tallulah'"].
6. District Attorney to Governor, Louisiana, March 29, 1900, in ASMAE, Washington, "Linciaggio di Tallulah."
7. Italian Ambassador to Department of State, Washington, DC, April 24, 1900, in ASMAE, Washington, "Linciaggio di Tallulah."
8. Italian Ambassador to Dept. of State, Washington, DC, May 6, 1900, in ASMAE, Washington, "Linciaggio di Tallulah."
9. The United States government paid an indemnity in the amount of $25,000 to the Italian government to be divided among the families of those killed in Tallulah; Haas, "Guns, Goats, and Italians," 54. See also two unidentified newspaper articles, "Indemnity for Tallulah Victims," and "The Lynching of Italians," preserved in ASMAE, Washington, "Linciaggio di Tallulah."

10. Minister of Foreign Affairs, Rome to Italian Ambassador, Washington, DC, April 7, 1900, in ASMAE, Washington, "Linciaggio di Tallulah."

11. Some of the more important work on immigration and whiteness includes Eric L. Goldstein, *The Price of Whiteness: Jews, Race, and American Identity* (Princeton, NJ: Princeton University Press, 2006); Jennifer Guglielmo and Salvatore Salerno, eds., *Are Italians White: How Race is Made in America* (New York: Routledge, 2003); Thomas A. Guglielmo, *White on Arrival: Italians, Race, Color, and Power in Chicago, 1890–1945* (New York: Oxford University Press, 2003); Matthew Frye Jacobson, *Whiteness of a Different Color: European Immigrants and the Alchemy of Race* (Cambridge, MA: Harvard University Press, 1998); Robert Orsi, "The Religious Boundaries of an Inbetween People: Street Feste and the Problem of the Dark-Skinned Other in Italian Harlem, 1920–1990," *American Quarterly* 44 (1992): 313–47; David R. Roediger, *Working Towards Whiteness: How America's Immigrants Became White. The Strange Journey from Ellis Island to the Suburbs* (New York: Basic Books, 2005); Roediger, *The Wages of Whiteness: Race and the Making of the American Working Class* (London: Verso, 1991); Roediger and James Barrett, "Inbetween Peoples: Race, Nationality and the 'New Immigrant' Working Class," *Journal of American Ethnic History* 16 (May 1997): 3–44; Rudolph Vecoli, "Are Italian Americans Just White Folks?" *Italian Americana* 13 (1995): 149–61.

12. During the period when lynching deaths were recorded, beginning in 1882, 85 percent of all victims in American South were black. The percentage is almost certainly higher in light of the many southern lynchings that went unreported. See Colin A. Palmer, *Passageways: An Interpretive History of Black America, vol. 1, 1619–1863* (New York: Harcourt Brace, 1998), 109–10.

13. Rooted in traditions of lawlessness associated with slavery and the strife of reconstruction, lynchings continued to occur in the South with regularity, long after they had become a rarity in other parts of the country. By the late nineteenth century, mob violence associated with lynching had become a distinct symbol of black oppression in the South and a prominent feature of the region's race relations. According to W. Fitzhugh Brundage, "to explain the prevalence of mob violence was to explain much about American attitudes about social order, justice, and race." (See Brundage, ed., *Under Sentence of Death: Lynching in the South* [Chapel Hill: University of North Carolina Press, 1997], 2, 4, and 11). In proportion and significance, lynching remained unmatched outside of the South. The percentage of lynchings that occurred in the South as compared with other regions increased with each decade after the Civil War, rising from 82 percent of American lynchings during the 1880s to more than 95 percent during the 1920s; Palmer, *Passageways*, 1: 109–10.

14. *Times-Democrat*, July 24, 1899.

15. *Daily Picayune*, July 25, 1899.

16. *New York Sun*, August 4, 1899.

17. For work that focuses on the "inbetweenness" of European immigrants see Roediger and Barrett, "Inbetween Peoples"; George E. Cunningham, "The Italian, A Hindrance to White Solidarity, 1890–1898," *Journal of Negro History* 50, no. 1 (January 1965), 22–36; Jean A. Scarpaci, *Italian Immigrants in Louisiana's Sugar Parishes: Recruitment, Labor Conditions, and Community Relations, 1880–1910* (New York: Arno Press, 1980); and Scarpaci, "A Tale of Selective Accommodation: Sicilians and Native Whites in Louisiana," *Journal of Ethnic Studies* 5 (1997): 37–50; Orsi, "Religious Boundaries"; John Higham, *Strangers in the Land: Patterns of American Nativism, 1860–1925*, 2nd ed. (1955; New Brunswick: Atheneum, 1963), esp. 169; Ernesto Milani, "Marchigiani and Veneti on Sunny Side Plantation," in *Italian Immigrants in Rural and Small Town*

America, ed. Rudolph Vecoli (New York: American Italian Historical Association, 1987), 18–30; Vecoli, "Are Italian Americans Just White Folks?"

18. See Orsi, 316.
19. Frederick Douglass, *Autobiographies: Narrative of the Life of Frederick Douglass, and American Slave; My Bondage and My Freedom; Life and Times of Frederick Douglass* (New York: Library of America, 1994), 989.
20. See Higham, 65.
21. United States Immigration Commission, "Abstract," in *Reports of the Immigration Commission*, 41 vols. (Washington, DC, 1911) [hereafter abbreviated as "USIC, *Reports*"], 1:14.
22. USIC, *Reports*, 14:24. See also Thomas Kessner, *The Golden Door: Italian and Jewish Immigrant Mobility in New York City, 1880–1915* (New York: Oxford University Press, 1977), 24–26.
23. USIC, *Reports*, 1:250.
24. USIC, *Reports*, 9:125.
25. USIC, *Reports*, 1:17.
26. Quoted from Thomas Bailey Aldrich, *Unguarded Gates and Other Poems*, (Boston: Houghton Mifflin, 1895), 17. For the text of Lodge's statement, see John J. Appel, ed., *The New Immigration* (New York: Pitman, 1971), 125–32.
27. *New York Sun*, August 4, 1899.
28. *Richmond Planet*, August 26, 1896; *The American Citizen*, August 7, 1891.
29. *Richmond Planet*, August 5, 1899.
30. Jeannie M. Whayne argues that Italian immigrants on an Arkansas plantation were considered a "third race" between blacks and whites. Considered in this status were the fact that they were "poor, Catholic, and spoke little or no English." See Whayne, "Labor Relations and the Evolving Plantation: The Case of Sunnyside," in Whayne, *Shadows Over Sunnyside: An Arkansas Plantation in Transition, 1830–1945* (Fayetteville: University of Arkansas Press, 1993), 35.
31. Prescott F. Hall, "The Future of American Ideals," *North American Review* 195, no. 1 (January 1912), 94–102; especially 99. Discussing the racial composition of the southern Italian in particular, Hall added "the South Italian, which constitutes the largest element in our present immigration, is one of the most mixed races in Europe and is partly African, owing to the negroid migration from Carthage to Italy" (95).
32. Scarpaci, *Italian Immigrants*, 219.
33. *New York Sun*, August 4, 1899.
34. Cunningham, "The Italian," 34.
35. Scarpaci, *Italian Immigrants*, 222.
36. Ibid., 152.
37. Ibid., 277.
38. Florence Dymond, Box 453, Folder 10, titled "Grinding," in the Florence Dymond Collection, Howard Tilton Memorial Library, Tulane University, New Orleans, LA.
39. Cunningham, "The Italian," 32.
40. Scarpaci, *Italian Immigrants*, 211–12.
41. Ibid., 150.
42. Ibid., 254.
43. Ibid., 253–55. Richard Gambino also puts emphasis on the economic factors leading to the 1891 lynching of 11 Italians in New Orleans. See his *Vendetta: The True Story of the Largest Lynching in U.S. History*, 2nd ed. (1977; Toronto: Guernica, 1999).

3

"Utterly Faithless Specimens"

Italians in the Catholic Church in America

Peter R. D'Agostino

Discrimination takes on many shapes and sizes. Sorting out "types" of anti-Italian discrimination and stereotypes is no simple matter. Even with a particular focus on the Roman Catholic Church in the United States, as in this essay, it is difficult to ignore scientific racism, struggles within the U.S. labor movement, and demeaning images in popular culture. For the sake of clarity, however, I will limit my focus to two broad issues central to anti-Italian discrimination in the history of the Catholic Church in the United States: (1) discrimination within the American Catholic community resulting from the unification of Italy; and (2) anti-Italian discrimination within the American Catholic community resulting from particular aspects of the "religiosity" or devotional "style" of Italians.

The Risorgimento and the Roman Question

The unification of Italy, which is to say the Risorgimento movement of 1848–1870, inspired aggressive condemnations from Pope Pius IX (1846–1878), who ruled the Papal States of central Italy. Even before the movement for Italian unification, the papacy had condemned the content of liberal ideology central to the Enlightenment and the French and American Revolutions. Freedom of speech, freedom of the press, religious liberty, separation of church and state—all of these "modern" notions earned papal censure before Pius's ascension to the papal throne.

Italian nationalists were divided between relatively conservative liberal monarchists, many of whom were thoughtful and practicing Catholics, and republican anticlericals. Both factions eventually accepted that the Papal States were a "medieval" anachronism legitimated through outdated absolutist conceptions of sovereignty. Ultimately, the Kingdom of Sardinia under the House of Savoy conquered the Papal States, which were annexed into the new Kingdom of Italy, proclaimed in 1861. In 1870, on September 20, King Vittorio Emanuele II's army conquered papal Rome itself and soon thereafter the capital of the kingdom was transferred from Florence to Rome.

Pius, humiliated and infuriated, excommunicated all those involved in the unification of Italy. He refused to recognize the legitimacy of the new state, forbid Catholics to run for national office and vote in national elections, and called upon European powers to restore him to his kingship over the lost Papal States. Pope Leo XIII (1878–1903) shared the same goal. He bargained unsuccessfully with Germany, Austria, and France to restore the papacy's lands in central Italy. In fact, every pope from 1861 to 1929 refused to recognize the Italian kingdom and called themselves "prisoners of the Vatican," suggesting that their spiritual independence, necessary to run a world church, had been compromised by their loss of temporal power.

This "Roman Question" was central to papal and Italian diplomacy from 1861 to 1929, when the Kingdom of Italy (under fascism) and the papacy agreed to the Lateran Treaties, which created the Vatican City and won Italy formal recognition from the Vatican. But before 1929, succeeding popes made every effort to win back their lost temporal dominions. Their strategy had several parts. First, they called upon European powers to destabilize Italy (even if it meant a republican revolution) and to restore the pope's temporal power. Second, the popes called upon Catholics in all states to pressure their governments to support the pope's bid for temporal sovereignty. Third, the popes struggled to gain a hearing at international conferences (such as the Peace Conference at Versailles after World War I) in order to try to convince powers other than Italy to take up the "Roman Question." At such moments, the Vatican hoped, foreign states would have to accommodate their outspoken Catholic populations calling for the pope's temporal power. Ultimately, none of these strategies worked, but the effort to employ them is germane to our concerns.

The second strategy in particular is central to the rise of anti-Italian discrimination in the U.S. Catholic Church. The papacy and the Church underwent a profound transformation in the nineteenth century, generally called the "Catholic revival." The papal concern for the temporal power deeply shaped this revival that revolutionized church doctrine and practice. Because the Vatican contended that the modern liberal world was pagan and had fallen to satanic influence, the papacy took unprecedented steps to promote Marian devotions, pilgrimages, public expressions of belief in the supernatural, devotions to saints, and Catholic educational and welfare institutions (and in some instances political parties). The creation of a veritable subculture of Catholic life would protect Catholics from the dangers of modern liberal societies, and cultivate a profound and intense loyalty to the institutions of the Church and their Holy Father, the prisoner of the Vatican, the pope. The theological expression of this altogether new and modern (or rather antimodern) cult to the papacy was the proclamation of papal infallibility in 1870.

Within this worldview, Italian statesmen and loyal subjects of the Italian king were prison wardens, using Italian nationalism as a pretext to crucify the sacred pontiff on a Calvary called the Vatican. Dramatic public displays and rituals to remind Catholics throughout the world about the evil events of the Risorgimento became institutionalized, and over a generation anti-Risorgimento attitudes became part and parcel of the modern Catholic identity. In short, the Catholicism familiar to an older generation who came of age before Vatican Council II (1962–1965), so thick with parochial schools, hospitals, parish sodalities, Catholic fraternal societies, Catholic Youth Organization (CYO) programs, devotional practices to saints and the Virgin, dietary restrictions, and a distinctive neo-Thomistic philosophy, was constructed between 1861 and 1929 to promote the pope's liberation from evil Italian liberals, Masons, Jews, and revolutionaries.

The Catholic revival had a profound impact on European and American liberals, Protestants, and Jews, who feared that Catholic power might disrupt liberal democratic institutions. Although the impact of the Catholic revival was not uniform, the Church in the United States was deeply transformed by the revival. Within a generation, before the 1880s when large numbers of Italians arrived in the United States, most of the American hierarchy was composed of Irish and Germany bishops deeply loyal to the pope and committed to his struggle against his Italian enemies.

I do not have the space here to demonstrate how thoroughly Catholics loyal to the papacy (of all nationalities) took up cudgels against any and all expressions of Italian national identity. But it is fair to say that every Italian holiday, patriotic demonstration, and display of solidarity with the *patria*, especially those that hosted an Italian consul, was met with *Catholic* resistance. On occasion, Italian Catholics (particularly priests) organized that resistance, but generally Irish Catholics embodied the Catholic ideological position against liberal Italian nationalism. As John Talbot Smith explained in 1905, "nothing more hateful to American Catholics could be named than the 20th of September, which the Italian colony [of New York] celebrated as the consummation of national glory ... For very slight cause the Irish would at any moment have attacked the annual procession, eager to drive the Garibaldians off the face of the earth ... and as for considering [Italians] Catholics and aiding them to keep their faith alive, that was out of the question."

Several points must be stressed to conclude our discussion of this type of discrimination. This was an ideological battle, not an ethnic conflict, which is generally how scholars have portrayed this form of discrimination. That is, Irish American *Catholic* animosity should not be confused with Irishness in general. Many Americans of Irish descent in the United States were Protestants, who consistently sided with Italian liberals against Catholics in these skirmishes. Furthermore, those Irish Americans who had radical commitments—to socialism, to violent forms of Irish nationalism not condoned by the Church, to the Wobblies, and so on—were also not interested in upsetting Italian American festive culture. If this implies that there were a variety of Irish national identities—Protestant, Catholic, socialist, and so on—the same was true of Italians.

For instance, the papacy encouraged many Italian national celebrations so long as those celebrations were expressions of Italian *Catholic* nationalism, and not Italian *liberal* nationalism. In some instances, Italian Catholic parish societies were permitted to march with the Italian tricolor flag so long as the flag was employed as a symbol of a region of Italy. Or the Italian tricolor flag was permissible for Catholics in a celebration that had nothing to do with the Italian *state*, but only represented the Italian *nation*, that is, the people themselves. (The situation can be likened to Cubans in Florida today, who certainly are Cuban nationalists, although the Cuban nation they claim to represent is not properly represented by the communist state of Fidel Castro).

The discrimination Italians in the U.S. Church often encountered was a result of the inability or unwillingness of American clergy and laity (often, but not always, of Irish descent), disrupting or refusing to permit Italian *Catholic* national celebrations, celebrations that the pope himself permitted in Italy. For instance, some American bishops refused to allow Italians in the United States to celebrate a high requiem Mass for their slain monarch, King Umberto I, in 1900. These American Catholics simply would not countenance the presence of Italian national symbols in their parish churches or cathedrals, in honor of a king whose father had "usurped" the papal dominions. But Pope Leo permitted those same services in Italy and the Vatican informed the American Catholic Church leaders that requiem Masses were permissible.

Italian Catholic Religiosity

Many historians have pointed out, and many Italian Americans themselves can recount, how their particular "style" of religiosity met with harsh criticism from fellow Catholics in the United States. What was this "style"? It consisted of a strong devotion to the cult of saints, a deeply Marian piety that was therefore less Christocentric, an absence of sacramental regularity in favor of familial and lay religious practices such as home altars, Mediterranean penitential rites, mourning rituals, healing techniques, elaborate public *feste*, extensive use of candles to aid in prayer, and lastly, the presence of heterodox forms of magic.

Until a generation ago, many historians and anthropologists suggested that the Mezzogiorno—southern Italy, the origin of most Italian immigrants to the United States—was an ahistorical, unchanging land. Recently, social historians and historical anthropologists have challenged static notions of religion and society in the Mezzogiorno. But previously, two theories of southern Italian Catholicism had developed that posited an unbridgeable gulf between "official Catholicism" and the peasantry. The first theory contended the real religion of the Mezzogiorno was an atavistic remnant of Greco-Roman paganism with a superficial veneer of Catholicism. The Christian veneer was merely a *religiosità esteriore* (exterior religiosity), form without authentic moral (i.e., Christian) content. This argument, I would suggest, was deeply flawed. Taken to its logical conclusion, this theory implies that Christian meanings imparted to Christmas trees, episcopal vestments, the Latin language, ancient church architecture, many hymns, exorcism Masses, and much of the orthodox Church calendar, to mention only a few examples, are actually cloaked paganism. This Protestant (and puritanical) critique of Catholicism has been replicated by social scientists.

The second theory contended that the southern Italian religion consisted of two unrelated, parallel systems practiced by two antagonistic and independent social groups: magic among subaltern classes, and "official Catholicism" among elite. This theory asserted that clergy and elite inhabited a culture distinct from the peasants. Two parallel universes, two different cultures—one elite, one peasant—never met, and never influenced one another.

A strange company of bedfellows promoted variations of these two theories. Scientific racists, Romantic folklorists, American students of immigration, conservative post-WWII anthropologists, and outspoken Italian American advocates of the "ethnic revival" of the 1970s all adopted notions that southern Italians were radically "other" and that their religiosity deviated fundamentally from that of other Catholics. Most famously, Carlo Levi's memoir, *Cristo si è fermato a Eboli* (1945), popularized an ahistorical rendering of the Mezzogiorno. Described as a "people without history," southern Italian villagers appeared as European Orientals in Levi's seductive prose. Translated into English in 1947 and made into a popular film, *Christ Stopped at Eboli* remains a favorite among scholars attached to romantic notions of Mezzogiorno peasants, and writers eager to convey the "otherness" of southern Italians isolated for millennia in an unchanging world of myth. This is not the place for an historical survey of the role of the Church in southern Italy from the early modern era to the period of mass migration. Needless to say, great strides have been made by historians in the last three decades to shatter the image of an unchanging, Mezzogiorno untouched by the Reformation, the Enlightenment, industrial capitalism, secular ideologies, and the Italian state after 1861.

But knowing what we do, it remains interesting that Italian penitential rites, mourning rituals, healing techniques, *feste*, and extensive use of candles to aid in prayer, generated a heated, public debate over the "Italian Problem" for two generations among English-speaking American Catholics. One wonders why were there no debates among Polish, French, Slovak, or Italian-speaking Catholics about the orthodoxy of Irish wakes? Answering these questions means addressing ethnic perceptions and power relationships within American Catholic culture.

Italians entered a Catholic Church in the United States plagued with ethnic conflicts. English-speaking Catholics controlled positions of power and aspired to reign over a middle-class Church and acquire the respectability it afforded. Italian migrants, however, came with no plans to settle permanently in the United States. Largely "birds of passage," they refused to invest resources in churches. Furthermore, they ignored parish boundaries (drawn and redrawn in distinctly American ways) which excluded them from participation in familiar *feste* and devotions in parishes other than their own. The frustration, embarrassment, and anxiety Italians created among their clergy and English-speaking Catholics generated harsh rhetoric deployed to discipline the newcomers. This rhetoric conflated resistance to pay pew rents or church entrance fees with heterodoxy, and it confused a style of worship with an inability to meet standards of hygiene that upwardly mobile Catholics aspired to.

Herbert Hadley, in the Jesuit magazine *America*, offers a typical example of this harsh rhetoric in an attack on Italian religiosity published in 1914: "Thousands upon thousands of boys and girls beyond the age of sixteen know nothing of their prayers, nothing of their catechism and have never even been instructed for or made their First Communion or Confession. The Italian . . . outside of a display at baptisms, marriages and funerals . . . has little attachment to the Church, its services or its sacraments."

"Piety," Hadley catechized, "does not consist in processions or carrying lighted candles, in prostrations before a statue of the Madonna, in processions in honor of the patron saints of villages." Instead, ". . . true piety consists in the daily fulfillment of the religious duties exacted of us by God Almighty and His Church and it consists in a love for that Church and her ministers. In these points . . . the Italian immigrant seems very deficient."

When others asserted that these Italian practices expressed an authentic piety, an anonymous priest, frustrated by his 15-year failure to "arouse [Italians] from their religious lethargy," joined the editorial fray in support of Hadley. "Their religion, what there is of it, is exterior." He recounted a visit to an Italian church: "Devotees came to visit, as I first imagined, the Most Blessed Sacrament, but to my surprise and, will I say my disgust, their devotion consisted in lighting candles, prostrating themselves before statues, going from shrine to shrine from side altar to side altar, side-tracking altogether the main altar wherein reposed the Saviour." U.S. bishops controlled and frequently forbade Italians' noisy, emotional, public spectacles of piety. In Boston, anxious priests requested episcopal permission for these breaches of propriety. "My parishioners are going to have a May procession. Really I am against it, but I wish to avoid troubles. Humbly I beg you to give the permission." In this case, authorization came on the condition that "this procession may be carried out with due religious decorum." An Italian Franciscan serving Sicilians on Boston's North End complained of such frequent requests. "To the Sacraments they do not care to go, but feasts and processions, yes, with panagiric [sic] every Sunday so much so that the Priests have no chance to preach the Gospel to the people wich [sic] is of grator [sic] necessity then all the panangiric [sic] and feasts of the Saints." The diocese of Providence granted permission for outdoor processions, "provided . . . that the procession is to be around the [parish] Church, and not around the [public] square." A Philadelphia pastor apologized to Archbishop Dennis Dougherty for failure to keep a timely schedule for Masses. "Owning to the big crowd, particularly when the different Italian societies celebrate their different saints . . . we are compelled to wait a few minutes, so that the people go in and out of the church . . . The Italians are not much in keeping time, those especially from south Italy."

Italian disobedience did not sit well with coreligionists and generated dehumanizing rhetoric. In order to resist the suppression of Our Lady of Good Counsel parish in 1933, South Philadelphia Italians kidnapped an Augustinian priest and physically occupied the church building. An irate "Catholic Lady" reported to Archbishop Dougherty,

> these uncivilized Italians, had taken down the doors of the Church, women were standing in the entrance of the Church with NO HATS ON THEIR HEADS, men standing in the entrance with LIT CIGARS in their mouth. Those in the Church yard were acting like a crowd of WILD CATTLE . . . It is a pity that Americans in the Catholic Faith are forced to listen to all kinds of SLURS from NON CATHOLICS in places of employment, in grocery stores, etc because of these UNCIVILIZED, IGNORANT, ITALIANS who call themselves CATHOLICS. As everyone knows only too

well that class of Catholics give [*sic*] little or NO financial support to any of the Catholic Churches in the city. (emphasis in the original)

In the midst of the conflict, one Mrs. O'Donnell from a nearby parish warned Dougherty of death threats against him: "This subject is the talk of the whole town . . . Why must you endanger your life for that little parish . . . You do not know the Italians when they are angry they are wild . . . especially those Sicilian men, they are likely to do any harm . . . You're a marked man."

Efforts to extract money from Italians generated English-speaking Catholics' greatest frustration. Ironically, as they violated their own canons, U.S. bishops and their diocesan clergy condemned Italians as ignorant, stubborn, and heterodox. Italian immigrants protested the enforced pew rents and entrance fees to American churches so frequently in letters to the Vatican that Apostolic Delegate Diomede Falconio issued a circular letter to U.S. bishops. Falconio reminded the U.S. episcopacy that the Holy See's Sacred Congregation of Propaganda Fide in 1869, Pope Pius IX in 1862, and the Second (1866) and Third (1884) Plenary Councils of Baltimore regulating the Church in the United States, had all condemned pew rents and entrance fees.

In short, Italian religiosity generated revulsion among English-speaking Catholics striving for middle-class respectability in the United States. American Catholic leaders refused, for the most part, to address these particular difficulties. Ignoring the problems in their midst, U.S. bishops at the Third Plenary Council of Baltimore (1884) refused to comply with the Vatican's recommendations to engage the issues Italian migration had raised for the Church. As Bishop Thomas Becker of Wilmington (Delaware) complained, "It is a very delicate matter to tell the Sovereign Pontiff how utterly faithless the specimens of his country coming here really are. Ignorance of their religion and a depth of vice little known to us yet, are their prominent characteristics."

Note

This essay is indebted to two of my works to which I refer readers interested in pursuing the sources from which this discussion was developed: Peter R. D'Agostino, *Rome in America: Transnational Catholic Ideology from the Risorgimento to Fascism* (Chapel Hill: University of North Carolina Press, 2004); and Peter R. D'Agostino, "Orthodoxy or Decorum? Missionary Discourse, Religious Representations, and Historical Knowledge," *Church History* 72 (2003): 703–35.

4

Perversions of Knowledge

Confronting Racist Ideologies
behind Intelligence Testing

Elizabeth G. Messina

The force of American racism fell with all its accustomed ferocity on the recent immigrants, making them ideological scapegoats . . . Italian American protest against the unjust stigma of their identity was silenced. The grandparents and parents who had experienced the brunt of the worst injustices of American cultural racism refused to speak of their experience, let alone to explore the burdens racism had unjustly imposed on their sense of themselves, including their ambitions and aspirations. Their grandchildren in consequence know little of this history . . . But failures to make sense of important cultural memories . . . thus deprive one of the resources better to understand [the past] and . . . to refuse complicity with comparable injustices today.

—David Richards, *Italian American: The Racializing of an Ethnic Identity*

The plight of Italian American immigrants is one of a list of prejudicial abuses affecting immigrants of many cultures trying to make their home in America as we'll see through our exploration of one the darkest chapters in the history of American psychology. Nearly a century ago, race psychologists stigmatized Italian Americans as a *genetically* inferior identity group. The success of Italian Americans today is complicated by the persistence of negative stereotypes of Italian Americans in the media industry as ignorant buffoons or criminals who are not particularly well developed intellectually (as in *The Sopranos*; the Italian protagonists of the *Oz* series, who are called "the Guineas"; the movie *My Cousin Vinny*; and the syndicated television recycling of *Who's the Boss?*, *Taxi*, and *Welcome Back Kotter*).[1] Many have failed to take notice, or to take seriously, the discrepancies between the success of Italian Americans today and the ongoing widespread negative portrayals of them in the media. No other European ancestry group in America who migrated at the turn of the century continues to be so blatantly defamed and stigmatized.

The purpose of this essay is to generate awareness of one of many origins of the stigmatization and pernicious stereotyping of Italian Americans as an innately intellectually inferior identity group that has persisted into the twenty-first century. In this chapter, a systematic critique of psychology's early intelligence testing research on Italian Americans and the dynamic interaction between politics, history, and psychology in the early part of the twentieth century that created the myth and stereotype of the innate intellectual inferiority of Italian immigrants and their children will be examined. The role of Italian American social activist, Leonard Covello, in challenging eugenic orthodoxy about Italian immigrants will be discussed briefly. Finally, the impact of psychology's early intelligence testing research on the intergenerational educational experiences of Italian Americans will also be explored. It is my hope that by identifying gaps in our knowledge of the history of Italian Americans, untruths will be supplanted by accurate memories of the experiences of many of those who came before us.

The Origins of a Stigma

Social science researchers have observed that stigmatization is a universal and socially defined feature of human life. In ancient Greek society, criminals and traitors were physically stigmatized by marks (created by slicing the skin with a knife or by using hot irons to brand the skin). Such a mark was called a "stigma" to alert Greek citizens that an individual bearing a stigma was to be "scorned and avoided."[2]

Contemporary psychologists consider such practices to be a behavioral manifestation of the more general practice of *psychological stigmatization*, which is defined "as the process of intellectually marking an individual as possessing a negative attribute so discrediting that it engulfs other views of the individual."[3] In various forms, and at different historical periods in American history, Italian Americans have been psychologically stigmatized as intellectually inferior, undesirable second-tier citizens.

Historically, those who are poor or racially and ethnically different have been the targets of stigmatization. Stigmatization may arise from motivations to justify or rationalize the status quo in a society that often involves institutional forms of discrimination and segregation that serve both individual and group functions.[4] Some theorists argue that one of the social purposes of stigmatization is to identify individuals who pose a threat to the status quo or who hinder the interests or success of their own group (i.e., control of political, social, and economic resources). The behavioral manifestations of stigmatization are motivated by the fear that the "other" (which is to say the "new immigrants") will deplete or usurp resources of the dominant group.[5]

Sociopolitical and Historical Contexts of the Stigmatization of Italian Immigrants

The enduring images and perceptions of Americans of Italian ancestry found in psychology's early intelligence testing literature mirrored many of the attitudes and feelings of American society during the period of the great migration (1890–1920). The extraordinary economic, technological, and cultural changes in the pre– and post–World War I era sent the nation tumbling into modernity, leaving Americans disoriented, confused, and anxious. Many Americans focused their anxiety on the millions of "new immigrants" from the southern and eastern European "races" who crowded their cities. Americans were coping with changes brought about by a rapidly growing urban, industrial capitalist society and Italian immigrants, among others, posed yet another threat to American's sense of national stability.

The impact of the *perceived threats* to changes in the status quo (politically, economically and socially) led Americans to *displace* their anxiety, hostility, and aggression onto the millions of immigrants entering the United States who were different than the "old immigrants." After 1890, the majority of "new immigrants" left southern and eastern Europe (Italy, Russia, Balkans) for the United States. In previous decades, most immigrants to America had been northern and western Europeans from Scandinavia, Germany, and the British Isles. Most of the "new immigrants" were neither Protestant nor wealthy; they were poor and less educated than the "old immigrants" that preceded them.

The rise in the belief in Anglo-Saxon superiority and society's fear that foreigners were invading their country justified a growing faith in "white supremacy"—the superiority of the northern European or "Nordic" American "race." Race-based nativism created a "generation of eugenicists, conservatives and reactionaries" in the United States who forged new theories of race and initiated studies of "the alien menace."[6] These new intellectual ideas predicted that inferior hereditary traits of "new immigrants" would lead to the nation's decline and to the demise of democracy itself.

In order to justify the unjust treatment and exploitation of those who are racially or ethnically different, people form a variety of "justification ideologies" to justify and rationalize their increasing hostility and discrimination against "new immigrants." By escalating the rhetoric of threat of the "alien menace," eugenicists could both justify and rationalize their increasingly hostile and discriminatory behavior against "new immigrants." Justification ideologies endorse prejudice and discrimination that social norms would suppress and ordinarily find unacceptable.[7]

Eugenicism and Psychology's Intelligence Testing Movement

"Eugenics" is a term coined by Francis Galton in 1883, derived from a Greek root meaning "good birth" or "well born."[8] Galton believed that heredity, not environmental opportunity structures, determined human behavior and intelligence. Although eugenics was a broad coalition of groups promoting similar and divergent scientific, social, and political policies, most shared a belief that obtaining scientific control over processes governing human heredity would provide benefits to society.[9] Eugenicists believed that all men *are not born equal* and that white Americans and northern and western Europeans, in particular, were superior to all other racial groups. In the early 1900s, American eugenicists, scientists, and policy makers embarked on the pursuit of "racial purity" goals similar to those embraced by the Nazis.[10] Eugenicists believed that a biologically bad "stock" of "new immigrants" would create a nation of people "whose multiplying here is likely to lower the average [White population and intelligence] of our people."[11]

Pioneers of the American intelligence testing movement—Lewis Terman of Stanford University, Robert Yerkes of Harvard University, and Henry Goddard of the Vineland Training School of New Jersey—were involved in the eugenicist movement prior to the development of intelligence tests. These racist psychologists generally accepted the idea that there was a hierarchy of races with northern and western Europeans at the top, and southern and eastern Europeans at the bottom. The "Aryan" and "Nordic" races were thought to be racially distinct from and superior to the "Latin" and "Mediterranean" races.

They believed that the intelligence test could provide a fixed measure of innate intelligence. In their view, the average difference in IQs between the "races" was determined by "genetic" factors. They believed that the intelligence test could be used to detect genetically inferior racial groups whose high birth rates posed a "menace to the future of the state."[12] Moreover, eugenicist psychologists advocated for the preservation of the "racial purity" of American society by supporting policies restricting immigration of racial groups who were shown to have innately inferior intelligence.

Eugenicist Psychologists and the Development of the Army Alpha and Beta Intelligence Tests during World War I

During the pre– and post–First World War period the Army Alpha intelligence test (a written paper and pencil test) and the Beta intelligence tests (a nonverbal performance test that did not require the draftee to read) were developed by psychologists led by Robert Yerkes of Harvard University, who was then president of the American Psychological Association.

The Army's Alpha and Beta tests were designed to determine innate differences in intelligence between American-born citizens and foreign-born draftees. Although the tests were allegedly intended to aid in job placement of draftees they were, in fact, not used for placement of men.[13] W. E. B. Dubois (1920) commented that these tests were just one more effort to prove "scientifically" that northern Europeans were superior to all others.[14]

During World War I, approximately 1,726,000 draftees and recruits stationed across 24 camps across the nation were used to try out these new intelligence tests. The Army Alpha and Beta Tests were typically administered in open-air Army tents with soldiers sitting side by side at long tables. Test administrators stood on platforms at the front of the tent with whistles in hand. The whistles were used to signal when to begin and end each subtest. Test instructions were given in the form of commands (e.g., "When I call attention, stop instantly . . . Do just what you are told to do. Ask no questions . . .").[15] The draftee was required to answer as many questions as possible, within a given amount of time. Each successive question within each subtest increased in its degree of difficulty. Every subtest was rigidly timed.

The Army Alpha Tests consisted of eight timed subtests as described below:[16]

1. Alpha Test of Following Directions: The person is presented with a row of circles and is asked by the examiner to mark a cross in the first circle and the number one in the third circle. The person then completes the same sequence of symbols across a row of circles. Time limit: five seconds

2. Alpha Arithmetic Test: a series of 20 arithmetic questions ranging from easy ones to more difficult ones involving mental computations and reasoning problems. (For example, "If you save $7 a month for four months how much will you save?" Time limit: five minutes.)

3. Alpha Test of Practical Judgment: Items in which a person must explain why certain practices are desirable or what course of action is preferred under certain circumstances. The test is a multiple-choice format. (For example, "Why do we use stoves?" (1) They look well. (2) They keep us warm. (3) They are black. "Why are doctors useful? "Why is tennis good exercise?" "Why ought every man to be educated?" (1) Roosevelt was educated. (2) It makes a man more useful. (3) It cost money. (4) Some educated people are wise. There are 16 items. Time limit: 1.5 minutes).

4. Alpha Synonym-Antonym Test: In order to assess vocabulary, the person is asked to identify whether a series of ten paired words are alike or opposite in meaning The person is presented with ten pairs and is asked to underline whether or not each pair has the same or opposite meaning. (For example, "perfunctory—meticulous": same or opposite?; "vesper—matins": same or opposite? Time limit: 1.5 minutes)

5. Alpha Disarranged Sentence Test: The person is presented with 20 sentences in which the words are scrambled. The person is asked to rearrange the words into a coherent sentence and mark whether the statement is true or false. For example, "property floods life and destroy" True or False. (Floods destroy property and life.)

6. Alpha Number Checking Test: A person is asked to look at a row of numbers and to complete the two numbers that should follow a particular sequence. (For example, 9, 1, 7. 1. 5. 1. _ _. Twenty items were to be completed within three minutes.)

7. Alpha Test of Verbal Analogies: Pairs of words have the same or opposite meanings. (For example, tears: sorrow:: laughter: joy:: *smile, girls, grin.* Forty items were to be completed within three minutes.)

8. Alpha Test of General Information: presented a series of *40* questions that assessed a range of information most Americans were expected to possess. The questions were presented in a multiple-choice format. (For example, "Nabisco is a: patent, b: medicine, c: disinfectant, d: food-product, e: toothpaste"; "Identify the color of chlorine gas" [green]; "the author of *Robinson Crusoe*" [Defoe]).

The Army Beta Test was a picture test developed for illiterate draftees. Illiteracy was determined by a variety of methodologies: in some camps, anyone who could not read any English at all was determined to be illiterate; in others, anyone who could not write their name within 30 seconds or who had not completed fourth grade was determined to be illiterate.

The Beta Test is a nonverbal pictorial measure that did not rely on reading skill or familiarity with the English language. Performance tests, like the Army Beta, try to avoid some of the more obvious biases of verbal materials by, for example, asking the draftee to complete incomplete drawings, or by identifying relationships between various geometric forms. Test administrators displayed pictorial test items on a blackboard and demonstrated through gestures how to respond to a sample test item. The Army Beta Test consisted of seven subtests that were also timed. The Beta subtests are described below.

1. Beta Picture Completion Test: The person is presented with 20 pictures and has to identify which part is missing in each picture. (For example, there is a picture of a rabbit with one ear. The missing part is the second ear. The examinee has to draw the missing ear on the figure. Maximum time: three minutes)

2. Beta Substitution Test: The person is required to complete a series of 12 different patterns made up of crosses and zeroes. (For example, there is a box across the width of the page beginning with the following pattern: xox . The examinee is required to reproduce the pattern across the width of the paper (e.g., xox xox xox etc.) Maximum time: two minutes.

3. Beta Digit Symbol Test: A task in which symbols are to be matched with numbers on the basis of a code given to a person on the examination paper. Maximum time: three minutes.

4. Beta Mazes Test: The person must trace the correct route from a starting point to home on a series of five mazes. Maximum time: two minutes.

5. Beta Cube Analysis Test: The person is presented with 16 sets of small blocks drawn on the examination paper. The person has to count the number of blocks in each set. Maximum time: 2.5 minutes.

6. Beta Geometrical Construction Test: Paper Form Board Problems: The person is presented with a square on the examination paper. To the left of each square are three different geometrical forms (e.g., a triangle). The person has to draw a line in the square to show how it could be constructed from varying geometrical forms. There are ten squares accompanied by various adjacent geometrical figures. Maximum time: 2.5 minutes.

7. Beta Number Checking Test: The person is required to check 50 pairs of numbers and mark an "X" against those that are not exactly the same. Maximum time: three minutes.

Readers may decide for themselves whether these specimens from the Army Alpha and Beta intelligence tests fairly measured the intelligence (IQ or "intelligence quotient") of the literate or illiterate foreign-born draftees.

Most of the verbal and nonverbal content of the Army Alpha and Beta tests was culture specific and culturally biased. Test scores were heavily influenced by familiarity with American culture and language, even when "nonverbal" performance tests were used. Moreover, most of the foreign-born draftees had not been exposed to formal schooling, and lacked test taking experience and, therefore, had not acquired the academic abilities or experiences necessary to perform well on either of these tests.

In short, these tests measured what one has learned in school rather than how one *uses* his or her intelligence. To attribute racial differences in intelligence to genetics, rather than to whether or not a person has had an opportunity to acquire the skills, knowledge, and experience necessary to perform well on these tests, is not a conclusion of science but rather a perversion of it. The army test results had clear political implications for the foreign born.

The Relationship between Intelligence Testing and Exclusionary Immigration Laws

The "new science" of intelligence testing generated data of profound social and political significance. Shortly after the war, psychologists conducted an analysis of intelligence test data of a sample of 12,407 foreign-born draftees. A letter grade from "A" to "E" was awarded to each draftee based on their test performance: "A" draftees scored the highest score,[17] "C" was average, and "E" the lowest score.[18] Their analysis confirmed that northern European draftees ranked highest, while draftees from southeastern Europe ranked lowest.[19] *Italian draftees ranked second lowest ("D" grade) to all other foreign draftees, except the Polish.*[20] The army data became known to Congress with the assistance of several "scientific" committees formed by psychologists to provide "relevant scientific information" to government agencies. The proportion of Grade A through D men of various national origins was depicted in a series of charts that were displayed during Congressional hearings on the restriction of immigration. This ranking of human groups on the Army Alpha and Beta Tests obtained political and scientific legitimacy in the United States Congress.

In 1920, the Eugenics Research Association, under Yerkes's leadership, formed the Division of Anthropology and Psychology and the Committee on the Scientific Problem of Human Migration.[21] Several experimental psychologists and biologists joined the association and one of its members, a biologist, Harry H. Laughlin, PhD, was appointed by the committee to the position of "Expert Eugenic Agent" of the House Committee on Immigration and Naturalization of the United States Congress.

In 1921, the National Academy of Sciences published the results of the analysis of Army data in a book edited by Robert M. Yerkes. The book was published during the same year that the United States Congress passed legislation that placed an immigration quota on southeastern European immigrants (The Emergency Quota Act of 1921). Yerkes's report had a significant impact on the national debate on immigration as well as the debates in Congress led by the Committee on Immigration and Naturalization. In a chapter written by Yerkes, he reported that the highest percentage of "D" grades was found among southeastern European immigrants (Italian, Polish, and Russians).[22] Yerkes, along with several other eugenicist psychologists, drew broad conclusions from the low scores earned by these foreign draftees and used data to confirm the innate inferiority of foreign races and to argue for new laws restricting immigration by national origin.

In a political climate already predisposed toward restricting immigration by country of origin, several works by other psychologists were published confirming popular prejudices. For example, Carl Brigham, a former army tester, then a Princeton University psychologist, reanalyzed the Army test data in great detail. He used the scores of African American draftees as a baseline for comparison of the intelligence of different racial groups. Brigham's interpretation of the data showed that 42 percent of Italian draftees scored at or below the scores of "Negroe" draftees.[23] Eugenic scientists reported that the intelligence of "new immigrants" was "nearer the intelligence of the average negro . . . than to the intelligence of American Whites."[24]

Numerous social scientists connected theories of racial differences in intelligence with the need for immigration restriction. In his book, *American Intelligence* (1923), published by Princeton University Press, Brigham wrote that we can "assume we are measuring native or inborn intelligence [and] we are forced to . . . accept the hypothesis that . . . [there is] a gradual deterioration in the class of immigrants examined in the army who came to this country." To Brigham, the decline in immigrant intelligence, as assessed by the Army intelligence tests, "supported Mr. Madison Grant's thesis of the superiority of the Nordic type."[25] American intelligence was, according to Brigham, in danger of declining in direct proportion to the number of new immigrants who arrived in the country possessing "inferior blood." There was concern that "new immigrants" were multiplying in numbers that would threaten the survival of white Americans and eventually lower the average intelligence of American citizens.

Brigham urged that a law be devised to reduce the number of "new immigrants." Brigham argued that "steps should be taken . . . dictated by science and not by political expediency . . . looking toward the prevention of the continued propagation of defective strains in the present population."[26] The book's foreword was written by Brigham's mentor, Robert Yerkes, who wrote that Professor Brigham had "rendered a notable service to psychology . . . and above all, to our lawmakers." Yerkes warned Americans not to "ignore the menace of race deterioration or the evident relations of immigration to national progress and welfare."[27]

Brigham's interpretation of Army IQ data was presented to committees of the Congress concerned with the formulation of immigration policy. As the debate in Congress unfolded regarding the Immigration Restriction Law of 1924, Brigham's findings were cited repeatedly in Congressional hearings, chaired by Senator Alfred Johnson of the House Committee on Immigration, lending "scientific" support for the necessity of immigration restrictions.

The findings of Dr. Arthur Sweeney's 1922 journal article, "Mental Tests for Immigrants," were incorporated in the appendix to the Hearings of the House Committee on Immigration.[28] Sweeney cited Brigham's reanalysis of the Army Alpha as scientific evidence of the intellectual inferiority of the "Slav" (Polish) and "Latin" (Italian) races. Sweeney proffered that Italian immigrants belonged to a "degenerate horde so depraved they hardly belong to our species"[29] He characterized Italian immigrants as "imbeciles" with primitive brain structures, who were "uneducable." They are, writes Sweeney, "imbeciles who think with their spinal cords [a phylogenetic characteristic of reptiles] rather than their brain."[30] Their intelligence, states Sweeney, is "scarcely superior to that of the ox."[31] Sweeney's metaphor, unintentionally, tells more of the story of the hard laboring immigrants whose basic human rights were denied, rather than their subhumanity. Sweeney reduced Italians to subhuman nonpersons. Such blatant racism directed against Italian Americans became public policy.

The overt racism, contempt, and disdain for Italian immigrants articulated by Sweeney and others is stunning. The eugenicist movement personified the fervor of a pseudoreligion: always at stake was the intellectual vitality and racial purity of the "Nordic" American people. Sweeney cautioned that "we [must] strenuously object to immigration from Italy with its proportional lower end of the scale of 63 percent ["D" class] . . . It is largely from this [group] that the stream of intelligent citizenship is polluted."[32] For eugenicists like Sweeney, Italian immigrants were the embodiment of ignorance, moral decay, and racial contamination.

Psychologist Kimball Young concurred with Sweeney that "What we want . . . is such a selection of European peoples that they will add variety to our population but not lower its intelligence."[33] Embedded in eugenicist ideology was the belief that Americans possessed a special destiny. The superior intelligence of the "American Nordic race" permitted America to eternally pursue progress. Culturally entrenched racial prejudices supported by dehumanizing stereotypes of Italian immigrants permitted Americans to exclude them from benefiting from the nation's prosperity on equal terms. The alleged underlying intellectual deficiency of Italian immigrants was used as a rationalization to use them and exclude them from the body politic.

The need to stratify the labor market to meet the needs of industrial capitalism gave rise to the moral and psychological justification of the subjugation and exploitation of Italian immigrants. Italians immigrants acquired "value" in American society solely as cheap sources of labor. Sweeney sums up the burden of incorporating immigrants into the labor market and the dilemma posed by their presence in American society. He writes, "The economic exploitation of cheap, unintelligent labor from abroad has fastened a serious racial as well as social-economic problem upon us."[34] Further, he debases Italian immigrants as incapable of assuming any other occupational role because of their limited intelligence. Sweeney states, "Men of D class [predominantly Italian immigrants] are physically well developed. A large number of them are attractive and pass in a crowd as normal. In this class belongs the *moron*, whose intellectual level seldom exceeds that of eleven years . . . with pick and shovel [they] build roads . . . They lack initiative. The educational possibility was limited."[35] Sweeney constructed humiliating images of Italian males that reduced them to the terms of marketable beasts of burden.

There was also widespread public debate about the mental fitness of Italian and other "new immigrants" for American citizenship. As early as 1915, President Theodore Roosevelt declared that there is "no such thing as a hyphenated American who is a good American."[36] Echoing Roosevelt's sentiments, on January 24, 1923, Sweeney was quoted in the permanent record of the House Committee on Immigration and Naturalization as follows:

How can it be expected that these of low intellectual grade can become good citizens . . . They are incapable of becoming good citizens by reason of intellectual deficiency, and they should be allowed no place in this country and no voice in its affairs. We cannot hope to make worthy citizens of the sub-normal . . . Education can be received only by those who have intelligence to receive it . . . That is what one is born with . . . the intelligent can receive education only in proportion to their capacities . . . we must protect ourselves against the degenerate horde.[37]

Eugenicist orthodoxy proposed that genetic deficiencies of Italian immigrants not only rendered them incapable of fulfilling the basic duties and responsibilities of American citizenship, but also that these alleged deficiencies limited their potential to attain more than a rudimentary level of education. Italians were viewed as having limited intelligence and, hence, low educability.

Psychology's extrascientific agenda helped Congress to pass racist immigration laws.[38] The interactions between psychologists, members of the Eugenics Association, and Congress ultimately enabled Congress to gather "scientific support" for anti-immigration legislative initiatives. In blatant violation of basic democratic principles, federal legislation of the 1920s articulated eugenicists' hostile sentiment toward Italian immigrants who were thought to be inassimilable immigrants endangering the future racial purity of the American race. These laws established an annual quota for each southern and eastern European nation based on the percentage of people residing in the United States during the lowest periods of immigration. The first Emergency Quota Act (1921) permitted the admission of only 3 percent of the numbers of each group reported for the census of 1910.[39] The second act, the Johnson-Reed Act of 1924, cut the previous quota to 2 percent by assigning each country an allowable quota based on the census of 1890. The Johnson-Reed Act dramatically reduced the volume of Italian immigrants allowed to enter the United States to below 29,000 per year after a peak of 349,042 in 1920.[40]

This was racially discriminatory legislation in that people from northern and western Europe could migrate at will. These exclusionary legislative acts limited the immigration of Italians to the United States to 29,000 annually. The persistence of racial and ethnic assumptions allowed these restrictive immigration policies to remain unchanged until it was repealed in 1965.

The Dawn of Antiracist Testing

The ability of exclusionary legislative acts to facilitate and escalate discriminatory actions against Italian immigrants and their children not only sanctioned the social devaluation of Italian immigrants, but also contributed to the development of stigmatizing and unjust social and educational policies that had extremely negative psychological, social, and economic consequences for their children and grandchildren.

By the early 1920s, the innate intellectual inferiority of Italian immigrants had been established by the Army intelligence test data. However, as early as 1914, before intelligence tests were fully developed, there was widespread belief that the children of the foreign-born were uneducable. Writing in *Century Magazine* in 1914, sociologist Edward Alsworth Ross stated that literacy tests had shown that children of Italian immigrants were the most intellectually retarded compared to other children among the "new immigrants." According to Ross, they lacked both motivation and ability to remain in school. Ross commented that "Italian children are lacking in the conveniences [i.e., capacity] for thinking . . . they hate study, make slow progress . . . 56 per cent are retarded [that is, perform below grade level] and perform below the Hebrews, Portuguese and Poles . . . it appears that these children [Italian] with the dusk of Saracenic or Berber ancestors showing in their cheeks, are twice as apt to drop behind other pupils of their age."[41]

Hereditarian pronouncements about people of color were seminal to the discourse of the intelligence testing movement. Ross's reference to "Saracenic or Berber . . . cheeks" of Italian immigrant children subtly linked their dark-skin pigmentation to their alleged "mental retardation." In 1913, in the first reported study of "White-Negroe" differences in intelligence, A. C. Strong invoked the "mulatto hypothesis," concluding that Negro children of lighter complexion outperformed their darker-skinned peers.[42] Ross incorporated a variant of the "mulatto hypothesis" in his commentary: lighter-skinned Poles, Hebrews, and Portuguese children outperformed their darker-skinned Italian peers. Ross implied that the true cause of the Italian child's alleged intellectual retardation was deeply rooted in their biological similarities to dark-skinned Negroes.[43] The tone of this sweeping assessment of the alleged genetic deficits in mental abilities of Italian children would reverberate in race psychologists' assessments of Italian children's intellectual abilities during the 1920s. Significant variables that might affect the performance of the foreign-born on an intelligence test were ignored. There was no attempt to critically analyze the impact of the culture and history of immigrants that deprived the people of southern Italy respect for their basic human rights, including the right to an adequate education. Unjust cultural assumptions uncritically interpreted their illiteracy and lack of English language literacy as a reflection of their underlying genetic incapacity.

Throughout the 1920s, group-administered tests of intelligence (instruments that could be given to a group of participants in a single setting) were systematically used by racist psychologists to accrue evidence for a genetic-evolutionary explanation of inherent racial differences in intelligence.[44] From a eugenicist perspective, gathering empirical evidence to document the innate intellectual inferiority of the immigrant's child would leave no doubt that intelligence is heritable. In the following section, I will examine representative studies of the 1920s in which American-born and Italian children and youths were study participants. This time period contains some of the principal examples of racist research on intellectual performance.

In 1920, Columbia University instructor, Katherine Murdoch, conducted a comparative study of the intelligence of the "brightest" immigrant children (identified as such by their teachers). These public high school students resided in New York City. Utilizing the Pressy Group Intelligence Test (a test similar in content to the Army Alpha Test), Murdoch assessed the intelligence of Jewish (n = 500), Italian (n = 500), American (n = 500) boys, and "Negroe" (n = 225) boys (quotation marks have been place around the term "Negro" because that was the nomenclature used during this period in history). Based on the mean score of each racial group, the study showed that Italian children scored considerably below the mean scores of American-born and "Hebrew and Negro" children in intelligence. Murdoch wrote that "On the whole the colored boys [African Americans] seem to be halfway between the Hebrews and the Italians. The Italians maintain their position at the foot of the four races."[45] Murdoch's conclusions about the children of Italian immigrants were unequivocally racist. Murdoch and other race psychologists firmly established the second-tier position of dark-skinned Italians and African American youth in the country. Psychologist Kimball Young invoked the "selective migration" hypothesis to explain Murdoch's finding that "Negroes" scored higher than Italians. He conjectured that the higher IQ scores of African Americans were due to the migration of more intelligent Negroes from the South to the North.[46]

Professor Kimball Young, of the University of Oregon, compared racial differences in intelligence, as measured by the Army Alpha and Beta Tests, between American-born children and children of Italian, Portuguese, and Spanish-Mexican ancestry who attended public schools in California. Overall, the test results demonstrated that "Latin" students had "extensive school retardation" (that is, performed below grade- level for their age). "Latin" ancestry students scored below American-born children and Italian students, in particular, scored significantly lower than their American counterparts.[47]

Young reported that on the Army Beta test (the nonlanguage pictorial test), American-born children scored in the high end of the sixtieth percentile, while the Latin-born children scored in the mid- to low end of the fiftieth percentile. The differences in IQs between the two groups were relatively small. However, Young negated the significance of the Beta test results and stated that the Alpha examination IQ scores was a significantly more valid indicator of their respective intellectual endowment. Young's conclusion was racially biased because it inaccurately reflected the study results. Young stated that "If the mentality of the southern Europeans who are flooding this country is typified by the mentality of the three groups studied [Italian, Portuguese, and Mexican children] . . . the future standard of living, high-grade citizenship and cultural progress is in serious trouble."[48]

By limiting his comparisons to the verbally loaded test of intelligence (Army Alpha), Young deliberately removed from his analysis the issues of differences in measured intelligence due to lack of English language proficiency. Young's selective interpretations of the study results obviously supported eugenicist ideology. Young, a former graduate student of Lewis Terman, adhered to Terman's racist ideology in his interpretation of racial differences in intelligence. Kimball's autobiography, written later in his career, revealed that professional gain, and not a belief in eugenicist ideology, motivated him to draw racially biased conclusions in his studies of differences in racial intelligence. Young wrote, "I was pretty fed up with Terman's doses of intelligence being inherited as a biological trait. But he made a tremendous impression on the educational world. So I played it cool and didn't say much about this in my dissertation [the above study was part of his dissertation], though I wanted to. I had to get that union card, as we all know."[49]

Maud A. Merrill analyzed "mental differences," as measured by the Stanford Binet, between American and foreign-born children (mean age = 11.5) who resided in Santa Clara, California. Merrill found that the majority of IQ scores of the foreign-born children were in the below average or mentally retarded range.

She also found that 8 percent of their IQ scores fell into the average or above average range. In addition, there was a small but significant correlation between the parent's SES (socioeconomic status) and the IQ scores of American-born and foreign children. Unfortunately, eugenicist ideology perverted Merrill's interpretation of the data. She ignored evidence (e.g., relationship between SES and the fact that 8 percent of the foreign-born children's scores fell in the average or below average range) that contradicted hereditarian assumptions. Merrill concluded that genes, not environmental influences, were the determinants of intelligence. She wrote that the "foreign group is more retarded than the American group and this inferiority seems to be due to native endowment . . . of the foreign group the Italians constitute the largest per cent . . . the retarded children of the group have been pushed beyond their mental capacity."[50] According to hereditarian assumptions, a child's ability to benefit from education and training was commensurate with his or her innate intelligence. In her conclusion, Merrill singled out Italian children as the least intellectually endowed of all study participants. In her view, their potential to benefit from education was limited by their intellectual genetic deficiencies. Guided by Terman's eugenicist ideology, Merrill concluded that foreign-born students in general, and Italian students in particular, "have been pushed beyond their mental capacity."[51] To acknowledge that social class differences affect IQ is to suggest that environmental differences, and not heredity alone, accounted for racial differences in intelligence. Similarly, to acknowledge that 8 percent of the "foreign group" scored in the average range is to suggest that genes or race alone were not controlling intelligence. Clearly, Merrill's selective interpretation of the study results demonstrate that eugenicist orthodoxy, and not scientific objectivity, guided her conclusions.

The participants in V. T. Graham's study of 1926 were American-born Jewish and Italian children who resided in Boston and its environs. She compared racial differences in intelligence, as measured by the Revised Stanford-Binet and the Pinter and Patterson Performance Tests, between three "racial" groups: Jewish children ranked highest (IQ = 105), American children ranked second (IQ = 99) and Italian children ranked lowest (IQ = 85). Because both the verbal and nonverbal versions of the intelligence tests were used, Graham concluded, "While Italians made a poor showing in every respect . . . all possible language factors were ruled out, so that the consistent inferiority of the Italians to the Jews cannot be explained away as a function of language."[52]

The Jewish and American children scored in the average range (90–100), and the Italians in the low average range (80–90). In Graham's study, small differences were found between Italian, American, and Jewish children, yet Graham's conclusions exaggerated the significance of these differences. Moreover, the performance of foreign-born children on the Stanford-Binet was compared to a "normative sample" of one thousand white, middle-class, and English-speaking children. Foreign-born children were not represented in the standardization group of the Stanford-Binet. Consequently their performance was unfairly compared to native-born children.

To summarize the findings of the studies examined in this section, racist psychologists concluded that foreign-born and Italian children's depressed performance on intelligence tests was due to "genetic differences" in "inherent intellectual ability." Explanations for the observed low IQ scores compared to that of their white peers were consistently racially biased and hereditarian based.

Verbal tests of intelligence, such as the Stanford-Binet and the Army Alpha Test utilized by racist psychologists, penalized children whose mother tongue was not English. Yet these tests were routinely administered to children of immigrants who were limited in or nonproficient in English or were developing bilingually. In addition, verbal tests were also administered in the absence of first assessing the language status of foreign-born study children.

Moreover, these studies, as documented by Otto Klineberg in 1935, were seriously methodologically flawed. Klineberg challenged the validity of intelligence tests administered by entrenched hereditarians. A professor of psychology at Columbia University, he reviewed a number of these and other studies in which IQ data were available for diverse racial groups (e.g., Italian) on both linguistic tests (verbally loaded tests like the Stanford-Binet, which was used in Graham's study) and performance tests (nonverbal tests such as the Army Beta Test). Klineberg then compared the grand mean IQ of the linguistic tests to the grand mean IQ on the performance tests and found that the mean IQ on the performance tests was higher than the mean IQ on the linguistic tests. Klineberg concluded that language and other key variables (such as SES, English language proficiency, acculturation, etc.) presented serious methodological flaws in comparative studies of intelligence between racial groups. In Klineberg's view, any research-based statements about white superiority in innate intelligence were unwarranted.[53]

Powerful racist attitudes toward Italian immigrants and their children were supported by race psychology's eugenicist orthodoxy, which failed to take seriously the immigrant's culture and history. Citing the questionable cyclical nature of the scientific search for the between group's differences in IQ based on race, contemporary psychologist Marvin Zuckerman posits that "some researchers on race seem dedicated to establishing the racist ideology on a scientific basis while denying the political beliefs associated with it."[54]

Antiracist Intelligence Testing

During the 1920s, not all social scientists agreed that genetic factors alone were responsible for the foreign-born children's low performance on intelligence tests. Critics of these highly controversial studies thought that the conclusions drawn by these psychometricians were racist. Activist academic social scientists, anthropologists, and psychologists, including Franz Boas, Margaret Mead, Ruth Benedict, and Otto Klineberg, among others, argued that racial differences did not, on face value, constitute evidence for a genetic interpretation of racial differences in IQ. They and other social scientists who were ideologically committed to notions of equality and the application of research to social problems thought that social inequities, lower SES, length of parental residence in the country, parent's occupation, and the amount of English spoken at home accounted for the racial differences in intelligence found in comparative studies of intelligence between children of the foreign-born and American-born children.[55]

A study published by anthropologist Margaret Mead in 1927 is most representative of this body of research.[56] She compared the intelligence of American-born children and the Italian-born children of Italian immigrants who attended public high schools (in grades 6 through 10) in Hammonton, New Jersey. On average, Italian children scored 27 points below the Americans on the Otis Group Intelligence Test. Analysis of the relationship between Italian children's IQ scores and the language spoken at home (English or Italian) revealed that IQ scores of Italian children increased in direct relation to the amount of English spoken at home: the more English was spoken at home, the higher the child's IQ score. Similarly, Mead found a positive correlation between the child's IQ score, the SES level of the parents, and the family's length of residency in the United States. In sum, Mead found that a child's IQ score was higher if English, rather than Italian, was spoken at home. In addition, the longer the length of residence in the United States and the higher the father's SES, the higher the child's IQ score. Mead concluded that "classification of foreign children in schools where they have to compete with American children, on the basis of group intelligence test findings alone, is not a just evaluation of the child's innate capacity."[57]

Unfortunately, the opinions and scientific evidence accrued by these scientists had little, if any, impact on educational policy makers or the public's attitudes about Italian American children's academic abilities.

Leonard Covello (1887–1982): Antiracist Educator and Social Activist

There was a cadre of African American scholars of the 1920s who joined the rising heterodoxy to challenge the allegations of hereditarian thinkers who asserted that African Americans were innately inferior intellectually.[58] During this same historical period there was a singular Italian American scholar, Leonard Covello, who challenged the allegations of eugenicists and psychologists that Italian American children and youth were also innately inferior in intelligence.

Dr. Covello, a visionary educator and community activist, spent 45 years of his career fighting to abolish educational discrimination against *all* immigrant and minority groups residing in the impoverished ghetto of East Harlem.[59] He devoted his life to the education of boys at De Witt Clinton High School and later as principle of Benjamin Franklin High School, who in "in the estimation of the outside world . . . [were part of] a pariah community."[60] He understood, from his personal educational experiences, the profound negative emotional impact American schools had on the child and the parent and how school engendered "feeling[s] of scorn and shame."[61]

During the 1920s and 1930s, Covello rejected anti-immigrant discourse and the rhetoric of "Americanization" that meant "casting off everything that was alien," especially the language and culture of national origin. He rejected social scientific claims that Italian American children had genetically inferior intellects. Outraged at scientific pronouncements of the alleged intellectual inferiority of his students, Covello stated rhetorically "How is this? I argued. Do you mean to tell me this [intelligence test] is supposed to be conclusive evidence that my boys have less brains? I don't believe it. My experience does not bear this out. I am not convinced."[62] Covello recognized that factors such as the child's familiarity with the testing setting and the child's ease in the testing situation also affected his or her performance. He understood the pressures and anxieties that Italian and other foreign-born children experienced during the "period of intelligence test insanity" at De Witt Clinton High School in New York. Covello recalled, "I will never forget one of those testing periods [during the 1920s]. Several hundred boys were tested at the lunchroom tables. The tests all had a time limit. The examiner stood on the platform with a stopwatch and a whistle, ready to signal the beginning and end of each test . . . There were students who could work under pressure, but others were unable to concentrate, became panicky, and as a result get low scores."[63] Covello cogently argued that Italian students were intellectually capable people who did not have access to the same opportunity structure as other privileged American-born children. Covello wrote that "in general these tests measured only the opportunity a student had to learn. They proved that a boy from a slum area whose parents spoke broken English usually did not have the vocabulary to express himself and did not have the opportunity to absorb the fundamentals of education as thoroughly as a student from a better economic class."[64]

Covello knew from his own experience that American society was not always fair, and our schools not always democratic. In Covello's view, teachers and the school should assume major responsibility for what happens to a student, and he asked teachers to view themselves as counselors. Covello repeatedly demonstrated how taking this approach resulted in greater student success rather than failure. The "solution" to the Italian American school problem, wrote Covello, "must be found in the school itself [and] the stigma of failure must be placed on a boy as seldom as possible."[65]

Racial biases ascribing the cause of difference in the educational performance of Italian children to genetic deficiencies justified an educational system that built inequalities within schools tracking Italian students to vocational and technical fields. Covello, a vigorous champion of social justice and egalitarianism in the education of all children and youth found the idea of an intellectual aristocracy repugnant. During the 1930s, the Board of Education planned to build a vocational technical institution for Italian American boys. Covello strenuously objected to creating an industrial high school to make "our boys trade workers." Such a plan, he stated, "suggests that the boys of East Harlem are not capable of doing academic work."[66] Covello wrote, "The stigma attached to an industrial high school, the psychological effect upon the pupils and community! Sure, people say on the outside 'The proper school for them dumb immigrants. They don't deserve any better.' It's wrong. A high school here must have all the dignity of a seat of learning. It must reflect its influence into the community and be the center for its improvement."[67]

Covello challenged the conventions of society that insisted on excluding Italian American youth from receiving an academic education. Through the intervention of then-Mayor Fiorello La Guardia, Covello ultimately succeeded in his goal of establishing an academic high school. In 1934, Covello was appointed principal of Benjamin Franklin High School.

Covello understood that the problem of labeling a child and an entire ethnic group as intellectually inferior was a critical one: it influenced his or her academic placement and influenced teacher expectancies and attitudes toward him or her in the classroom and also in his or her peer group in the community. Covello's prescient understanding of the impact of teacher expectancies on student performance was subsequently validated by experimental studies in social psychology conducted by psychologists Robert Rosenthal and Lenore Jacobson.[68] Rosenthal and Jacobson did their work in an elementary school where IQ tests were administered to all of the students. Students had been chosen at random by the researchers to create the expectation in the minds of the teachers that some students IQs were so high they were expected to be academic "bloomers." In fact, this was not true: confederate students were designated "bloomers" but were no smarter than the "non-bloomers." The students who had been designated as "bloomers" showed significantly higher gains in their IQ scores at the end of the year. The study demonstrated that teacher expectations of students had become reality.[69]

Covello's creation of an egalitarian school environment in East Harlem demonstrated what the above-named psychologists documented through their research: when educators implement a pedagogical approach in the classroom that eliminates prejudice and promotes educational equality among *all* children and youth, teachers will succeed in raising the self-esteem and achievement of students. Through his personal and community-based activism, Covello succeeded in raising the self-esteem and academic achievement of Italian American students by accepting them, respecting them, and teaching them in the same way as more privileged children. His pioneering work went a long way in dispelling the myth that Italian American youth were incapable of attaining higher levels of education.

Moreover, Covello anticipated the social science philosophy of multiculturalism by several decades. As the population of East Harlem continued to shift and change during the 1930s and 1940s—with Italian Americans moving to the suburbs and an influx of African Americans and Puerto Ricans—Covello instituted multicultural studies (then called "Intercultural Education") in every classroom at Benjamin Franklin. At the time, the student population at Benjamin Franklin encompassed 34 nationalities. The purpose of the multicultural curriculum was to promote racial tolerance in school and to increase students' understanding of their peers who were of different racial and cultural backgrounds. Questionnaires assessed students' attitudes toward various racial and ethnic groups at the beginning and end of each school year. The studies showed a decrease in prejudicial attitudes toward the various racial and ethnic groups within the student body.

Covello's passionate social activism on behalf of minority children had an enduring impact on his students and on every ethnic group in the East Harlem community at large during his tenure. Despite Covello's groundbreaking pedagogical contributions to the field of education, his work does not appear in educational textbooks nor is it included in the curriculum of undergraduate or graduate schools of education.

The Impact of Intelligence Testing on the Educational Opportunity Structure of Italian American Children and Youth

During the 1930s and 1940s, research related to racial and ethnic differences in intelligence lost prominence among American hereditarians and eugenicists because they did not want to be associated with the racist beliefs of Nazism.[70] Nevertheless, the deficit thinking of eugenicists and race psychologists continued to have serious social and educational implications for immigrant children: used in schools, intelligence tests identified ability, prescribed curricula, and determined students' futures.[71] Disparities in measured intelligence between races resulted in educational placement of children of the foreign-born in classes that severely limited their subsequent educational and occupational opportunities. Based on IQ data accrued from research during the 1920s, it is likely that most Italian ancestry children were placed in classrooms for slow learners or in nonacademic vocational education tracks that emphasized low-level skills.

"Curriculum differentiation" was used in ways that stratified students along ethnic and racial lines. Writing in 1920, Lewis Terman believed that using intelligence tests for curriculum differentiation would make it possible for students to have a "grade of school work which a child could do . . . [based] upon the level of development [intelligence] he has attained."[72] Italian American children were perceived by educators to be lacking in basic intellectual capacities to pursue a college education and were "tracked" into vocational programs for training in jobs requiring manual labor or to prepare them for factory, domestic service, secretarial work, and housework. It is reasonable to hypothesize that academic placement, teacher expectancies, and attitudes toward Italian American children in the classroom and in his or her peer group in the community in many cases discouraged most Italian American students from pursing higher levels of education.

Italian American students frequently entered learning situations accurately assuming that their instructors thought less of them as students. A thin body of research has examined how the self-esteem of Italian children and youth was negatively affected by their experiences in American classrooms and schools.[73] For example, William D. Tait found that second generation Italian American students (n = 734) who attended school with white American children (n = 734) struggled with heightened feelings of inferiority, felt rejected by their American-born peers, and reported greater awareness of negative attitudes held by their peers toward Italian Americans.[74] Similarly, Covello observed that the Italian school child's sense of inferiority in the American school system was nurtured by the "high prestige of American norms," and by an "awareness of the disrepute into which the non-Italian group places the parental background of the Italian children."[75] Irvin Long Child found that the task of reconciling distinctly different orientations of American and Italian culture had a significant impact on the retention or rejection of an Italian American identity. Many study participants withdrew from an emotional connection to their Italian ancestry and denied the significance of their social or cultural background.[76] These studies demonstrate that internalization of American ideals and devaluation of Italian culture negatively affected the self-esteem of the Italian American school child and possibly his or her aspirations for higher levels of educational attainment.

Racism in the Social Sciences and the Emergence of the Italian American Voice in Literature

In the social sciences (sociology, psychology, and anthropology) negatively stigmatizing attitudes about Italian Americans' intellectual and cultural inferiority persisted well beyond the 1920s and 1930s. Some social scientists explained the "Italian school problem" by using a widely applied "deficit model approach" (i.e., Italian Americans lack motivation, intellectual ability, and cultural values to achieve higher levels of educational attainment compared to other European ancestry groups).[77] Deficit thinking is a variant of the "blaming the victim" mindset; it is a fusion of ideology and science positing that educational deficits of Italian American students are rooted in specific cultural values and personal attributes. This approach did not take into account the structural inequities that confronted Italian American students. What has been little emphasized, except by scholars such as Leonard Covello and Francesco Cordasco, is that school for the Italian American, in the words of Covello, too often proved to be a "cruel stepmother," a place where humiliation and failure was the rule, rather than the exception.[78]

Social scientists ascribed Italian Americans' low educational aspirations and academic underachievement to their working class values and fatalistic attitudes toward life. In their view, Italian American cultural values led this identity group to perceive higher education as nonutilitarian. For example, Strodbeck and Rosen supported such perceptions by "proving" that Italian Americans have "low achievement motivation."[79] Shibutani and Kwan found that Italian Americans are "fatalistic" and regard intellectual interests as "effeminate." Sowell asserted that Italian American "traditional peasant culture" is a "barrier to higher education."[80]

The enduring impact of stigmatizing and racist attitudes about Italian Americans' inferior intellectual abilities are surfacing in the literary works of contemporary Italian American writers.[81] The psychological effects of the American school system's racist attitudes toward Italian American children are illuminated, for example, in the poetry of Maria Mazziotti Gillan. During the 1940s when anti-Italian sentiment was still quite virulent in the American school system, Gillan describes in her poem, "Public School No. 18: Paterson, New Jersey," the deep feelings of shame and humiliation instilled in her by her teachers. Gillan writes how

Without words, they tell me
to be ashamed.
I am.
I deny that booted country
even from myself
want to be still
and untouchable
as these women
who teach me to hate myself.

Year later, in a white
Kansas City house,
the Psychology professor tells me
I remind him of the Mafia leader
On the cover of *Time* magazine.

Gillan's poem charts an inner journey of psychological liberation from internalized feelings of inferiority. She awakens to a self that is confident and viscerally rejecting of stigmatizing representations of her Italian American self. Gillan's understandable outrage toward those teachers, who had taught her to hate her "foreign" self, is emotionally palpable in the final stanza of the poem:

Remember me, Ladies,
the silent one?
I have found my voice
and my rage will blow
your house down.[82]

Gillan speaks for many Italian Americans past and present. To have maintained an interest in education and beliefs in the rewards of learning required individual acts of faith and inner confidence on the part of many Italian Americans. They have had to cling to their own views of themselves and defend themselves against the institutional depreciation of Italian Americans in this country for several generations.

Coming into Our Own

Institutional racism is frequently not recognized as being unjust because it is embedded in social norms and accompanied by racial ideologies and stigmas that justify it. In this chapter, I have examined the history of psychology's institutional racism that stigmatized Italian Americans as an innately intellectually inferior identity group. The unjust and prejudicial educational policies and institutional practices that flowed from racist psychology's pseudoscientific research and its negative intergenerational impact on the educational experiences of Italian Americans was laid bare. The body of research discussed in this chapter indicated that Italian Americans, collectively, did not possess the innate capacity to attain the same educational levels and social or political power and status of other white European ethnic groups who entered the United States a century ago.

The Italian American story of injustice and discrimination discussed in this chapter does not exist in isolation from other groups. Whole groups of people carry the collective wounds of discrimination and oppression. People of color carry the history of racism. Jews carry the scars of anti-Semitism. Italian Americans carry the history of racism and subjugation by their country of origin and by the country to which they emigrated. In psychology, however, there has been little or no recognition of the fact that Italian Americans have suffered prolonged burdens of racial prejudice. In part, this is the result of a tendency in the social sciences to treat white European Americans as a monolithic group who have uniformly enjoyed the power and privilege of their "whiteness."

As a result, psychology's scholarly community is unaware of the many contemporary perspectives and issues of concern to Italian Americans (such as the ongoing and overtly denigrating representations in the media industry of Italian Americans as intellectually inferior "street smart" individuals who have not attained levels of education similar to other European ancestry groups). There is also preliminary evidence suggesting that "processes of ethnic exclusion" or subtle forms of discrimination may be impeding Italian American scholars, scientists, and artists, who are elected members of the American Academy of Arts and Science, from gaining entry to the elite strata of the association.[83]

Psychologists are in a unique position to breach the gap in our knowledge about the link between historical and contemporary experiences of racism and discrimination and its profound effect on the others' perception and the self-perception of Italian Americans, individually and collectively. Empirical and narrative research methodologies are powerful scientific tools that can be used to document the existence and impact of discrimination against Italian Americans. Sometimes we have to see unequivocal evidence to believe it.

Notes

The opening epigraph comes from David Richards, *Italian American: The Racializing of an Ethnic Identity* (New York: New York University Press, 1998), 227, 237.

1. For an in-depth psychological analysis of the history of stereotyping of Italian Americans in the United States, see Elizabeth G. Messina, "Psychological Perspectives on the Stigmatization of Italian Americans in the American Media," in *Saints and Rogues: Conflicts and Convergence in Psychotherapy*, ed. Robert B. Marchesani and E. Mark Stern (New York: Haworth Press, 2004), 87–122.

2. John F. Dovidio, Brenda Major, and Jennifer Crocker, "Stigma: Introduction and Overview," in *The Social Psychology of Stigma*, ed. Todd F. Heatherton, Robert E. Kleck, Michelle R. Hebl, and Jay G. Hull (New York: Guilford, 2003), 3.

3. Steven L. Neuberg, Dylan M. Smith, and Terrilee Asher, "Why People Stigmatize: Toward a Bicultural Framework," in *The Social Psychology of Stigma*, ed. Todd F. Heatherton, Robert E. Kleck, Michelle R. Hebl, and Jay G. Hull, 31–61.

4. Dovidio, Major, and Crocker, 9.

5. Neuberg, Smith, and Asher, 49.

6. Matthew Pratt Guterl, *The Color of Race in America, 1900–1940* (Cambridge, MA: Harvard University Press, 2001), 8, 31.

7. Christian S. Crandall, "Ideology and Lay Theories of Stigma: The Justification of Stigmatization," in *The Social Psychology of Stigma*, ed. Todd F. Heatherton, Robert E. Kleck, Michelle R. Hebl, and Jay G. Hull, 126–52: quote from page 128.

8. Leila Zenderland, *Measuring Minds: Henry Herbert Goddard and the Origins of American Intelligence Testing* (New York: Cambridge University Press, 1998), 7.

9. Zenderland, 7–9.

10. Richie Perez, "From Assimilation to Annihilation: Puerto Rican Images in U.S. Films," in *Latin Looks: Images of Latinas and Latinos in the U.S. Media*, ed. Clara Rodriguez (New York: Westview Press, 1997), 146.

11. Mark Haller, *Eugenics: Hereditarian Attitudes in American Thought* (New Brunswick, NJ: Rutgers University Press, 1963), 146.

12. Leon J. Kamin, *The Science and Politics of IQ* (Potomac, MD: Erlbaum, 1974), 6.

13. For analyses of the Army's response to testers see Daniel J. Kevles, "Testing the Army's Intelligence: Psychologists and the Military in World War I," *Journal of American History* 55 (1978): 565–81; Joel Spring, "Psychologists at War: The Meaning of Intelligence in the Alpha and Beta Tests," *History of Education Quarterly* 12 (1972): 3–15.

14. W. E. B. Dubois, "Race Intelligence," *The Crisis: A Record of the Darker Races* 20, no. 3 (July 1920): 118–19.

15. Robert M. Yerkes, ed., *Psychological Examining in the United States Army*, Memoirs of the National Academy of Sciences 15 (Washington, DC: Government Printing Office, 1921), 347–55; Cyril Burt, *Mental and Scholastic Tests*, 2nd ed. (1921; New York: Staples Press Limited, 1947), 123–28.

16. For a description of the content of the Army Alpha and Beta tests see *Psychological Examining*, 347–55; Burt, *Mental and Scholastic Tests*, 143–49.

17. Twelve percent of white Americans compared to four percent of foreigners were classified in the "A" or "B" range. All of the men in this classification had completed some years of college. Although four percent of foreign draftees scored in the "A" and "B" range, eugenicists did not comment on this finding. To do so would challenge underlying assumptions about the genetic nature of intelligence.

18. Yerkes, ed., 421–24.

19. Psychologists were shocked by the high rate of illiteracy among white American draftees. The average "mental age" of the white draftee (determined by comparing Army Alpha with scores on the individual Stanford-Binet tests, a number of which had been gathered during the course of standardization of the army tests) was 13.5. The average "mental age" of the foreign born "D" men was 9.5. The norms for the Stanford-Binet were based on results from a few hundred California school children. See Yerkes, ed., 785–89.

20. Kamin, 290; emphasis added.

21. Ibid., 19.

22. Yerkes, ed., 359.

23. Carl Brigham, *A Study of American Intelligence* (Princeton, NJ: Princeton University Press, 1923), 20.

24. *Hearings before the Committee on Immigration and Naturalization, House of Representatives, December 26, 27, and 31, 1923, and January 3, 4, 5, 22, and 24, 1924* (Washington, DC: Government Printing Office, 1924), 837.

25. Brigham, 182. Madison Grant, *The Passing of a Great Race* (New York: Scribner, 1916), summarized American's fears about the influx of immigrants. Grant wrote that "with this human flotsam . . . the whole tone of American life, social, moral and political has been lowered and vulgarized by them" (89–90).

26. Brigham, 210.

27. Robert Yerkes, "Foreword," in Brigham, *A Study*, v–viii.

28. Kamin, *The Science and Politics of IQ*, 23. For the original article see Arthur Sweeney, "Mental Tests for Immigrants," *North American Review* 215 (May 1922): 600–12.

29. *Hearings before the Committee on Immigration and Naturalization, House of Representatives, January 3, 4, 5, 22, and 24, 1923* (Washington Government Printing Office), 589–94.

30. Ibid.

31. Ibid.

32. Ibid., 592.

33. Kimball Young, "Mental Differences in Certain Immigrant Groups: Psychological Tests of South Europeans in Typical California Schools with Bearing on the Educational Policy and on the Problems of Racial Contacts in this Country," *University of Oregon Publications* 1, no. 11 (July 1922): 432.

34. Ibid.

35. Sweeney, 603.

36. Quoted in Richards, 175.

37. *Hearings . . . January 3, 4, 5, 22, and 24, 1923*, 605–6.

38. Most psychologists who have written about the history of this period agree that the claims of psychologists about racial differences in intelligence test scores played an important role in the passage of the immigration restriction acts, although Mark Snyderman and Richard J. Herrenstein, "Tests and Immigration Act of 1924," *American Psychologist* 38 (1983): 980–95, have emphasized other forces at play to support the legislation.

39. See Carol J. Bradley, "Restrictive Immigration Laws in the United States: The Literacy and National Origins Quota Act," in *The Italian American Experience: An Encyclopedia*, ed. Salvatore J. LaGumina, Richard J. Cavaioli, Salvatore Primeggia, and Joseph A. Varcalli (New York: Garland Press, 2000), 543–44.

40. Ibid., 544.

41. Edward Alsworth Ross, "Italians in America," *Century Magazine* 87 (1914): 443–45.

42. A. C. Strong, "Three Hundred Fifty White and Colored Children Measured by the Binet-Simon Measuring Scale of Intelligence," *Pedagogical Seminary* 20 (1913): 485–515.

43. The "whiteness," and therefore the racial purity of Italian immigrants, became an issue of concern to eugenicists and to the American public. Newspapers and magazines of the day described Italians as "swarthy" and "kinky haired." The public subjected Italian immigrants to racial epithets such as "black dagoes" and "black guineas." As a racial group, Italian immigrants were stigmatized as "nonvisible blacks" or as "white negroes" further denigrating both races. Scholars agree that the genetic ambiguity of the racial status of Italian immigrants constituted their racial "inbetweenness." See Donna R. Gabaccia, *Italy's Many Diasporas* (Seattle: Washington University Press, 2000), 125; Clive Webb, "The Lynching of Sicilian Immigrants in the American South, 1886–1910," *American Quarterly* 44, no. 3 (2002): 314.

44. Katherine Murdoch, "A Study of Race Differences in New York City," *School and Society* 11 (January 31, 1920): 147–50; Kimball Young, "Intelligence Tests of Certain Immigrant Groups," *Scientific Monthly* 15 (1922): 103; Rudolf Pintner, "Comparison of American and Foreign Children on Intelligence Tests," *Journal of Educational Sociology* 14 (1923): 292–95; Dorothy Wilson Seago and Theresa Shulkin Kolden, "A Comparative Study of the Mental Capacity of 6th Grade Jewish and Italian Children," *School and Society* 22 (October 31, 1925): 564–68; Clifford Kirkpatrick, "Intelligence and Immigration," *Intelligence and Immigration*, Mental Measurement Monographs, vol. 2 (1926): 127–35; Maud A. Merrill, "Mental Differences in Children Referred to a Psychological Clinic," *Journal of Applied Psychology* 10 (1926): 470–86; Virginia Taylor Graham, "The Intelligence of Italian and Jewish Children in the Habit of Clinics of the Massachusetts Division of Mental Hygiene," *Journal of Abnormal and Social Psychology* 20 (1926): 371–76.

45. Murdoch, "Educational Research," 150.

46. Young, *Mental Differences*, 425.

47. Ibid., "Intelligence Tests," 105.

48. Ibid., *Mental Differences*, 422.

49. Fred B. Lindstrom, Ronald A. Hardert, and Laura L. Johnson, eds., *Kimball Young On Sociology in Transition, 1912–1968: An Oral Account of the 35th President of the ASA* (Lanham, MD: University Press of America, 1995), 16.

50. Merrill, "Mental Differences in Children Referred to a Psychological Clinic," 485.

51. Ibid., 470–86.

52. Graham, 373.

53. Otto Klineberg, *Race Differences* (New York: Harper, 1935); Richard R. Valencia and Lisa A. Suzuki, *Intelligence Testing and Minority Students* (Thousand Oaks, CA: Sage Publications, 2001), 19.

54. Marvin Zuckerman and Nathan Brody, "Oysters, Rabbits and People: A Critique of Race Differences in Behavior by J. P. Rushton," *Personality and Individual Differences* 9 (1988): 1025–33; especially 1028.

55. Gilbert L. Brown, "Intelligence as Related to Nationality," *Journal of Educational Psychology* 5 (1922): 324–27; G. A. Feingold, "Intelligence of the First Generation of Immigrant Groups," *Journal of Educational Psychology* 15 (1924): 65–82; Nathaniel D. M. Hirsch, *A Study of Natio-Racial Mental Differences*, Genetic Psychology Monographs 1, no. 3–4 (1926), 394–97; Margaret Mead, "Group Intelligence Tests and Linguistic Disability Among Italian Children," *School and Society* 25 (April 16, 1927): 465–68.

56. Mead, "Group Intelligence Tests," 465–68.

57. Ibid.

58. Valencia and Suzuki, 19.

59. "Leonardo Coviello," whose name was changed by an American teacher to "Leonard Covello," was born in Avigliano, Italy. The eldest of three children, his family emigrated from Italy to the Italian section of East Harlem when he was nine years of age. Despite poverty, he excelled academically in New York City's public schools. Winner of a Pulitzer Scholarship, Covello attended Columbia University where he received his BA degree (1911) and Master's Degree in Romance Languages and was elected to Phi Beta Kappa. Covello obtained his EdD from New York University in 1943. His dissertation on *The Social Background of the Italo-American School Child: A Study of the Southern Italian Mores and Their Effect on the School Situation in Italy and America* was published in the Netherlands by E. J. Brill in 1967 and is still considered a standard in the field. Subsequently, New York University invited Dr. Covello to teach a course to educators about the culture of the Italian American school child. Covello's course may have been the first course in Italian American Studies to be offered at an American university.

   In 1927, East Harlem comprised 90 thousand Italian Americans and was considered the largest Italian ghetto in the nation. See Leonard Covello with Guido D'Agostino, *The Heart is the Teacher* (New York: McGraw Hill, 1958).

60. Covello with D'Agostino, *The Heart is the Teacher*, 171.

61. Ibid., 127.

62. Ibid., 150.

63. Ibid.

64. Ibid., 152.

65. Ibid., 174.

66. Ibid., 203.

67. Ibid., 181.

68. Robert Rosenthal and Lenore Jacobson, *Pygmalion in the Classroom: Teacher Expectations and Student Intellectual Development* (New York: Holt, Rinehart and Winston, 1968).

69. The findings of Rosenthal and Jacobson have since been replicated by other researchers including E. Babad, "Pygmalion—25 Years after Interpersonal Expectations in the Classroom," in *Interpersonal Expectations: Theroy, Research and Expectations*, ed. P. D. Blanck (New York: Cambridge Unitersity Press, 1993), 125–53; Stephanie Madon, Lee Jussim, and Jacquelynne Eccles, "In Search of the Powerful Self-Fulfilling Prophecy," *Journal of Personality and Social Psychology* 72 (1997): 792–809; A. E. Smith, L. Jussim, and J. S. Eccles, "Do Self-Fulfilling Prophecies Accumulate, Dissipate, or Remain Stable over Time?" *Journal of Personality and Social Psychology* 77 (1999): 548–65.

70. See Douglas E. Foley, "Deficit Thinking Models Based on Culture: The Anthropological Model," in *The Evolution of Deficit Thinking: Educational Thought and Practice*, ed. Richard R. Valencia (Palo Alto, CA: Stanford University Press Series on Education and Public Policy [London: Palmer, 1999]): 113–31.

71. Foley, "Deficit Thinking," 122.

72. Lewis Terman, "The Use of Intelligence Tests in the Grading of School Children," *Journal of Educational Research* 1 (1920): 20–32; citation on page 21.

73. Leonard Covello, *A Study of the Southern Italian Social Mores and their Effect on the Social Situation in Italy and America* (1947; Leiden: Brill, 1967); Joseph William S. Tait, *Some Aspects of the Effect of the Dominant American Culture and Chilgren of Italian Parentage* (New York: Bureau of Publication Teachers College, Columbia University, 1942); Irvin Long Child, *Italian or American? The Second Generation in Conflict* (New York: Russell and Russell, 1943).

74. Tait, *Some Aspects*, 124.

75. Covello, *A Study*, 338.

76. Child, *Italian or American?*, 95.

77. Fred L. Strobeck, "Family Interaction, Values, and Achievement," in *Talent and Society*, ed. David McClelland (Princeton, NJ: Van Nostrand, 1958), 135–94. Also see B. C. Rosen, "Race, Ethnicity and the Achievement Syndrome," *American Sociological Review* 24 (1959): 47–60; Richard Ulin, "Ethnicity and School Performance: An Analysis of Variables," *California Journal of Educational Research* 19, no. 4 (1964): 190–97; Tamotsu Shibutani and Kian M. Kwan, *Ethnic Stratification: A Comparative Approach* (New York: Macmillan, 1965); Thomas Sowell, *Race and Economics* (New York: McKay, 1975).

78. Covello, *Social Background*; Francesco Cordasco, ed., *Studies in Italian American Social History: Essays in Honor of Leonard Covello* (Totowa, NJ: Rowman and Littlefield, 1975); Lawrence Oliver, "'Great Equalizer' or 'Cruel Stepmother'? The Image of the School in Italian American Literature," *Journal of Ethnic Studies* 15, no. 3 (1983): 113–30.

79. Strodbeck and Rosen, "Family Interaction," 190.

80. Shibutani and Kwan, *Ethnic Stratification*, 152.

81. See also the memoirs of Marianna De Marco Torgovnick, *Crossing Ocean Parkway* (Chicago: University of Chicago Press, 1994), 13–14; and Louise De Salvo, *Vertigo* (New York: Penguin, 1996), 156.

82. Maria Mazziotti Gillan, *Where I Come From* (Toronto: Guernica, 1995), 12–13.

83. Richard Alba and Dalia Abdel-Hady, "Galileo's Children: Italian Americans' Difficult Entry into the Intellectual Elite," *Sociological Quarterly* 46 (2005): 3–18.

5

Frank Sinatra and Notions of Tolerance

The House I Live In

Anthony Julian Tamburri

"With equal pleasure I have as often taken notice that Providence has been pleased to give this one connected country to one united people—a people descended from the same ancestors, speaking the same language, professing the same religion, attached to the same principles of government, very similar in their manners and customs."

—*The Federalist*

"It is Billie Holiday who was, and still remains, the greatest single musical influence on me. Lady Day is unquestionably the most important influence on American popular singing in the last twenty years."

—Frank Sinatra, *Ebony* (1958)

In an unscientific poll among colleagues and graduate students, some of whom were enrolled in a PhD seminar entitled "Problematics of Italian/American Culture," I asked what were the first words that come to mind at the sound of "Frank Sinatra." Their responses included: Italian, music, mob, singer, actor, blue eyes, Kennedy, "My Way," Mia Farrow, Ava Gardner, and so on.

What we need to remember, with regard to the subject of this discussion, is that Frank Sinatra was indeed a social activist of various sorts throughout his lifetime. Initially a liberal, Sinatra eventually moved to the right.[1] Nevertheless, throughout his lifetime he engaged in philanthropy of all sorts, from doing public service announcements against bigotry early in his career, to insisting his black entertainer colleagues stayed in the same hotel and enjoyed the same privileges as he, to having given away more than one billion dollars in his lifetime to charities, especially those concerned with children's welfare. Such activity was ultimately recognized in 1997, when the 105th Congress passed Public Law 105-14, which underscored both his entertainment contributions as well as his more civic activities. I cite in this regard section (3) of the bill, which reads, "the humanitarian contributions of Frank Sinatra have been recognized in the forms of a Lifetime Achievement Award from the NAACP, the Jean Hersholt Humanitarian Award from the Academy of Motion Picture Arts and Sciences, the Presidential Medal of Freedom Award, and the George Foster Peabody Award."[2]

The House I Live In is a short film that, while unknown to many people and difficult to find in any good version, won a special Oscar for Sinatra in August 1946, the year following its debut.[3] The Oscar was a trophy that would sit in Sinatra's house alongside his later Oscar for *From Here to Eternity*. In one of Edward R. Murrow's television interviews, in fact, Sinatra was quick to point out this second Oscar, stating unequivocally that he was indeed "very proud of this, too."[4] While the call for ethnic, racial, and religious acceptance is the underriding theme, and a strong one at that, when viewing the film from today's perspective, we must keep in mind the year in which the film was made, 1945, immediately following the Second World War, when Nazi Germany and Japan, especially, ganged up, so to speak, on a good part of the Western world. I would also preface this discussion at the outset by saying that while "tolerance" is the word of the day in this turn-of-the-century moment, I have opted for the term "acceptance." I read "acceptance" as a much more inclusive sign, since "to accept" is "to receive . . . willingly"; "to admit to a group or place"; "to be favorably disposed to"; "to regard as usual, proper, or right." Conversely, definitions of "to tolerate" prove less inclusive, indeed limiting to some degree, however slight such limitation may seem to some: "to allow without prohibiting or opposing: permit"; "to recognize and respect, as the rights, opinions, or practices of others, whether agreeing with them or not"; "to put up with; to bear; endure."[5] Inclusiveness indeed subtends Sinatra's own thoughts on the subject, as he articulated them in 1945. In concluding a talk that was published in the *Spectator*, he stated, "It is up to all of us to put aside our *unfounded* prejudices and make the most of this wonderful country—this country that's been built by many people, many creeds, nationalities and races in such a way that it can never be divided, but will always remain the United States—one nation, indivisible, with liberty and justice for all."[6] Phrases such as "many people, many creeds, nationalities" and the by now proverbial "one nation, indivisible, with liberty and justice for all" underscore Sinatra's sense of inclusiveness and desire for difference.

The House I Live In

This short movie stars Frank Sinatra, as himself, during a recording session of what we might consider a typical ballad of the time, a love song that underscores its narrator's unconditional love for his beloved.[7] Finishing the recording, Sinatra decides to step out back momentarily for what we can assume to be a simple cigarette break while the orchestra leader sets up for the subsequent song.[8] Instead of spending what we would again presume to be a moment alone, he finds a group of ten boys chasing another, all because they do not "like his religion."

What follows is a short "lesson" on accepting difference, which first originates from an episode of religious bigotry but soon transforms itself into a larger discourse on racial and ethnic acceptance, joined then together with a good dose of nationalism. In fact, Sinatra delivers a small lecture to the boys, a lecture that becomes *de facto* a sort of Socratic experience for the members of the group, since they are required to participate in Sinatra's "lesson."

Ten boys chase after one of their peers clearly with the intention of "beating him up," as they used to say in the old neighborhood, because they simply "don't like his religion," as one states defiantly to Sinatra. We are never told the potential victim's religion, but his identity as Jewish is clear from his ear curls and the cap he is wearing. Sinatra thus refers to the bullies as "Nazis," and this becomes the ultimate insult throughout the narrative. In addition, as we shall see, toward the end of the film, immediately following the Pearl Harbor narrative, the two "different" religions mentioned are "Presbyterian" and "Jewish"—indeed, the only two religions mentioned in this short film. Such a dichotomy should not go unnoticed, as the former is surely a mainstay group of the United States religious historical map, whereas the latter has experienced a centuries-long discrimination.

Sinatra's subsequent "lesson" on difference and acceptance opens with a time-sensitive statement: "You must be one of those Nazi werewolves." And when the conversation continues, one of the boys protests being called a Nazi, as opposed to an American, and he immediately references his father—a sergeant in the army—having been wounded. It is at this point that Sinatra has the first opening to deliver his message, and the following conversation occurs:

> "Say, he must have gotten some of that blood plasma," Sinatra muses.
> "He was wounded so bad he had to get it three times," the boy retorts.
> Turning to the potential victim, still fearful, on the window-sill, Sinatra asks: "Son, anyone in your family ever go to the blood bank?"
> "Sure, my mother and my father both."
> "Hey," Sinatra says, turning to the potential bigot, "I bet you his pop's blood helped save your dad's life. That's bad."
> "What's bad about it?", the boy responds.
> "Well, don't you see?", Sinatra continues, "Your father doesn't go to the same church his father does. That's awful."

As Sinatra's "lesson" continues, he asks all the right questions: Would the boy's father have refused the blood if he had known its origin? Would the boy want to have his father die so as not to take blood from someone of a different religion? And so on. The answers, as well expected, are all negative. Of course not, the boy responds.

The idea of blood thus becomes universal, which only underscores the universality—read, oneness—of the human race. Though not explicitly stated at this time in the visual narrative, this becomes the overriding message. Then, Sinatra launches a shot at the Nazis; for, to continue to think as the boys do, one would have to be "either a Nazi or stupid," he states, because, after all, "religion makes no difference." One significant fact here, again, is that we are in 1945, at the close of World War II, and anti-Nazi feelings were perhaps strongest then within the

U.S. populace, although we should not forget anti-Japanese and, to a comparative degree, anti-Italian sentiment, since the Japanese directly attacked the United States, and Italy soon after declared war on the United States unprovoked. An irony here is that Sinatra's own feelings against bigotry had their origins in his having grown up hearing and being the victim of anti-Italian epithets.[9] Equally pertinent, to return now to the threatened boy's religious affiliation, is that the potentially victimized boy's Jewish identity reminds the viewer of the Holocaust, the dimensions of which were only now, in 1945, becoming known to the U.S. public.[10]

To be sure, here we might readily extend the tribal notion of "blood is thicker than water" from that of a familial or clannish semiotic to one that is significantly much more universal. That message was already communicated above, when Sinatra asked the rhetorical question of whether the boy's wounded father would refuse blood from someone of a different religion. Indeed, this is then underscored when Sinatra states the following: "Your blood's the same as mine. Mine's the same as his. Do you know what this wonderful country is made of? It's made up of a hundred different kinds of people, and a hundred different ways of talking, and a hundred different ways of going to church. But they're all American ways." What we see here is the insistence, on the one hand, of oneness and universality: "Your blood's the same as mine. Mine's the same as his." The sameness underscored here is blood, the body's literal life source and thus physical well-being, as we were told above, when the boy referred to his father's wounds and his subsequent blood transfusions. On the other hand, at the same time there is an underscoring of difference. For we live among "a hundred different kinds of people" who talk in "a hundred different ways," all of whom engage in "a hundred different ways of going to church," which, for the boys, brings the conversation back to their immediate conundrum, namely what to make of the boy who is "different."

The closing of this part of Sinatra's "lesson" is most intriguing, as it completes a sort of circle; it traces a trajectory, a round trip, from oneness to a sense of multitude, only to return to another sign of oneness.[11] And the sign of oneness at this point in the film is one that is both, now, particular and universal: "But they're all American ways." This final sign is "particular" in nature insofar as it is neither Nazi nor, as we shall soon find out, Japanese; and the ever-present sense of patriotism and nationalism, at this time in U.S. history, is duly underscored. On the other hand, the "universality" of the adjective "American" is readily signaled by that which immediately precedes it: the list of various "hundreds" of sorts of ethnicities and races, languages, and religions.

Nationalism, ethnicity, and religion are again brought together in a formula similar to what we have seen above. As Sinatra continues, he engages in a series of rhetorical strategies that set up an intriguing semiotic, one that underscores nationalism ("My dad came from Italy, but I'm an American."), religion ("Presbyterian," "Jew"), and, if we consider ethnic acceptance as a state of togetherness, then we can see his third term as a synonym of racial and ethnic acceptance and thus interaction—that is, what he calls "teamwork."

All this comes together in his story about Pearl Harbor, which now brings to the fore the Japanese, thus combining the two major foreign powers that were enemies of the United States at this time. Whereas earlier in the film events were described and narrated, for this part of Sinatra's "lesson," the film switches to a clip of an actual bombing, all of which underscores in an ironic manner, I would submit, the difference between the Japanese and Americans.[12] We see, that is, the vindication of the United States against the Japanese, a non-Western nation, whose "difference," along with the Nazis, seems to stand out, as "every American threw his head back that day and felt much better."

"Guts, know-how, and teamwork" are the operative words in this episode. Indeed, the story of the bombing complements the earlier episode of the wounded soldier, but a soldier as someone who is dependent on another—and here we might slightly modify this last word as "an other." The pilot, we come to know, was "Meyer Levin, an American and a Jew"; the bombardier, "Colin Kelly, an American and a Presbyterian." Together, these two "Americans" succeeded in sinking the Japanese ship, in spite of, Sinatra intimates, their different religions: "Do you think they should have called the bombing off because they were of different religions?"[13]

At this point in the film, Sinatra turns to the boys and tells them never to "let anyone make suckers out of" them, bidding his good-bye on his way back to work. In hearing that Sinatra's job is singing, the same little boy who had earlier blurted out that they "did not like his religion," responds, "Ah, you're kidding?", at which Sinatra takes up the challenge and begins to sing the movie's title song, which asks,

What is America to me?
A name, a map, or a flag I see;
. . .
The children in the playground,
The faces that I see,
All races and religions,
That's America to me.

Interestingly, the song's last three stanzas were omitted, presumably because they refer explicitly to African Americans ("My neighbors white and black").[14] In 1945 the praise for diversity could extend only so far.

"The House I Live In" had already become a sort of national anthem, a patriotic pronouncement, after it first appeared in 1943 and, understandably it still retained that status at the end of World War II. The lyrics constitute a series of signs, metonyms at times, that reference and describe those things we readily cherish about living in a "democracy": a plethora of images that underscore the most likeable of places, people, things, and professions, all seemingly equal. The most significant refrain is "But especially the people / That's America to me," which appears at the end of the film's shortened version of the song, so that the song underscores the previous conversation—the singer's "lesson" I called it at the outset—that Sinatra had had with the movie's boys. "All races and religions"—its people—constitute the ideal "America" in this short film. In fact, to underscore the religious freedom the film espouses, when Sinatra sings the words "All races and religions," the camera focuses in on the "Jewish" boy who had been threatened by the other children.

In finishing his song and turning to reenter the building, Sinatra bids his adieu with "So long, men!"[15] In the closing scene, as the boys leave the alleyway, the sergeant's son picks up the potentially victimized boy's books. In turn, as the music of "America the Beautiful" plays, the aforementioned smallest of the group—he who first yelled "We don't like his religion!"—turns to look into the camera, which now occupies the perspective of Sinatra's previous position in the alley, and momentarily smiles, only then to turn away and exit the alley in pursuit of his friends, as the lyrics come to an end and the screen fades to black.

Afterthoughts

Sinatra remained steadfast to his views against bigotry of all sorts. As his career progressed, especially after its low point in the early 1950s, he always championed the so-called "underdog," often that person who was not part of the socially accepted establishment (read, especially, "white" and "Christian"), however that was defined at the time. Indeed, in the 1960s, Sinatra was offered the national chairmanship of what was then characterized as the "militant year-old American-Italian Anti-Defamation League," a position he considered a "working appointment,"[16] but which was immediately perceived as controversial by some.[17] In accepting the chairmanship, he immediately announced a major event for the following fall (October 19) in Madison Square Garden, an evening to commemorate and promote the league in an attempt to build its membership to reach one million in numbers,[18] adding that "No American can rest easily until all vestiges of discrimination are erased from our society" and that the American-Italian Anti-Defamation League was in fact "the right step in the right direction in one area."[19]

Similar thoughts of his anticipated these comments in an essay published in the *Scholastic* magazine that was cited in the first section of this essay.[20] In a similar vein, at a later moment in the 1962 *Playboy* interview mentioned earlier above,[21] Sinatra combined his disgust for the religious bigotry we find in *The House I Live In* with an opening reference to an historical event of racial bigotry. To the question posed by the *Playboy* interviewer—"Hasn't religious faith just as often served as a civilizing influence?"—Sinatra responded,

> Remember that leering, cursing lynch mob in Little Rock reviling a meek, innocent little 12-year-old Negro girl as she tried to enroll in public school? Weren't they—or most of them—devout churchgoers? I detest the two-faced who pretend liberality but are practiced bigots in their own mean little spheres. I didn't tell my daughter whom to marry, but I'd have broken her back if she had had big eyes for a bigot. As I see it, man is a product of his conditioning, and the social forces which mold his morality and conduct—including racial prejudice—are influenced more by material things like food and economic necessities than by the fear and awe and bigotry generated by the high priests of commercialized superstition. Now don't get me wrong. I'm for decency—period. I'm for anything and everything that bodes love and consideration for my fellow man. But when lip service to some mysterious deity permits bestiality on Wednesday and absolution on Sunday—cash me out.

Notes

The first quote comes from *The Federalist*, no. 2, "Concerning Dangers from Foreign Force and Influence."

1. For more on Sinatra's leftist political leanings, see Gerald Meyer's acute essay, "Frank Sinatra: The Popular Front and an American Icon," *Science & Society* 66, no. 3 (2002): 311–35; and Jon Weiner, "When Old Blue Eyes Was 'Red': The Poignant Story of Frank Sinatra's Politics," *New Republic* (March 31, 1986), 21–23.

2. Public Law, (May 14, 1997), 105–14.

3. Mervyn LeRoy, director; written by Albert Maltz; RKO Radio Picture (1945). Albert Maltz, by the way, would later become one of the Hollywood Ten during the McCarthy anti-Communist era.

4. Interview with Edward R. Murrow, on the DVD *Frank Sinatra Memorial* (Passport Video, 1999).

5. For definitions of both terms, I quote from *The American Heritage Dictionary*, ed. William Morris (Boston: Houghton Mifflin, 1980), s.v. (sotto voce). Although it is a discussion for another forum, I would nevertheless query the reader to ponder whether, as I seem to recall, the term "acceptance" was the preferred noun during the 1960s and 1970s, whereas "tolerance" seems to have crept into our vocabulary and supplanted the former sometime around the onset of the 1980s.

6. Frank Sinatra, "What's This about Races?" in Leonard Mustazza, ed., *Frank Sinatra and Popular Cullture: Essays on an American Icon* (Westport, CT: Praeger, 1998), 25. The essay was first published in *Scholastic* (September 17, 1945) and also published in the *Spectator*.

7. The song Sinatra sings for the recording session is "If You Are But a Dream." One might, to be sure, see some sort of pre-announcement in the song's title, since the bigotry that presents itself in the film is not an easy one to remedy, if not indeed more of a "dream" than a reality. Cowritten by Moe Jaffe, Jack Fulton, and Nat Bonx, it was recorded four times by Sinatra (October 23, 1944, November 14, 1944, May 8, 1945, December 11, 1957). Short, the lyrics are as follows: "If you are but a dream / I hope I never waken, / It's more than I could bear / To find that I'm forsaken. / If you're a fantasy / Then I'm content to be / In love with lovely you, / And pray my dream comes true. / I long to kiss you / But I do not dare, / I'm so afraid that / You may vanish in the air, / So darling, / If our romance would break up, / I hope I never wake up, / If you are but a dream."

8. From this point on, when I mention Sinatra within the context of this film, I am referring to Sinatra qua sign, as beholder of those meanings that a viewer might attribute to the filmmaker's or script writer's semiotic intentionality. My reason for making such a distinction is that Sinatra, as civic individual, has decided to collaborate in this specifically based ideological enterprise; conversely, as actor and interpreter, his performance is mediated through that of the script, scriptwriter, and director.

9. For more on Sinatra's *italianità*, see Pete Hamill, *Why Sinatra Matters* (New York: Little, Brown, 1998), passim; and Gil Fagiani, "The Italian Identity of Frank Sinatra," *Voices in Italian Americana* 10:2 (1999), 19–32.

10. The lyrics of title song were written in 1943 by Abel Meeropol under the pseudonym of "Lewis Allan." A Jewish, hard-core liberal with ambivalent feelings toward America, Meeropol defended constitutional rights and freedoms, but he deplored bigotry toward people of other races, religions, and political views. While surely valiant, Meeropol's liberalism often placed him under government scrutiny. To post–World War II history buffs, he may be best known for his interest in the case of Julius and Ethel Rosenberg,

whose two sons Meeropol and his wife adopted when the Rosenbergs were executed. In addition to "The House I Live In," Meeropol wrote "Strange Fruit," a song decrying the horrors of lynching that later became Billie Holiday's signature song. On his career see Nancy Kovaleff Baker, "Abel Meeropol (a.k.a. Lewis Allan): Political Commentator and Social Conscience," *American Music* 20 (2002), 25–79, and especially 54–56 (on "The House I Live In").

11. Here I would note that the multitude is natural to a sense of oneness, insofar as we are speaking of the human race.

12. As I mentioned before, we have the three major players in the German, Italian, and Japanese Axis. The irony, to be sure, is twofold: the Italians (defeated earlier in the war) are not presented in a negative manner in this brief film, while Sinatra underscores his own Italian ethnicity as difference, placing the accent on American with the adversative conjunction "but," as we saw earlier.

13. To understand better Sinatra's notions of religion, we might look to his interview with *Playboy* 17 years later (February 1962):

> Playboy: Are you a religious man? Do you believe in God?
>
> Sinatra: Well, that'll do for openers. I think I can sum up my religious feelings in a couple of paragraphs. First: I believe in you and me. I'm like Albert Schweitzer and Bertrand Russell and Albert Einstein in that I have a respect for life—in any form. I believe in nature, in the birds, the sea, the sky, in everything I can see or that there is real evidence for. If these things are what you mean by God, then I believe in God. But I don't believe in a personal God to whom I look for comfort or for a natural on the next roll of the dice. I'm not unmindful of man's seeming need for faith; I'm for anything that gets you through the night, be it prayer, tranquilizers or a bottle of Jack Daniel's. But to me religion is a deeply personal thing in which man and God go it alone together, without the witch doctor in the middle. The witch doctor tries to convince us that we have to ask God for help, to spell out to him what we need, even to bribe him with prayer or cash on the line. Well, I believe that God knows what each of us wants and needs. It's not necessary for us to make it to church on Sunday to reach Him. You can find Him anyplace. And if that sounds heretical, my source is pretty good: Matthew, Five to Seven, The Sermon on the Mount.
>
> Playboy: You haven't found any answers for yourself in organized religion?
>
> Sinatra: There are things about organized religion which I resent. Christ is revered as the Prince of Peace, but more blood has been shed in His name than any other figure in history. You show me one step forward in the name of religion and I'll show you a hundred retrogressions. Remember, they were men of God who destroyed the educational treasures at Alexandria, who perpetrated the Inquisition in Spain, who burned the witches at Salem. Over 25,000 organized religions flourish on this planet, but the followers of each think all the others are miserably misguided and probably evil as well. In India they worship white cows, monkeys and a dip in the Ganges. The Moslems accept slavery and prepare for Allah, who promises wine and revirginated women. And witch doctors aren't just in Africa. If you look in the L.A. papers of a Sunday morning, you'll see the local variety advertising their wares like suits with two pairs of pants.

14. It has been reported that when Meeropol first saw the film he became enraged when he realized that the last three stanzas of his song had been omitted. (See *Songfacts*, http://www.songfacts.com/detail.lasso?id=2306).

15. Again, but best treated in another forum, I would suggest to the reader that although the film speaks to ethnic and religious harmony and acceptance, there is a subtle tone of what today's viewer, especially, would perceive as a type of masculinism that subtends the text at certain points. Sinatra first refers to the group as "boys," but once they have learned his "lesson," they are now, here at the end, "men." Indeed, he, too, as mentioned above, was initially dubbed a "kid" when the group first knew of his job as singer. For perceptive observations on these themes, see Karen McNally, *When Frankie Went to Hollywood: Frank Sinatra and American Male Identity* (Urbana: University of Illinois Press, 2008).

16. See Peter Kihss, "Sinatra to Head Antibias Group," *New York Times*, May 4, 1967, 1, 27.

17. Kihss's article in the *Times* (preceding note) was the first in a series of articles by a number of people who questioned not only this appointment but also the name, if not existence, of the American-Italian Anti-Defamation League. First, there was the dispute with the Anti-Defamation League of the B'nai B'rith because the names were too similar and therefore would lead to confusion among the general public. Similar confusion was signaled by the older National Italian-American League to Combat Defamation. Second, the very next day, the *Times* published an editorial that stated, "If the new American-Italian group wants to raise money by staging a big show in Madison Square Garden, Frank Sinatra will serve its purpose well. If, however, the idea is genuinely to improve the Italo-American image, which the new organization seems to think is too closely linked to the Mafia and Cosa Nostra, there are professors, artists, musicians, scientists, a Governor from Massachusetts, a senator from Rhode Island—any number of distinguished citizens of Italian descent who might have been chosen. The American-Italian Anti-Defamation League, in picking Sinatra for their national leader, has chosen to add fire to fire." (See the editorial "Image in a Curved Mirror," *New York Times*, May 5, 1967, 37). See also Charles Grutzner, "Sinatra Assailed as Ethnic Leader," *New York Times*, May 12, 1967, 65; and "Judge Defends Sinatra as Antidefamation Head," *New York Times*, May 13, 1967, 36.

For more on the rift between the Anti-Defamation League of the B'nai B'rith and the American-Italian Anti-Defamation League because of the phrase "Anti-Defamation League," see the following: Charles Grutzner, "B'nai B'rith Anti-Defamation League Threatens Suit over a Similar Name," *New York Times* (May 18, 1967), 36, and Paul Hofmann, "Italians and Jews Go to Court," *New York Times* (June 4, 1967), 74. The Anti-Defamation League of the B'nai B'rith won an injunction on October 5, 1967 that prohibited the American-Italian Anti-Defamation League from using its then-current name. At this point, the American-Italian Anti-Defamation League changed its name to "Americans of Italian Descent, Inc." and it began discussions with the National Italian-American League to Combat Defamation, Inc. to join forces. For more on this development, see Paul Hofmann, "2 Italian Groups to Study Merger," *New York Times*, February 18, 1968, 55; and "Italian Group Plans to Change Methods for Positive Action," *New York Times*, April 3, 1968, 49.

18. The rally indeed took place, with Sammy Davis, Jr., as master of ceremonies, and close to 20,000 people attended. For more on the event, see Paul Hofmann, "Italo-Americans Hold Rally Here," *New York Times*, October 20, 1967, 57.

19. Kihss, "Sinatra," *New York Times*, May 4, 1967, 27.

20. See note 7.

21. See note 14.

6

What Luigi Basco Taught America about Italian Americans

Dominic L. Candeloro

In the long view of history, racism, prejudice, and distrust of foreigners have been the standard rule of conduct. In the early history of their migration to the United States, Italians, though considered "white on arrival" were relegated to somewhere near the bottom of the racial pecking order that placed "Aryans" on top and blacks on the bottom. Only since the 1920s and the work of sociologist Franz Boas and later the anthropology of Margaret Mead have even the intelligentsia entertained the notion of cultural relativism and the equality of races and nationalities.

Despite the negative feelings generated toward Italian immigrants by Italy's status as an enemy in World War II, popular culture in the postwar period experienced what I see as an "Italian American Trend." Led by Frank Sinatra, this sustained fad included the works of Perry Como, Vic Damone, Rose Mary Clooney, Louis Prima, Tony Bennett, Dean Martin and the sports exploits of Joe DiMaggio and many others. More than ever before, American mass media was exposed to Italian American culture. When combined with previous public images (such as the gangster portrayals), the message that this movement brought to American consciousness of Italian ethnics became the basis for the treatment of Italian Americans for the rest of the century.

One of the key elements in the Italian Trend was the fictional character, Luigi Basco of the hit radio (and later television) program *Life with Luigi*. Each week from 1948 to 1954, millions of listeners tuned in to be entertained and "educated" about Italian immigrant life. The program was produced by non-Italian Cy Howard and starred Irishman J. Caroll Naish. This was the golden age of radio, when everyone was listening and choices were limited to two or three network presentations. The public impact of *Life with Luigi* was far greater than that of best-selling novels about Italian Americans, such as Pietro Di Donato's *Christ in Concrete*. I cannot think of any other Italian American themed publication or production that got wider dissemination than *Life with Luigi* in that era. In short, Luigi explained Italian American life to the general public. Luigi also provided a mirror to Italian Americans that validated their experiences.

In many ways, *Life with Luigi* was to Italian Americans what *Amos 'n' Andy* was to African Americans: a comedic depiction of a subculture in which the lines between laughing *with* and laughing *at* the ethnic group were often blurred. It was also a show in which respect for the ethnic group or lack thereof lay in the mind of the beholder. Other ethnic programs on radio and television in that era include *I Remember Mama*, a show about a Norwegian family in San Francisco and *The Goldbergs*, which depicted a Jewish family in New York. And though many among us might urge that we all "lighten up, it's only a comedy," the history of mass media and advertising reminds us that the repeated impact of sounds and images *does* make a difference. We can get a notion of what America thought about Italian Americans by analyzing in some detail the structure and content of this popular (but fictitious) show.

The creator and producer of *Life with Luigi* was Cy Howard. In 1947, Howard's *My Friend Irma* radio series became one American radio's top shows. In 1948, Howard launched the *Luigi* show. Growing up with early television, he was also a writer for Milton Berle and Danny Thomas, worked for Desilu Studios, and in 1970 made his film directorial debut with *Lovers and Other Strangers,* a film with strong Italian American themes.

The series was originally called *The Little Immigrant*, but the name was changed before the first broadcast. "Luigi Basco" (played by J. Carroll Naish) was a recent Italian immigrant. An established relative, "Pasquale," owner of Pasquale's Spaghetti Palace on Halsted Street in Chicago, had paid Luigi's $38 boat fare to America in hope of getting Luigi to marry his portly daughter, "Rosa." Alan Reed (later the voice of Fred Flintstone) played Pasquale, and Jody Gilbert played Rosa. Most of the plot lines and the dramatic tension of the radio plays revolve around Luigi's unwillingness to marry Rosa as Luigi attempts to make his way in his new American environment.

The late 1940s was an era of wholesome entertainment, which by today's standards seems corny. Like most radio shows, Luigi had a live orchestra that provided music to set the mood. The show opened with "Chicago, That Wonderful Town" to provide a geographic setting. The dialogue began with "Oh Mari," as a background for Luigi reading his weekly letter to Mamma. This was an introduction that laid out the topic for each episode and introduced a problem that Luigi had to confront. In describing the folkways and culture of America, Luigi would make a series of humorous, but gentle, malapropisms. Enter Pasquale, who would make several statements that illustrated his basic stupidity and duplicity. The two would then engage in amusing "who's on first" type of banter in impeccable broken English. Often Pasquale would stumble into describing himself in such a way ("I'ma heada da block"), that Luigi could innocently sum up his comments with something like, "Ia alwaysa know that youa bigga block head." Whatever problem Luigi was wrestling with in the episode, Pasquale promised to fix it, if Luigi would only promise to marry Rosa. Luigi would then demur with the line "No, Rosa isa too fatta for a me." This segment would end with Luigi going off to night school singing, "America, I love you! You like a papa to me. From ocean to ocean."

Introduced by a few up-tempo bars of "School Days," the next scene would begin with Miss Spaulding taking roll at night school. In keeping with the light-hearted, melting-pot spirit of the show, Luigi's fellow students in the citizenship night school classes were immigrants. Hans Conreid played "Schultz," an outspoken German with rheumatism and a bossy wife. Mary Shipp played "Miss Spaulding," the teacher of the night class. Joe Forte played "Horowitz," and Ken Peters played "Olsen." The class members usually advised Luigi, recommending a straightforward and honest solution to his problem.

In the middle of the show, Luigi would continue his letter to Mamma and carry the story line a little further. Next, there would be some interaction with a government bureaucrat or businessman that would land Luigi in hot water. In the following scene, Luigi would agree reluctantly to a solution presented by Pasquale—in exchange for Luigi's promise to marry Rosa—"Alla righta Pasquale, I marry Rosa." And each week, miraculously, there would be some turn of events that would take Luigi off the hook. And the orchestra would strike up "Oh, Mari" under the monologue of Luigi finishing his letter to Mamma. The Luigi formula repeated many of the same gags each week and listeners smiled with delight as they anticipated familiar punch lines. The sponsors of the program, Wrigley's Spearmint Gum, described the show as a good-natured program for Americans from all walks of life.

Using the above format, *Life with Luigi* explored scores of topics. In the 70 episodes that I surveyed, most of the storylines depended on the "greenhorn" experience common to all newcomers and to native-born Americans alike. In a sense, we are all outsiders, uninitiated, and inexperienced in the ways of our fast-changing urban world. Listeners could readily empathize with Luigi's trials and tribulations in getting insurance, buying a first car, going on a date with an American girl, getting a driver's license, signing up for dance lessons at Arthur Murray, coping with the vagaries of returning gifts to Marshall Field's, dealing with telephone and electric bill problems, filing income tax forms, and going to the dentist. Many times, Luigi was taken in by a con man or given a hard time by lazy, self-important bureaucrats. In each episode, language problems and bad advice from Pasquale added up to difficulties with which all listeners could identify. In one episode, Luigi was taking an induction exam for the Marine Corps. When asked if the object in a picture was a U-Boat, his answer was, "No thatsa notta my boat." And so it went.

Some of the episodes amounted to propaganda for good causes. For instance, Luigi was portrayed as a good citizen and strong supporter of the Big Brothers of America, the Boys Club, local civil defense, and as a blood donor. At least 10 of the 70 episodes sampled had some kind of patriotic, community-minded message. Luigi was also very well informed about heroes of American history like Paul Revere, George Washington and Abraham Lincoln. The citizenship class gave the writers plenty of opportunities to insert patriotic factoids about the founding fathers. On July 10, 1949, a program epilogue urged listeners to "Vote regularly. Freedom is everybody's job." During election season in early November 1949, the program focused on Luigi's "electioneering" on behalf of a proposition to expand school funding.

The episode that seemed most direct in its advocacy was the May 19, 1950 program that promoted the "Crusade for Freedom." In that show Luigi, enlisted in a nationwide Cold War campaign to gather signatures endorsing freedom and the principles of the U.S. Constitution. The purpose here was to gather the signatures and place them in a monument in West Berlin as a witness to America's commitment to protect the freedom of West Berlin in the aftermath of the blockade of Berlin by Russian communist forces. Another aspect of the campaign was to supply the people in nations behind the Iron Curtain with radios. After being turned down by almost everyone, Luigi gave a down-hearted speech that shamed hundreds of his fellow citizens to sign. As an epilogue to that *Life with Luigi* episode, General Lucius Clay, the military governor of the American zone of Occupied Germany, thanked Luigi for his warm support and urged the rest of America to get on board.

In an episode dated February 20, 1951 and entitled "Luigi Puts a Negro in His Play" the message is patriotism and brotherhood. Assigned to write a play for the night school class to perform, Luigi determined that he would focus on the American Revolution, President Washington, and brotherhood. The script mentions that it was "Brotherhood Week." Newspaper sources confirm that February 18–25 had been so designated by the National Conference of Christians and Jews.[1] The skit that Luigi came up with portrayed the many nationalities that had played a role in helping George Washington (played by Luigi) to win the War of Independence. On his own initiative, Luigi also asked Henry Clock (a war veteran and student in another night school class referred to politely as a "Negro fellow") to play the role of Crispus Attucks, the martyr of the Boston Massacre of 1770. Though two teachers and Pasquale warned Luigi not to get too "preachy" with his audience, Luigi went ahead with his plan to include the African American in his play. The play was a success, even gaining some grudging compliments from one of the nay-saying teachers. When Luigi did the closing phrases of his letter to Mamma at the end of the show, he concluded "Itsa greata day for me an America, Mamma. About 150 years ago Thomas Jefferson issa say, 'Alla men are created equal' and the mosta wonnerful thing Mamma mia issa that every day more anda mora people are beginninga believe thata." This was pretty strong stuff for 1951!

The head writer for *Life with Luigi* was Mac Benoff, who was later among the media makers blacklisted during the McCarthy period. Why someone who wrote material for *Luigi* that was so patriotic and idealistic would be blacklisted is unclear.

A number of the shows featured guest stars. Most notable was the appearance of Frank Sinatra in the episode of October 10, 1950, in which Luigi won a "mystery voice" radio contest. The prize was a weekend in New York City with Frank Sinatra. Luigi was very excited. As he put it "Sinatra atza gooda italiano name." "I'ma gonna shaka handz with Franka Sinatra." When Luigi arrived at the train station, Sinatra was there to greet him and offer him a tour on New York's glamour spots—Toots Shor's, 21, and El Morocco—but Luigi preferred the public library, the Empire State Building, and the Statue of Liberty. That this episode aired right about the time that Sinatra debuted his new television show was no coincidence.

In the October 11, 1950 *Chicago Tribune*, Larry Wolters wrote, "J. Carroll Naish and Sinatra joined hands to unfold for TV viewers a scene from the *Life with Luigi*, a radio favorite."[2] That Sinatra's handlers saw an appearance on a radio show with an Italian immigrant theme tells us something about the perceived power of the show. Ironically, Sinatra related to Pete Hamill, "You know what radio show I hated the most? It was called "Life with Luigi," with J. Carroll Naish—there's a good Italian name for you—and it was all about Italians who spoke like-a dis, and worried about ladies who squeeze-a da tomatoes on-a da fruit stand. The terrible thing was, it made me laugh. Because it did have some truth to it. We all knew guys like that growing up. But then I would hate myself for laughing at the goddamned thing."[3]

The broken English of J. Carroll Nash and Alan Reed was spot-on. When I listened to the programs when I was a boy of ten, they sounded just like my father and grandfather. And when I listen to the programs on tape 50 years later, they still sound authentic. In our family were new immigrants from Italy, going to night school and signing long-term contracts for dance lessons with Arthur Murray. One reservation here is that the dialogue lost some authenticity in that real Italian words were only used in two episodes that I surveyed—the visit from Italy by Luigi's cousin Mario, and the guest-appearance of Mario Lanza plugging his movie, *Midnight Kiss*. Though a comedy, *Life with Luigi* was more real to me than anything on radio.

Naish was able to project Luigi as *molto simpatico* (a term the show never used), and his delivery of Luigi's lines evoked simplicity, charm, and sincerity. Everybody loved Luigi long before everyone loved Raymond. He was honest, generous, thoughtful, loyal, patriotic, and public-spirited. He sent remittances of $5, representing a fourth of his $20 a week income, each week to his mother. He organized a block party because American people didn't seem to know each other the way people knew each other in Italy. And in the "Age of Anxiety," when the public feared that Russia would drop an atomic bomb on Chicago, Luigi volunteered for the Civil Defense Board.

Though he was a greenhorn and spoke broken English, he was intelligent. He was more noble than the "American" bureaucrats and businessmen with whom he came into contact. In my survey of the *Luigi* programs, I found not one scintilla of a reference to organized crime. Luigi was a hero. He was everyman—every immigrant—trying to play by the rules and become a success in America.

The image of Pasquale, on the other hand, was mostly a negative one. He was ignorant, two-faced, cunning, and dishonest and he was always trying to trick Luigi. He can also be seen as a *padrone* who wanted to maintain control of Luigi's life. The only mitigating factor in Pasquale's character was the nobility of his underlying motive for all his trickery—he was a good father trying to marry off his fat daughter. In some of the episodes when Pasquale's actions go too far and hurt Luigi, and when Luigi threatens to leave, the writers of the show made Pasquale regretful and apologetic, and he asked forgiveness of Luigi, to whom he affectionately referred as "my little cabbage-a head" or my "little banana nose." Deep down, that blowhard, know-it-all, overbearing fool loved Luigi.

Another negative image was that of the Italian female, Rosa. Even allowing for the fact that 1940's radio trivialized women like (*My Friend*) Irma and Molly (of *Fibber McGee* fame) and Gracie Allen, in almost every *Luigi* episode the 250-pound Rosa and her giggly high-pitched voice was a one-dimensional joke. As Luigi said many times, "Rosa sheesa too fatta for me." The fat jokes were piled on in this supposedly gentle comedy in a manner that is offensive to our present day sensibilities. Thus, the program that celebrated Luigi as a heroic Italian American man depicted the only Italian American female character as ridiculous. In short, *Life with Luigi* made cruel fun of Italian American women. This becomes even more dramatic when one remembers that the true love of Luigi's life and the ideal woman in the series was Miss Spaulding, the night school teacher.

As positive as the image of Italian Americans is in *Life with Luigi*, and as authentic as is the broken English, the world around Luigi Basco leaves us with some questions. Except in the episode in which Luigi's cousin Mario visits from Italy, no actual Italian words are used in the show's dialogue. We are never told why Luigi is in the antique business. Why isn't he a construction worker, a bricklayer, or a fruit-seller? Why are his night school classmates Luigi's only peers? Why doesn't Luigi have any Italian friends his own age? How and why did the writers decide that the address of his antique shop should be 21 N. Halsted, about ten blocks north of the real Taylor-Halsted Little Italy? Other local references to Marshall Field's, Michigan Avenue, the Pump Room, the Chez Paree night club, and the Aragon Ballroom seem to be accurate.

A more important question concerns religion. There is no mention of religion or the friendly parish priest in the episodes I surveyed. Even the episode where Luigi *almost* marries Rosa depicts the ceremony before a justice of the peace. And no episodes focused on Pasquale trying to get Luigi to take Rosa to the *Festa della Madonna*. Perhaps it was the convention in mass media entertainment at that time to ignore religion and perhaps a non-religious, non-Catholic Luigi made him more acceptable to the audience.

Understandably, in the postwar era, Italy was portrayed as being very backward. There were running gags about the exploits of Uncle Pietro's goat and chickens back home in Castlemare and many of Luigi's letters to Mamma had him explaining airplanes, city traffic, and American newspapers as wondrous marvels unheard of in the Old Country. The recent war, which we assume had triggered Luigi's move to the United States, is never referenced.

Life with Luigi enjoyed a healthy 5-year run on CBS Radio until March 3, 1953, with some 15-minute daily versions broadcast in 1954. In the early 1950s, many of the hit radio shows moved to television. In 1952, most of the original *Luigi* cast switched to television. But apparently, they were too "hot" for the medium and the exaggerated stereotypes that played so well on the radio offended Italian Americans. (This issue of Italian Americans using pressure against the producer needs further research.) In an attempt to save the franchise, the television version was radically revised. Naish and Reed were dropped from the cast and the writing was toned down. Luigi lost his mustache and his broken English improved dramatically with an Italian American actor, Vito Scotti, now playing the title role. Luigi got along a lot better with Pasquale. Rosa was not nearly so fat and silly as in the original version, and Luigi seemed willing to date her in the new version. By 1954, Luigi was gone, never to appear again even in reruns. Though they surface from time to time on

Old Time Radio shows and many episodes are available in recordings online, *Luigi* is gone.

After being engaged in Italian American studies for the past 25 years, I found this nostalgic journey through 35 hours of the *Life with Luigi* radio shows of my youth a delightful experience. Despite everything—the non-Italian cast and production team, the negative depictions of Pasquale, Rosa, and even of Italy itself, and despite the omissions and inaccuracies in depicting little Italy—*Life with Luigi* remains important as the single most widely disseminated portrayal of Italian Americans prior to the publication of *The Godfather.* Moreover, I believe that this program transmitted to its massive audiences (the exact size of which requires further research) an extremely positive image of young Italian immigrants. Italian American protest notwithstanding, the show gave to young Italian Americans, like ten year-old Dominic Candeloro in Chicago Heights, Illinois, a sense of validation and belonging. Identifying with the intelligence and integrity of Luigi helped to balance out the shame that had been imparted to us children of immigrants. To conclude then, this fluffy radio comedy helped create greater toleration and acceptance of Italians in the larger society and at the same time helped to empower Italian American youth.

When combined with other developments during the 1940s and 1950s "Italian Trend," even while using stereotypes, *Life with Luigi* helped to erase reasons for distrust of Italians and, perhaps, prevented countless acts of discrimination against them, allowing them to advance in economic and social status at a faster pace than they might have. In my book, we all owe J. Caroll Naish and the *Luigi* crew a "Bigga Thanka You."

Notes

1. *Sunday Herald*, Bridgeport, CT, February 18, 1951.
2. Larry Wolters, "Surprise! On TV Frank Sinatra Is Really Good," *Chicago Tribune*, October 11, 1950.
3. Pete Hamill, *Why Sinatra Matters* (Boston: Little, Brown, 1998), 48–49.

Appendix to Chapter 6

The following radio episodes of "Life with Luigi" are available on the Internet from such vendors as http://www.audio-classics.com, eBay, and http://www.classicbroadcasts.com/

Date (y-m-d) / Program Title
1948-02-20 "Making A Speech With A Fever"
1948-06-15 "The Little Immigrant"
1948-07-03 "Luigi Buys a Car"
1948-11-09 "Finds Stolen Diamond Ring"
1948-11-16 "Luigi Attends PTA Meeting"
1948-11-30 "Luigi Joins Hospital Plan"
1948-12-07 "Damage Claim on Broken Mirror"
1948-12-14 "Paul Revere"

1948-12-20 "Pasquale Thinks No Gift For Luigi"
1949-01-09 "First Date With American Girl"
1949-02-06 "Luigi Gets Erroneous Phone Bill"
1949-02-20 "Luigi Needs Driver's License"
1949-03-13 "The Raffle"
1949-03-20 "The Car"
1949-03-27 "Luigi Goes To Dance School"
1949-04-03 "Luigi Return a Nightgown"
1949-04-10 "Rosa Must Lose Weight"
1949-04-24 "Luigi Gets A Big Electric Bill"
1949-05-01 "Plans A Block Party"
1949-05-08 "Luigi's Toothache"
1949-05-15 "Super Salesman"
1949-05-29 "The Wedding"
1949-06-05 "At The Racetrack"
1949-07-10 "The Registered Letter"
1949-07-17 "At The Beach"
1949-08-14 "Sore Thumb"
1949-08-28 "Go West, Young Man"
1949-09-10 "Luigi Tries To Become a Singer"
1949-09-24 "Statue Of George Washington"
1949-10-04 "Out of Water"
1949-10-11 "Columbus Day Play"
1949-10-25 "The Zoning Commission"
1949-11-01 "Football Game"
1949-11-08 "No Electioneering"
1949-11-22 "Thanksgiving Celebration"
1949-11-29 "Money For The Kids"
1949-12-20 "Pasquale Takes Luigi's Xmas $"
1949-12-27 "New Year's Phone Call"
1950-01-03 "Pietro Needs An Overcoat"
1950-01-17 "The Cold"
1950-01-31 "Beautiful Miss Spaulding"
1950-02-14 "Movie Date"
1950-02-21 "Washington Radio Contest"
1950-02-28 "Miss Spaulding's Party"
1950-03-07 "Income Tax Season"
1950-03-14 "Big Brothers of America"
1950-03-21 "Rosa or the Park"
1950-03-28 "Luigi Finds A Wallet"
1950-04-04 "Traffic Light"
1950-04-25 "Donation for Gym Equipment"
1950-06-06 "Party Line Troubles"
1950-07-04 "Independence Day Parade"
1950-08-15 "Luigi Has a Fire in the Store"
1950-08-22 "Business Trip to Buffalo"
1950-09-05 "Luigi Sells Ice Cream"
1950-09-12 "Luigi Is Lonely"
1950-09-19 "Crusade for Freedom Speech"
1950-09-26 "Trolley Transfer"

1950-10-03 "Luigi Gives Blood" 1951-02-13 "Luigi Puts a Negro in His Play"
1951-02-20 "Luigi's Washington Play"
1951-02-27 "Luigi Becomes a Gas Station Attendant"
1951-03-06 "Business Deal With A Millionaire"
1951-03-20 "The Spring Walk"
1951-03-27 "April Fool's Joke"
1951-04-17 "Basco-Pasquale Lifetime Shoelace Company"
1951-05-15 "Want to Be an American Day"
1951-05-22 "Rosa's Makeover For Antique Dealer's Dance"
1951-05-29 "How to Make Minestrone Soup"
1951-06-12 "Luigi Becomes a Soda Jerk"
1951-06- ?? "Luigi Decides to Paint His Own Safety Zones"
1951-06-26 "Luigi Throws a Party for Salesmen"
1951-07-03 "Fourth of July Parade"
1951-08-28 "Schultz and Olson Not in Luigi's Class"
1951-09-04 "Naming the O'Reily's Baby Contest"
1951-09-18 "Luigi Isn't in the Phone Book"
1951-09-25 "Go West, Young Man"
1951-10-02 "Mama Thinks Luigi Is a Millionaire"
1951-10-09 "'Why Was My Face Red' Contest"
1951-10-23 "Luigi, Square Dance Caller"
1951-10-30 "Trick or Treat"
1951-11-06 "Luigi Opens up New Antique Store"
1951-11-13 "Miss Spaulding Off for a Week"
1951-11-20 "Luigi's Thanksgiving Dinner for America"
1951-12-25 "A Christmas Present for Pasquale"
1952-01-01 "Insurance for Everything"
1952-01-08 "Luigi Takes Rosa to the Movies"
1952-01-15 "Rosa Attends Luigi's Night School Class"
1952-01-22 "Rosa Goes to the Head of the Class"
1952-01-29 "High Standard of Living"
1952-02-05 "Homesick"
1952-02-12 "Toledo Weigh Machine & Honest Abe"
1952-02-26 "Joins Local Civil Defense Group"
1952-03-04 "Pasquale Threatens to Evict Luigi"
1952-03-11 "Income Tax Problems"
1952-03-25 "Essay Contest"
1952-04-01 "April Fools Joke"
1952-04-08 "Easter Birthday Party"
1952-04-15 "Luigi Can't Sleep"
1952-04-22 "Takes a Date to Antique Dealers Dance"
1953-01-09 "Luigi Leaves for California"
The undated final episode was titled: "Cousin Mario Comes to America."

7

Affirmative Action for Italian Americans

The City University of New York Story

Joseph V. Scelsa

On December 9, 1976, the Chancellor of the City University of New York (CUNY), Robert J. Kibbee, took the unprecedented action of "designating Italian Americans as an affirmative action category for the University in addition to those so categorized under existing federal statutes and regulations."[1] Why did the CUNY chancellor take this action at that time, and what has it meant for Italian Americans at the City University of New York, then and now? In order to understand the chancellor's motives, we will examine a number of factors: (1) the role and function of The City University of New York in relation to emerging groups historically; (2) the effect of the Civil Rights movement on Italian Americans; (3) institutional racism in the academy; and, finally (4) the governance and financing of CUNY.

The affirmative action status of Italian Americans at CUNY was established by the chancellor's memorandum to the CUNY College Presidents. In it, the CUNY chancellor cites his numerous discussions over the previous few years with legislators, and with other persons, both within and outside the university. He also notes that he has had the opportunity to review and consider several studies dealing with the presence of Italian Americans among university staff.

Italian Americans first started to avail themselves of a college education in significant numbers in the 1960s and 1970s. These were the children and grandchildren of the mass immigration from Italy at the end of the nineteenth century and first few decades of the twentieth century (1880–1922). The first goal of the immigrants was to survive economically—to get a secure job with which they could provide for their families. Once this was accomplished, the second and third generations turned their attention to upward mobility and, like all people seeking success in America, realized full well that higher education was the way to attain that goal.

At the City University of New York, prior to 1970, there existed a very restrictive admissions policy that reduced the number of Italian American students by virtue of the fact that so many had attended Catholic schools. The problem was not that they were Roman Catholics, but that these schools tended to grade their students more severely, with the result that often otherwise well-qualified students did not achieve the grade average of 85 (out of 100) needed for admission to the University. All of this changed in 1970, when CUNY established an open admissions policy for all students that eliminated the grade average barrier. Thus, from 1970 to 1975, more and more Italian American students began to apply for admission, and more were accepted than ever before. By 1975 a campus like Queens College, CUNY had a student body whose population was about 25 percent Italian American.

This was an unexpected result of the CUNY open admissions policy. The policy had been aimed at "traditional minorities," which, in the late 1960s, had been protesting the university's restrictive policies and demanding their rightful place. Once the new Italian American students arrived at CUNY, they found that notwithstanding the policy's inclusive intent, they were ill-served by the university's programs, which offered few courses that were designed to assist Italian American students who were among the first generations in their families to seek college degrees. In particular, they requested courses about their own ethnic and cultural background. As they often expressed it, they would go to class with well-meaning faculty members who would teach about the need to be more racially neutral and to be socially aware of the struggles of African Americans and Puerto Ricans (the largest Hispanic group in New York City), but there would be little material on Italian Americans and their history and culture. It was not that they, the Italian American students, were uninterested or insensitive, but rather they wanted to learn about themselves as well. The struggles of *their* ancestors and the rich cultural heritage of Italy had had a lasting impact on the United States of America that was worthy of study.

There were precious few Italian American professors to instruct them, and even fewer courses, both in Italian American Studies and Italian language, throughout the university. By 1975, CUNY had grown to comprise 20 campuses throughout the 5 boroughs of New York City. These new students became involved in campus life and organized student Italian clubs eventually on all 20 campuses. To do this, they enlisted the help of the interested Italian American faculty.

With the building of new campuses and the increase in the overall size of the student body necessitated by open admissions, the university's student population doubled between 1969 and 1975, when it reached 220,000 students. This in turn required the hiring of more faculty. Within the ranks of this new faculty were a number of young Italian American professors who became mentors to Italian American students and generally assisted them in the transition in a scholarly environment.

Italian American students and faculty members also reached out to community leaders who had been sensitized by the gains made by the African Americans to the need to be assertive in order to obtain the resources and consideration they felt should be properly theirs as a major minority group within the university. To this end, the Italian American community in New York collaborated with members of the university faculty to publish several studies between 1970 and 1975 that demonstrated the need to provide Italian Americans with more resources, especially in the area of higher education. They later turned their attention specifically to the hiring and promoting of Italian American faculty at CUNY.

Their efforts were not without some success, at least at the level of the chancellor's office. In 1975, Chancellor Kibbee wrote directly to all 20 of the CUNY college presidents, urging them to consider ways in which their respective colleges could address the particular needs of Italian American students on their campuses. Without citing the studies, the chancellor went on to say that it was important to these Italian American students and their community that the university represent a congenial understanding and sympathetic environment by respecting the traditions, customs, and beliefs of this large and important component of our academic community.[2]

The chancellor recognized Italian Americans as New York City's largest minority, and he suggested that the campuses encourage the development of programs relating to the cultural and folk traditions of Italy. Such programs were to include student and faculty organizations on each campus, academic programs and courses that reflected the contributions of Italians, outreach programs to encourage potential Italian American students to attend CUNY, orientation programs to sensitize college counselors to the needs of Italian American students, the creation of advisory committees to each CUNY president consisting of Italian American students and faculty, and a mechanism for the presidents to meet periodically with Italian American students and faculty organizations in order to be informed of "incipient problems" so that they could be addressed and resolved.

The chancellor's message was an important victory for all concerned faculty, students, and the community. Unfortunately, it was short lived. By the spring of 1976, the ranks of the Italian American faculty would be decimated due to the city's fiscal emergency. New York City was going broke and a Financial Control Board was put in place to restrict the city's budget. What this meant for CUNY was that with New York City no longer able to pay half the cost of the CUNY system (as it had been doing), the New York State government would pick up the financial burden of administering the system. The precise mechanism took one year to work out, and, in the meantime, the university was required to lay off faculty and staff in order to reduce overall expenses. CUNY is a university with a strong union contact, thus the last hires were the first to be let go. This meant that the newly hired Italian American faculty received letters saying that they would be let go owing to the financial emergency. This, however, did not apply to those university faculty members who belonged to federally designated minority populations.

Having recently received the chancellor's backing to support Italian Americans at CUNY, the remaining faculty and staff, together with the Italian American students, turned to their elected officials. In Albany, the state capital, they found a champion in the person of State Senator John D. Calandra, a leader of the Italian American Legislative Caucus.

At the insistence of legislators, community groups, faculty, and students, Chancellor Robert J. Kibbee made his landmark decision designating Italian Americans as an affirmative action category for CUNY. In explaining his decision, Chancellor

Kibbee referred to his discussions with legislators as well as members of the university and community at large.

But, the damage had already been done, and even though Italian Americans were now being given this preferred status, it was in many ways after the fact, since faculty and staff ranks were already depleted. The momentum that would have created an important core of Italian American faculty within the university was lost, and the progress that could have been achieved in a natural progression had it not been for the financial crisis in New York City being brought to a close.

To address issues of institutional racism, you must have an administration that is receptive to all groups, not a select few. In our society, we have a paradox in that our rules of law that are meant to protect "individual rights," not "group rights," with the exception of those protected groups under civil rights status such as African American, Hispanics, Americans with disability, Asian Americans, American Indians, and women. The basis for those groups so designated under Affirmative Action, can be found in Federal Executive Order 11246, which requires employers not to discriminate against employees or applicants for employment because of religion, national origin, age, disability, or gender and to take affirmative action to insure that they are protected. Italian Americans, although a cognizable group, are mostly left out from an institutional perspective.[3]

Until Italian Americans as a group obtain their own seat at the cultural roundtable, the academy, they will not have achieved parity with the other groups who have successfully done so. Whether affirmative action will be the vehicle that accomplished this goal for them remains an unanswered question. The CUNY story of Italian American affirmative action should not be seen as a blueprint for success but one strategy in a long road to achieving this goal. However, until Italian Americans have a say in the governance of these cultural institutes, the struggle will need to go on. Only time will tell how it will end. I remain optimistic, since for many years I was privileged to see first-hand the hard-working spirit of stick-toitiveness of CUNY's Italian American faculty, who have survived and overcome under adverse conditions. I believe they will eventually prevail and achieve their rightful place in the academy. It may take them more time than it should and will probably be accomplished without the benefit of affirmative action.

Notes

1. Chancellor Robert J. Kibbee, memorandum to CUNY Council of Presidents, December 9, 1976, published in the Appendix as Document 2.
2. See Document 1 in the Appendix: Chancellor Robert J. Kibbee letter's to CUNY College Presidents of March 17, 1975.
3. To learn more about what happened to Italian Americans at CUNY and their struggles over the next two decades, I suggest these publications: Francis N. Elmi, *The Invisible Minority: A History of The Italian American Struggle for Justice and Equality of The City University of New York* (New York: John D. Calandra Italian American Institute, 1996); and Joseph V. Scelsa, "The 80th Street Mafia," in *Beyond The Godfather: Italian American Writers on the Real Italian American Experience*, ed. A. Kenneth Ciongoli and Jay Parini, (Hanover, NH: Universities of New England Press, 1997), 289–306.

Appendix to Chapter 7

Document 1. Chancellor's letter concerning Italian Americans at CUNY, March 17, 1975.

Letter of Robert J. Kibbee, Chancellor, City University of New York, to CUNY College Presidents.
Source: photocopy in the papers of Joseph V. Scelsa
THE FOLLOWING LETTER WAS SENT TO ALL COLLEGE PRESIDENTS
March 17, 1975
Dear [blank]:

Over the past ten years the City University has moved aggressively to offer the possibility of a higher education to populations previously excluded. Beginning with College Discover, then SEEK and finally through open admissions the opportunities of the University were expanded to ever larger segments of the City's youth.

Among those who have entered the University in ever growing numbers are Italian-American young people from all sections of the City. I would like to call your attention to this expanding component of the University's enrollment and to urge you to consider ways in which their particular needs can be served better.

The young Italian-Americans come to us with a proud and rich cultural tradition in literature, music and the arts. They also carry with them customs, and values that flow from their ancestral homeland, their religious heritage and their American experience. It is important to them and to their community that the University represent a congenial, understanding and sympathetic environment. If this is to be so it behooves all of us, faculty, administration and staff to recognize, understand and respect the traditions, customs and beliefs of this large and important component of our academic community.

To this end I would encourage you and your staff to consciously and positively consider ways in which each college can evidence its concern for our Italian-American students, faculty and the larger community from which they come. Among the efforts you might consider are the following:

The development of a series of programs that draw upon both the cultural and the folk tradition of Italy and the Italian-American community.

The encouragement of student and faculty organizations on the campus that are oriented toward the preservation and promotion of academic, cultural or spiritual values of importance to Italian-Americans.

The development of academic programs and/or courses that appropriately reflect the contribution made by Italians to history, literature, science and the arts.

The encouragement of outreach programs to serve the special needs and aspirations of those Italian-American communities within the natural orbit of the college.

The development of orientation programs for counsellors designed to sensitize them to the cultural, social and spiritual heritage of Italian-Americans. In establishing such programs every effort should be made to draw upon the resources of the community and upon its leadership.

The creation of advisory committees to the President with which you can consult as to how the college and its various components can improve their services to Italian-American students and the communities from which they come.

Periodic consultation with the Italian-American faculty and student organizations ton the campus so that you can be alert to incipient problems and through which you may ascertain ways in which the college can more effectively fulfill its obligations to its students and faculty.

I urge you to consider additional measures that might be taken on your own campus to quicken the colleges [*sic*] response to the City's Italian-American communities and to heighten campus sensitivity to the special needs and concerns of Italian-American students. We are concerned here with the City's largest minority and one which, like other minorities, has over time suffered the degrading effects of bigotry, misunderstanding and neglect. One of the great purposes of the University, and particularly of this University, is to foster understanding, diminish thoughtless and emotional prejudice and to expand both the horizons of those we serve and the opportunities to achieve their aspirations. Unfortunately the realization of these aims does not just happen. We must make it happen and I commend your attention to this task.

I realize that many of the colleges have already instituted some of the activities described here or others. So that I can have some sense of the efforts being made I would like to have a report by June 1 describing the activities being undertaken.

Sincerely yours,
Robert J. Kibbee

Document 2. Affirmative Action Directive regarding Italian Americans at CUNY, December 9, 1976.

Memorandum from Robert J. Kibbee, Chancellor, CUNY, to CUNY Council of Presidents.
Source: photocopy in papers of Joseph V. Scelsa
December 9, 1976
To: CUNY Council of Presidents
From: Robert J. Kibbee

Last year I wrote to you at some length regarding the University's concern for the Italian-American community and for our many Italian-American students. The response of many of the Colleges to the concerns expressed in my letter was most encouraging and deeply appreciated by those representatives of the Italian-Americans with whom I shared them.

At that time, I did not speak to the question of Italian-American faculty and staff members at the University, about whom I have had numerous discussions over the past few years, with legislators and with others both within and outside the University. I have also had an opportunity to review and consider several studies dealing with the presence of Italian-Americans in the University staff.

It is my belief that the present situation requires the University to take positive action to assure that qualified persons of Italian-American ancestry are identified so that they can be considered fairly along with the other candidates for positions that might become available at the University. I am equally concerned that the processes of the University are such that Italian-Americans receive fair consideration in the processes that lead to promotion and tenure within the University.

To this end I am designating Italian-Americans as an affirmative action category for this University in addition to those so categorized under existing Federal statutes and regulations. I also have instructed the Affirmative Action Office to include Italian-Americans in the data collected for affirmative action purposes.

As you well know, the Italian-Americans constitute the largest single ethnic minority in the City of New York and one of the largest elements of the University's student population. They bring a rich heritage of learning and culture to our City and have contributed significantly to its growth and vitality. We must make every effort to assure that within our University, both students and faculty of Italian-American heritage are treated with fairness and sensitivity.

8

The Changing Roles of Italian American Women

Reality vs. Myth

Susanna Tardi

Using a sociohistorical approach, this essay examines the changing roles of women of Italian heritage in the context of (1) subcultural (Italian) norms and values, (2) dominant ("American") cultural norms and values, and (3) changing structural conditions (i.e., World War II, the labor market, and the women's movement). Media reinforcement of dominant cultural norms and values is also addressed.

I have been conducting research on Italian Americans since the mid-1970s, and have found that the type of research available concerning Italian American women has remained largely unchanged. Descriptions and explanations of the norms and values of Italian Americans, and in particular of women's roles, have been provided mostly through literature, poetry, anthologies, and autobiographies—genres that offer subjective "revelations" of cultural experiences. While these works contain rich histories, they do not provide concrete information that is readily generalizable to the population of Italian American women.

Italian American Women: Four Generations in Perspective

To provide a sociohistorical analysis of Italian American women, it is important to comprehend the role of women in Italy prior to peak migration (1880–1910). These women were embedded in a patriarchal (father-headed) but matricentric (mother-centered) society. In Italy, no distinction was made between labor inside or outside of the home. In Italy, household production was central to the economy of southern Italy. In the Italian family, contributions to the family and interdependence were valued, whereas "American" values focused on independence and self-fulfillment. As the familial socioeconomic status declined, the importance of the "mother" role increased in the Italian family.

In a world where the family was judged not by the occupation of the father but by the signs of family well-being which emanated from the household, the mother played an important role in securing their status.[1]

Consequently, for the peasants in particular, there was a power dimension to the mother role, since she was a contributor to the household production, and was largely responsible for creating perceptions of family well-being. This was achieved by her ability to "manage" the household and utilize creativity and ingenuity. In a culture steeped in family, food, and pride, never displaying "*mala figura*" (a bad impression) was of key importance.

When these immigrant women came to the United States, sometimes months or even years after their husbands, they were confronted with an economic necessity to earn more money for family survival and well-being. The *Mezzogiorno* (areas south and east of Rome) "code of honor" possessed cultural norms and values (cultural "baggage") that prohibited them from interacting with *gli stranieri* (outsiders, literally "the strangers"), particularly those of the opposite sex. During the wave of Italian immigration to the United States, male workers dominated the American labor market. This contributed to many Italian immigrant women earning additional money for the family by engaging in occupations that were home-based, such as laundering, tailoring, flower-arranging, and pasta- and bread-making. This working environment did not threaten family solidarity. Even taking boarders into the household was considered preferable to the Italian woman than leaving the home to work.[2] In New York, Italian immigrant women working in the garment industry was permitted because coworkers were female.[3]

Isolating cultural factors to account for the participation of Italian women in the labor market is inadequate. Miriam Cohen's research on Italian immigrants in New York City from 1900–1950 suggests that Italian patriarchal norms and values did not inhibit daughters from external participation in the American labor market.[4] Newly arrived male immigrants experienced more problems securing employment than other immigrant cohorts, so daughters in these families went to work out of necessity. However, the longer the male household head lived in America, the less likely it was for the daughter to be engaged in the labor market. It seems that for at least as long as the economic necessity for family stability existed, modified norms and values permitting women to work outside the home existed. The interaction between economic, demographic, and cultural factors must be considered in understanding female Italian American labor force participation.

While American society was and is patriarchal, similar to Italian society, it lacked the power dimension of the mother in Italian society. When Italians first immigrated to the United States, they tended to cluster together in urban ghettos (areas predominantly consisting of others from the same cultural background), out of choice (subcultural similarities), and necessity (jobs and affordable housing). Italian immigrant women frequently lived in ghettos, and if they did not work outside of the home, their exposure to the norms and values of the dominant culture was less than their male "working" counterparts. This segregation of Italian American women from the dominant culture was maintained until the 1950s.

Following World War II, ethnic communities decreased, especially among the second generation. The isolation of Italian American women from the dominant culture dramatically declined due to two factors. First, public schooling exposed both second generation Italian American children and their parents to the differences between Italian and American culture, which included the priority of the family over all institutions and the individual, the matricentric family versus the patriarchal family, and a culture of interdependence versus independence. Second, there was the growing trend of suburbanization, in which Italian Americans ventured away from the ghetto to take advantages of better job opportunities. However, suburbanization for Italian Americans often involved a two-generation move: the second generation and their immigrant parents. Inclusion of the parents in household moves preserved the role of the elders in maintaining the central importance of the Italian American family.[5] This is important because it helps explain why the Italian American family was able to maintain its stronghold over the individual members.

A comparative qualitative analysis of first, second, and third generation, working- and middle-class Italian Americans in New Jersey found a persistence of familial cohesiveness requiring (1) love and respect, (2) reciprocal obligation among nuclear and extended family members (particularly parents and siblings), (3) residential proximity (particularly regarding parents and siblings); and (4) emotional and, to a degree, financial interdependence (particularly regarding parents and siblings).[6] Ethnic identity was based on perceived differences between Italian family norms and values and those of *gli Americani* (the Americans), not ties to Italy or their use of the Italian language. The inability of individuals whose ethnic heritage is "Italian" to speak the Italian language, read Italian books or newspapers, or cook Italian dishes are signs of assimilation, but did not result in significant alterations in the basic norms and values that effect overall life patterns. The respondents in this study recognized both the positive and negative social and economic impact their ethnic heritage has had on their lives.

Among younger (under 40) third and fourth generation Italian Americans, assimilation may be greater than for their older counterparts. A study involving a non-probability sample of third and fourth generation college students from "pure" Italian, "mixed" Italian, and non-Italian ethnic backgrounds found no significant difference between ethnicity and the respondents' degree of ethnic cohesiveness (i.e., ethnicity as one of the primary means of self-identity). Most respondents chose to identify themselves as "Americans, nothing more, nothing less."[7] Findings also indicated that respondents from Italian ancestry were not found to have significantly higher levels of familial priority than those from non-Italian ancestry.[8] There were no gender differences regarding these relationships. Structural conditions and cumulative cultural factors that may contribute to the apparent lack of ethnic cohesiveness are (1) being born into middle-class families; (2) more limited contact with extended family; (3) mothers working outside of the home; (4) the absence of the relaying of the cultural oral histories within the family; and (5) an educational curricula lacking information on white ethnics in general, and Italian Americans, in particular. Research on third and fourth generation Italian Americans is extremely limited. To understand Italian American women, particularly those of the third and fourth generations, it is necessary to further elaborate on the structural changes and socialization processes that have influenced these women.

The Labor Market and The Socialization Process

World War II is one of the most important factors influencing the American labor market. This event had an enormous impact on women in American society. During World War II, media reinforced the changing needs of society. Until the end of the war, the media (magazines, advertisements, posters, newsreels, radio) message was "women, your men and the United States are counting on you to produce the goods necessary to maintain the war effort and help preserve your men's jobs." After the war, the same media that urged women to enter the labor force, then emphasized their role in the home. American society expected women to resume their "normal" roles as mothers and housewives. The personal needs, desires, and skills of these women were irrelevant.

From the 1960s until the present, economic necessity—the need for the dual income household—has required women to participate in the labor force. Studies have noted the increased importance of women's financial contributions to the household.[9] Frequently, poverty has been avoided because of their economic contributions. The economic stability, if not the survival of the family, has necessitated the dual income household. Women's statuses have expanded to include "employee" along with homemaker and mother. Irrespective of gender, "real," individual power in American society increases as socioeconomic status (income, education, and occupation) increases. However, familial expectations for women exist in the absence of power; they are simply one part of the expanded female role. The home-related workload of women has not decreased, despite their participation in the labor market. The labor participation rate of women in 2003 was 59.5 percent, which constituted 47 percent of the total U.S. labor force.[10] Over the past 30 years, women in the United States have economically progressed; they hold higher-paying, more prestigious jobs, own more businesses and have made strides to narrow the wage gap.[11] They "earn less," however, and "are less likely to own a business, and are more likely to live in poverty than men."[12] There still exists a gender wage gap and gender segregation regarding the distribution of labor.

In the United States, women's wages continue to lag behind men's. In 2002, the median wages of women who worked full-time, year-round were 76.2 percent of men's. In other words, among workers with the greatest employment effort, women earned about 76 cents for every dollar earned by men.[13]

Women also work in different occupations and segments (industries) of the labor market than men. The two industries with the largest percentage of women workers are "managerial/professional specialty" (33.2 percent) and "technical/sales and administrative support" (39.5 percent); men are more dispersed across six broad occupational categories: managerial/professional specialty (29 percent), technical sales and administrative support (9.7 percent), service (17.6 percent), farming forestry and fishing (3.6 percent), precision productions, craft, and repair (18.8 percent), and operators, fabricators, and laborers (18.8 percent).[14] Not only do women work in different labor sectors, but they also lack equal access to top-earning jobs.[15]

Gender socialization influences the occupations men and women choose, but given the opportunity, women will accept traditionally defined "men's work." It is through the socialization process that children learn the gender-based expectations of others, which form the framework for learning social roles.[16] Gender differences in socialization, wages, and occupation continue to have a negative impact on the social status and economic well-being of women. Feminists brought these issues of gender discrimination to the foreground, but the media, a key agent of socialization, has successfully distorted this reality.

Media Images and Feminist Issues

The media (film, television, magazines, advertisements, radio) have traditionally reflected and perpetuated the marginalization and objectification of women. A woman's contributions to the society and the family have been downplayed. This has supported the superiority of men and the subjugation of women.

The feminist continuum has not been adequately reflected in print media. Feminists have been portrayed as black widow spiders fixated on devouring men or as "anti-female, anti-child, anti-family, and anti-feminine."[17] Rita Simon, Cathy Young, and Katie Roiphe accused feminists of exaggerating sexual violence and inequality.[18] The media has contributed to the negative connotations associated with the word "feminism." Feminists have not been credited for attempting to create gender equality, but instead have been indicted for providing women with options internal and external to the home.

From the mid-1960s until the early 1990s, there have been demographic, social and economic factors that have influenced the representation of women in the media. There has been an increase in the representation of women among television network news reporters due to socioeconomic changes and the feminist movement.[19] However, studies indicate that women in the media are underrepresented in high status and power positions (i.e., editors-in-chief, news publishers, deans or directors of journalism programs), and overrepresented in low status positions.[20] In general, the reality of women's role in society has not been appropriately represented in the media. Women in contemporary society are still characterized in headlines and topics by their statuses as wives and daughters, rather than as independent agents with issues of public concern.[21]

Gender bias has also been found to exist in advertising. According to Lori Wolin, "advertisers often use color, shape, texture, packaging, logos, verbiage, graphics, sound and names to define the gender of a brand. Brand gender is thereby communicated through advertising."[22]

Males and females have been found to process information differently, and are therefore targeted through genderized communication.[23] To the marketing and advertising experts, the issue becomes identifying the market appropriate to the product and the means by which that product will be accepted. Whether or not the advertisements perpetuate societal gender, ethnic, or other stereotypes is not particularly relevant to the marketing task.

Studies have focused on broadcasts during prime time, "however, network practices remain largely a black box of little understood customs and conventions."[24] Time slots influence ratings on prime time television.[25] Furthermore, the culture of the organization is influenced by the group norms and values and personal likes and dislikes of those in control (i.e., network presidents, executive producers, etc.). Research notes a tendency for those cultures to become more stable and embedded as the age of the organization rises.[26] Since most of the individuals controlling prime time television are males who have been socialized in a sexist society, they are more likely to select programs that align their gender-biased socialization and personal tastes.

Ethnicity, Societal Attitudes, and Media: Where Do We Begin?

An October 2004 survey on ethnic attitudes in American society conducted by Raeleen D'Agostino Mautner, Research Director of the American Italian Defense Association (AIDA), offered a series of relevant results. Overall, Italian Americans appear to have a positive image in American society. Furthermore, a majority of the respondents (53 percent) agreed that the "media portrayal of Italian Americans is offensive." "The majority of those who agreed recognized that Italians are portrayed as Mafia, gangsters, and bad guys, instead of as hardworking, law-abiding citizens."[27] It is difficult to reconcile these largely positive results with the existing formal evidence, as well as informal and anecdotal information concerning discrimination against Italian Americans. Raeleen D'Agostino Mautner cites nationwide examples of court cases that offer substantial "documentation of discrimination and defamation of Italian Americans."[28] What individuals believe and what they purport to believe differ. What individuals say and what they do are frequently divergent. Furthermore, individuals may say things (express feelings) that contradict fact. A report commissioned by the Order Sons of Italy in America (OSIA), based on the 2000 census, indicated that individuals reporting Italian heritage were predominantly white-collar workers and that they were above the national average in education, occupation, and income.[29] Yet they continue to be stereotyped in the media as blue-collar workers, uneducated types, and mobsters. Another example of reality versus myth is a poll conducted in 2001 by Fairleigh Dickinson University's Public Mind. The poll found that of the respondents who reported having watched *The Sopranos*, 45 percent disagreed that the show had "sexually explicit scenes/dialogue"; 48 percent disagreed that it contained "offensive/vulgar language"; 55 percent disagreed that it contained excessive/graphic violence; 57 percent disagreed that it "glorified organized crime; and 65 percent disagreed that it "portrayed Italian Americans in a negative way."[30]

Bill Dal Cerro has conducted an ongoing study for the Italic Institute of America (Image Research Project) on images of Italian culture in films from 1928 to 2002. According to Bill Dal Cerro, the results indicate a significant increase in "mob movies" after the success of the *The Godfather* (1972). In 2003, the Order of the Sons of Italy presented a report, "Stereotypes in Advertising," which identified gender-based stereotypes in advertising that involved Italian Americans: men were portrayed as Mafia gangsters and the women as overweight housewives in black, or as gum-chewing bimbos.[31]

Media portrayals of individuals of Italian heritage have been primarily based on negative stereotypes. Italian American men and women have been depicted as gang "family" members, uneducated, inarticulate, and loud. Italian American men have been depicted as violent, aggressive, shady, sexual predators. Italian American women have been generally portrayed in a dichotomous manner; either as old, fat, and buxom, with dyed black (like shoe polish) or gray hair, matronly, dressed in black or a housecoat, or young, thin, and buxom, with dyed black or blonde hair, with tight-fitting, but fashionable clothing. The one exception in the dichotomous representation is the generalized characterization of Italian American women as "manipulative." The term "manipulative" has a negative connotation in American society. Women in general have been perceived as "manipulative," but men as "influential," for accomplishing or attempting to accomplish the same goals. Societal gender expectations and media reinforcement of these perceptions may contribute to the perpetuation of gender stereotypes.

The socialization process, which includes media as one of its agents, contributes to gender-based age discrimination. Aging lines near the eyes are referred to as "crows' feet" on women, but "lines of distinction" on men; women with gray hair are characterized as "old," while men are called "distinguished"; in midlife, women experience "menopause" (hot flashes, night sweats, mood swings); men have a "midlife crisis" (find a younger woman and buy a sports car). This gender-based age discrimination can be witnessed in all forms of media.

Current Media Images

Since norms, values, beliefs, and attitudes occur over time, examining the overall messages communicated by media and the source of that message is important. An examination of three recent, popular, Emmy Award–winning television programs, *Ally McBeal* (1997–2002), *Sex in the City* (1998–2004), and *The Sopranos* (2000–2007) reveals a number of common themes: women all play central roles in these programs; one or more of the women on each of these programs is a professional (i.e., lawyer, psychiatrist, journalist, etc.). Women are portrayed as emotionally unstable, and emotionally, if not financially dependent, calculating, manipulative, adaptive, but needing a man, a child, or both to be "complete." At least one woman in each episode is portrayed as a sexual "deviant."

For Italian Americans in general, and Italian American women in particular, *The Sopranos* has the most interest and impact, positive or negative. Unfortunately, it has gained its notoriety because it has all of the key components of societal interest: violence, vulgar language, sexism, racism, and ethnic discrimination. Most of the females are uneducated with the exception of the psychiatrist, Dr. Jennifer Melfi, who is herself seeing a psychiatrist because she is treating Tony Soprano, a mob leader, and she is attracted to this murderer who is somehow portrayed as a "teddy bear" character who just happens to be a murderer. Most of the women are depicted as financially dependent on their husbands, aware of their husband's association with the mob, but willing to overlook this fact to maintain a certain lifestyle. This supports the portrayal of women as "prostitutes."

Steven Spielberg's animated film *Shark Tale* continues a pattern of negative Italian American stereotyping and has received a significant amount of criticism from Italian American organizations. These organizations see the film as particularly damaging to children's perceptions of Italian Americans since, as a group, children are highly impressionable. Children are growing up in an increasing technological environment and with increasing access to technology in both the classroom and the home. Children may have a particular sensitivity to media influence. Research indicates that children's programs (i.e., cartoons) are approximately three times more likely to contain violence than prime time television.[32] According to a National Television Violence Study of 1997, children's television programs are often humorous and only on rare occasion shown to have long-term consequences.[33]

Children may be socialized by the media to engage in aggressive or violent acts, partially because they learn that there are no long-term negative consequences to this type of behavior. According to Robert Hodge and David Tripp, children see or hear violence in the media, but as a fantasy, not reality.[34] Despite conflicting research findings, one point is certain: media influence societal norms and values. While they are not sole determinants of behavior, they certainly influence and shape self-concept and societal world perspectives.

Do the children know enough about their ethnic heritage to recognize ethnic discrimination, covert or overt? The practice of providing oral histories has traditionally played an important role in transmitting ethnic heritage from one generation to the next, especially in traditional folk cultures such as that of the Italian peasants. In recent years, this practice has probably declined, if not been eliminated altogether. In families in which both parents are working outside of the home, eating meals together is not necessarily the norm. In the past, oral histories were a part of the dinnertime routine. For certain cohorts of Italian Americans, family, often extended family, gathered around the dinner table as the elders relayed the "when I was young" scenarios. Are these individuals who are not exposed to their ethnic history, neither in the home nor in the educational environment, growing up without ethnic consciousness?[35] It has been suggested that ethnic stereotyping may influence children to engage in self-loathing.[36] Raeleen D'Agostino Mautner points to a Heinberg, Thompson, and Stormer study indicating that in order for the media to affect attitudes, the message needs to be internalized.[37] However, I am suggesting that if one has not developed "ethnic consciousness," the ethnic "message" will be incomprehensible, and therefore will not be internalized. If parents, educators, and media do not pass down or teach ethnic history, it is unlikely that children will identify with, or even be cognizant of, ethnic discrimination.

***

There is no singular reality for Italian American women. An understanding of women of Italian heritage requires an integration of subcultural (Italian) and dominant cultural (American) norms and values in the context of the prevailing structural conditions. These conditions have had a very different impact on each generation. First generation Italian American women reflect traditional Italian norms and values. Second generation Italian American women are caught in cultural conflict trying to find a balance between the Italian and American cultures. The adoption of norms and values in the third generation may be split by age; the author's research suggests that older members retain ethnic cohesiveness and younger members and those of the fourth generation identify as "Americans, nothing more, nothing less."

All women, including Italian American women, seem to be socialized to adapt to changes, especially when they benefit the family. While women's roles are changing, discrimination continues because it is embedded institutionally. Sexism is not just an ideology; it is an institutional practice for controlling women.

Sociological research involving Italian Americans is very limited. Studies relating to Italian Americans need to be more rigorous with respect to the setting of explanatory research goals, use of more representative sampling, and the simultaneous examination of variables (i.e., sex, age, generation, socioeconomic status). This research agenda will provide a necessary foundation for a comprehensive understanding of Italian American women.

Notes

1. Frances X. Femminella and Jill Quadagno, "The Italian American Family," in *Ethnic Families in America: Patterns and Variations*, ed. Charles H. Mindel and Robert W. Habenstein (New York: Elsevier, 1976), 93.
2. Richard D. Alba, *Italian Americans: Into the Twilight of Ethnicity* (Englewood Cliffs, NJ: Prentice-Hall, 1984).
3. Virginia Yans-McLaughlin, *Family and Community: Italian Immigrants in Buffalo, 1880–1930* (Ithaca, NY: Cornell University Press, 1977).
4. Miriam Cohen, *Workshop to Office: Two Generations of Italian Women in New York City, 1900–1950* (Ithaca, NY: Cornell University Press, 1992). These findings are based on data from the 1900 census.
5. Zena Smith Blau, *Old Age in a Changing Society* (New York: New Viewpoints, 1973); C. Leahy Johnson, *Growing Up and Growing Old in Italian-American Families* (New Brunswick, NJ: Rutgers University Press, 1985); Susanna Tardi, "The Traditional Italian Family is Alive and Well and Living in New Jersey," *Italian American Review* 5 (1997): 1–14.
6. Susanna Tardi, "Family and Society: The Case of the Italians in New Jersey" (PhD diss., New York University, 1989).
7. Susanna Tardi, "Where Have All The Italians Gone? Familial Priority and Ethnic Consciousness Among White Ethnics" (unpublished conference paper, Eastern Sociological Society, Baltimore, Maryland, 2001).
8. Ibid.
9. Maria Cancian, Sheldon H. Danziger, and Peter Gottschalk, *Working Wives and Family Income Inequality Among Married Couples* (New York: Russell Sage Foundation, 1993); Anne E. Winkler, "Earnings of Husbands and Wives in Dual-Earner Families," *Monthly Labor Review* 121, no. 4 (April 1998): 42–48.

10. United States Department of Labor, Bureau of Labor Statistics, http://www.dol.gov/wb/factsheets/Qf-laborforce.force.htm.

11. Amy Caizza, April Shaw, and Misha Werschkul, *Women's Economic Status in the States: Wide Disparities by Race, Ethnicity, and Region* (Washington, DC: Institute for Women's Policy Research, 2004), 31.

12. Ibid.

13. Ibid., 9.

14. Ibid., 14.

15. Institute for Women's Policy Research, *Research-in-Brief: Restructuring Work: How Have Women and Minority Managers Fared?* (Washington, DC: Institute for Women's Policy Research, 1995); *The 2002 Catalyst Census of Women Corporate Officers and Top Earners in the Fortune 500* (New York: Catalyst, 2002).

16. Nancy Chodorow, *Femininities, Masculinities, Sexualities: Freud and Beyond* (Lexington: University of Kentucky Press, 1994); Chodorow, *The Reproduction of Mothering: Psychoanalysis and the Study of Gender* (Berkeley: University of California Press, 1978).

17. Sally Quinn, "Feminists Have Killed Feminism," *Los Angeles Times*, January 23, 1992, B7.

18. Rita J. Simon and Cathy Young , "Men Too Are Victims of Domestic Violence," *New York Times*, February 4, 1994, A22; and Katie Roiphe, *The Morning After: Sex, Fear and Feminism on Campus* (Boston: Little, Brown, 1993).

19. Marion T. Marzolf, "Deciding What's Women's News," *Media Studies Journal* 33 (1993): 36–44.

20. Kay Mills, "The Media and the Year of the Woman," *Media Studies Journal* 7 (1993): 19–31; Jean Otto, "A Matter of Opinion," *Media Studies Journal* 7 (1993): 157–66.

21. Maurine H. Beasley and Sheila J. Gibbons, *Taking Their Place: A Documentary History of Women and Journalism* (Washington, DC: American University Press, 1993); Deborah Rhode, "Media Images, Feminist Issues," *Signs* 20 (2001): 685–710.

22. Lori Wolin, "Gender Issues in Advertising-An Oversight Synthesis of Research: 1970–2002 ," *Journal of Advertising Research* 43 (2003): 111–29.

23. Ruth A. Borker and Daniel N. Maltz, "Anthropological Perspectives on Gender and Language," in *Gender and Anthropology: Critical Reviews for Research and Teaching*, ed. Sandra Morgen (Washington, DC: American Anthropological Association, 1989), 411–37.

24. Martha M. Lauzen and David M. Dozier, "Equal time in prime time? Scheduling favoritism and gender on the broadcast networks," *Journal of Broadcasting & Electronic Media* 46 (March 2002): 137–54.

25. Susan T. Eastman and Douglas A. Ferguson, *Broadcast/Cable Programming: Strategies and Practices*, 5th ed. (New York: Wadsworth, 1996); Bridget Byrne, "Public Opinion," *Variety* 19 (2000): 64–66.

26. Terrence Deal and Allan A. Kennedy, *Corporate Culture: The Rites and Rituals of Corporate Life* (Reading, MA: Addison-Wesley, 1982); Allan L. Wilkins and William G. Ouchi, "Efficient Cultures: Exploring the Relationship Between Culture and Organizational Performance," *Administrative Science Quarterly* 28 (1983): 468–81; Edgar H. Scherin, *Organizational Culture and Leadership* (San Francisco: Jossey-Bass, 1985).

27. Raeleen D'Agostino Mautner, *American Attitudes Towards Italian Americans: A Preliminary Investigation* (Stone Park, IL: American Italian Defense Association, October 2004), 16.

28. Ibid., 6–7.

29. Order Sons of Italy in America, *A Profile of Today's Italian Americans: A Report Based on the Year 2000 Census*, (online), http://www.osia.org/public/pdf/IA_Profile.pdf, (Washington, DC, Order Sons of Italy in America, 2003), 3.

30. Fairleigh Dickinson University, Public Mind Poll, *New Jersey and the Sopranos: Perfect Together?*, (online), http://www.publicmind.fdu.edu/badabing/index.html (Madison, NJ: Fairleigh Dickinson University, 2001).

31. Order Sons of Italy in America, *A Profile of Today's Italian Americans: A Report Based on the Year 2000 Census*, (online), http://www.osia.org/public/pdf/IA_Profile.pdf (Washington, DC: Order Sons of Italy in America, 2003).

32. Nancy Signorielli, *A Sourcebook on Children and Television* (New York: Greenwood Press, 1991).

33. Margaret Seawell, ed., *National Television Violence Study*, II (Thousand Oaks, CA: Sage Publications, 1997).

34. Robert Hodge and David Tripp, *Children and Television: A Semiotic Approach*, (Stanford, CA: Stanford University Press, 1986).

35. Susanna Tardi, "Out with the Old, In with the New? Into the Millennium: Norms and Values among Italian-American Students," in *Millennium Haze: Comparative Inquiries About Society, State, and Community*, ed. Mario A. Toscano and Vincent N. Parrillo (Milan: FrancoAngeli, 2000), 35–42.

36. Raeleen D'Agostino Mautner, *American Attitudes Towards Italian Americans* (Stone Park, IL: American Italian Defense Association, 2004).

37. Leslie J. Heinberg, J. Kevin Thompson, S. M. Stormer, "Development and Validation of the Sociocultural Attitude Towards Appearance Questionnaire (SATAQ)," *International Journal of Eating Disorders* 17 (1995): 81–89.

9

Prejudice and Discrimination

The Italian American Experience
Yesterday and Today

Salvatore J. LaGumina

"Tonight I am going after Wops. I am going to beat up Wops."

—One of the actors, while drunk, in *It's a Wonderful Life*,
directed by Frank Capra (1946)

"Still there seem to remain a few groups one can stereotype and slur with impunity, for instance, religious fundamentalists, Roman Catholics, and Italian Americans. As Italian-Americans are usually Catholics they get hit twice. The president of the Columbus Citizens Foundation has good reason to be sore. If Spielberg's film emphasized Italians' contributions to Western culture from the Roman Empire on down through the Renaissance, to modern engineering, science, the arts, and let us not forget such staples of American cuisine as pizza and pasta, who would object? But Spielberg's *Shark Tale* is fixated on the Mafia as an Italian enterprise, with no mention of the occasional German, Jew, or Irishman, who made their contributions to organized crime in America."

—R. Emmett Tyrell, "Ugly Jaws," *American Spectator*, September 16, 2004

I propose to discuss the topic of anti-Italian discrimination by treating it under three different headings. I shall begin by reviewing the vocabulary we now use to discuss discrimination. In the second part of my essay, I will treat historical anti-Italian discrimination. In the concluding section I shall discuss discrimination in the present generation.

Definitions

It would be helpful to explore and define various terms that are associated with discrimination: bias, bigotry, defamation, discrimination, prejudice, and stereotyping. "Bias" may be defined as having multiple meanings, however, in reference to intergroup relations, "bias" means "to have a slant or prejudice in favor or against." "Bigotry" involves "intolerance and prejudice," while "defamation" is defined as "attacking, slandering or injuring by false and malicious statements." "Discrimination", although in and of itself may not necessarily be pejorative given a possible definition as "distinguishing so as to divide, recognizing differences between, showing partiality," it is usually used in a derogatory sense when dealing with ethnic groups. "Prejudice" refers to a "judgment or opinion formed before facts are made" and accordingly may be favorable; nevertheless, it also is usually used in a biased, unfavorable way. "Stereotyping" implies "an unvarying pattern of behavior when dealing with ethnic groups."

This quick review of terms as they are normally employed in intergroup relations conveys clear attitudes that are demeaning, detrimental, divisive, and disruptive—in a few words, they are derogatory and offensive and indeed can be dangerous. These words are inherently loaded and disruptive catchwords that inflame and abuse by serving to emphasize the harmful and negative. Often offered in verbal contexts, frequently they are acted upon, becoming additionally injurious. Even in the absence of offensive action, these terms have the effect of instilling and reinforcing attitudes in peoples' minds. Does not the fact that recent polls (for instance from Zogby International) showing that over 70 percent of respondents associate Italian names with organized crime, support the interpretation that, notwithstanding the absence or intention of malice or meanness, the majority of people in today's society unconsciously believe that there is a link between the two?

Historical Anti-Italian Discrimination

It can be averred that historically, virtually every new group that has entered American society has had to endure periods of prejudice and discrimination—usually for two to three generations for most white ethnic groups, while for non-whites it has been an enduring phenomenon. The flow of masses of Italian immigrants began to enter this country in the 1880s, with their numbers peaking in the pre–World War I period and once again in the early 1920s, before it was seriously interrupted by immigration quotas. It resumed after World War II and lasted until the 1970s, when it dwindled to a relative trickle. If we accept the dictionary definition of approximately 30 years before one generation is succeeded by another, then we can assume that, after making allowance for the latter immigration period, currently Italian Americans are for the most part in the third or fourth generations—surely sufficient time for a waning of discrimination and prejudice. This proposition deserves further examination.

Research that I and others have undertaken confirms the existence of discrimination and hostility experienced by the first generation, especially; the second, considerably, and the third; partially. My book, *WOP! A Documentary History of Anti-Italian Discrimination in the United States*, published in 1973, became the first major publication on the topic of intolerance against Americans of Italian descent.[1] That work sought to delineate the record of antagonism and hostility that awaited Italian immigrants and their issue in this country by recording numerous discriminatory episodes that were for the most part blunt, curt, and flagrant. *WOP!* provides abundant examples of the existence of discrimination dating from even before the onset of mass Italian immigration unto the present. Using documentary evidence in the form of public statements, government reports, advertisements, organizational resolutions, and so forth, my research demonstrated that discrimination was pervasive not only among those usually regarded as ignorant and intolerant, but also in more respected circles of American society.

Until the mid-twentieth century, indolence, ignorance, religious superstition, and an inclination toward criminality were the standard terms that characterized nativist views regarding Italian newcomers, thus becoming the bases for discrimination. One or two examples would be in order. Consider what Edward Alsworth Ross wrote in *Century Magazine* in 1914:

> Italians rank lowest in adhesion to trade unions, lowest in ability to speak English, lowest in proportion naturalized after ten years' residence, lowest in proportion of children in school, and highest in proportion of children at work. Taking into account the innumerable "birds of passage" without family or future in this country, it would be safe to say that half, perhaps two thirds of our Italian immigrants are *under* America, not *of* it. Far from being borne along our onward life, they drift round and round in a "Little Italy" eddy, or lie motionless in some industrial pocket or crevice at the bottom of the national current.[2]

Ross, it must be pointed out, was not considered an intolerant redneck; rather he was known as a distinguished scholar.[3]

It is revealing to note the persistence and pervasiveness of ethnic prejudice well into the twentieth century even with respect to individuals who were on the way to becoming national icons. For example, as late as the end of the 1930s, a time when Italian Americans seemed to be on the cusp of acceptability after decades during which they endured unflattering characterizations as superstitious, ignorant, unintelligent buffoons, or, even worse, as gangsters, they still suffered from stereotyping. Thus, despite his evolving folk hero status as a New York Yankee, teammates referred to Joe DiMaggio as the "Big Dago." A *Life* magazine article reveals the casual bigotry that then existed. While perhaps not intending to demean DiMaggio as an Italian American, but rather to comment on his baseball achievements, the author indulged in prevailing stereotypes when he described the athletic son of Sicilian immigrants as follows: "Although he learned Italian at first, Joe, now 24, speaks English without an accent, and is otherwise adapted to most United States mores. Instead of olive oil or smelly bear grease he keeps his hair slick with water. He never reeks of garlic and prefers chicken chow mein to spaghetti."[4]

At approximately the same time, Frank Sinatra was on the way to becoming the premier male singer in the nation. He attracted the attention of popular band leader Harry James, who signed him on as his band's vocalist. When James suggested Sinatra change his name to the less Italian-sounding "Frankie Satin," the Hoboken singer adamantly rejected the notion: "I said no way, baby. My name is Sinatra. Frank fucking Sinatra."[5]

In this era, one could find confirmation in official government reports of the idea that Italian Americans were inherently inferior. United States Navy officers assigned to consider the feasibility of employing Italian American fishing boats and crews in California at the outbreak of the Second World War were unusually blunt in their appraisal: "They are volatile in nature and are therefore not completely reliable . . . The majority of the Italians are not good seamen, good fishermen, good navigators. They are not over intelligent."[6] The low esteem in which the ethnic group was held as the 1940s approached did not end abruptly with World War II. Instead, it persisted for perhaps another generation—that is until the 1970s, when significant strides had been made in American society along with legislation designed to curb racial and ethnic discrimination.

Discrimination in the Present Generation

Comparing the earlier period with our own times, it is clear that the character of current anti-Italian discrimination is quite different. In the pre–World War II era the deprecation of Americans of Italian origin was often blatant and unapologetic, but its modern counterpart is more subtle and elusive. The low regard for things Italian persisted during the Second World War, especially in the early period. Writing in the grave atmosphere of the war, Louis Adamic gave an example of severe pressure exacted on Italian Americans to change their names as necessary precursors for acceptance in the business, social, and political worlds. He relates the account of Joseph Pedrotti, a well-educated teacher whose application for a position at a prep school for boys in the late 1930s was frustrated because of his refusal to Anglicize his Italian name. The letter sent to Pedrotti by a representative of the school is revealing: "I am sure you will agree that although they have distinguished themselves in many other fields, the Italians have not done so well in education."[7]

Discrimination in our times is much less obvious and often only implied. Indeed, circumstances require that it be less apparent in view of society's greater sensitivity toward ethnic prejudice. Another factor is the greater societal prominence of Italian Americans in public life. Vigilance against defamation on the part of Italian American organizations like the Commission for Social Justice (of the Order Sons of Italy in America) and the National Italian American Foundation has also played an important role. But discrimination, stereotyping, and the demeaning of Italian Americans have not vanished. They remain in existence, albeit they are far less conspicuous.

The basis for anti-Italian discrimination in the present generation lies in stereotyping, guilt by association and noninclusion. Various television shows in the 1970s and 1980s, as well as the current popularity of *The Sopranos*, can be cited as promoting typecasting and caricatures of Italian Americans. The portrayal of a silly, boisterous, ignorant Italian American family in NBC's *Torellis* in the 1980s is a case in point. Utilizing all the tired, worn-out clichés of the past, this series lent credence to the idea that Italian Americans readily serve as the butt of society's jokes—that they are devoid of positive features that would deserve recognition or emulation. Television advertisements in which Italian Americans are depicted as crude and unrefined characters further illustrate a failure of ethnic sensitivity.

In some respects, the present climate is far different than that experienced by Italian Americans in the first half of the century when they were openly denied membership in organizations ranging from recreational clubs and fraternal associations to volunteer fire companies. While the time of openly stated exclusion is largely over, there are still some cases in which Italian ethnicity remains a basis for denial. Because it is frequently difficult to prove, such bias usually goes unchallenged. In some instances, however, the response is direct—even remarkably so. Thus avid golfer John A. Segalla, a wealthy Connecticut builder who was told, "Too bad you have an Italian name," when he was denied membership in a golf club, responded by building his own golf club in 1993.[8]

As in the past, linking Italian Americans with criminality remains the predominant feature of stereotyping. The run of popular commercial and television movies that included *The Godfather* (Parts I–III) and *The Untouchables*, has made the criminal stereotype so pervasive that even otherwise esteemed jurists have embraced it on occasion. In a decision that imposed life sentences on three convicted mobsters in May 1993, Senior United States District Judge Jack B. Weinstein made an observation that, while intended as instructive, was widely condemned for reinforcing negative images. After hearing testimony that individuals "had been lured into organized crime by the ethos of the neighborhood, as young twigs bent by their seniors," Weinstein stated, as reported in the *New York Post*, "I believe there is a large part of the young Italo-American community that should be discouraged from going into this line of work."[9]

The response was swift and condemnatory. The leaders of Italian American organizations bristled at the remarks. One commented, "It indicates the mindset people have about Italian-Americans—that somehow, Italian-American young people are intrinsically attracted to organized crime."[10] A critical *New York Post* editorial seconded the views of many: "It seems safe to assume the federal Judge Jack Weinstein was momentarily careless last week when—after sentencing three mobsters to life in prison—he pronounced from the bench that 'there's a large part of the Italian-American community that should be discouraged from going into this line of work.'"[11]

Guilt by association is another insidious anti-Italian pattern. The suggestion that a person with an Italian name is somehow connected with mobsters or illicit activity has sometimes resulted in censure and disapproval that are patently unfair. This was evident in 1992 when the New York City Comptroller, Elizabeth Holtzman, in an arbitrary and capricious decision, sent an official missive to Mayor David Dinkins recommending against granting a contract for a construction project to the Leon DeMatteis Construction Co., despite the fact that DeMatteis Construction presented the lowest sealed bid for the work and that the firm had executed projects satisfactorily for the city previously. Holtzman linked Frederick DeMatteis with such convicted mobsters as Anthony "Fats" Salerno, and she maintained that DeMatteis had interests in concrete companies linked to organized crime, citing testimony before the New Jersey Division of Gaming Enforcement to buttress her case. Revealingly, however, she dismissed a report by the same agency that had exonerated DeMatteis. After a thorough review of DeMatteis's activities, the New Jersey agency had approved his casino service industry license in January 1991, stating, "Mr. DeMatteis has never been convicted, indicted, arrested or targeted by a grand jury. He has never been identified by any law enforcement agency as a member or an associate of organized crime. He has worked for the family business since his discharge from the Army in 1945. He is a decorated veteran of World War II, has engaged in substantial charitable work and enjoys an outstanding reputation in his Long Island community."[12] Notwithstanding the previous scrutiny, Holtzman nevertheless used the power of her office to prevent DeMatteis from obtaining a city construction contract. Vindication for DeMatteis, and, by extension, for Italian Americans, came with DeMatteis's appeal to a higher court. In a strongly worded brief of October 7, 1992, a New York Supreme Court Justice rebuked Holtzman and the city administration for denying DeMatteis a contract on spurious grounds that reflected ethnic prejudice:

> Other than innuendo, speculation and guilt by association particularly by one with an Italian surname, there is simply no evidence of a probative value to show a link between petitioner and corrupt activity . . . Frederick DeMatteis has not only lost a contract here. He has also, because of the recommendation to debar his company from future work with the City, largely lost the opportunity to do business in and for New York. He has also lost his good name.
>
> I find that none of these losses were justified on the record before the Comptroller, before the Mayor, or before the Court. Therefore, summary judgement is granted in favor of the petitioner.[13]

In February 1993, the appellate court overruled the action of New York City that held DeMatteis not to be a responsible contractor. "The purported evidence conveyed no more than an impression of guilt by association rather than demonstrating any relationship, other the merely incidental, between petitioner and members of organized crime."[14]

It was guilt by association or, more accurately, the alleged sins of the father that formed the nexus of anti-Italian discrimination experienced by New York City Corrections Commissioner Catherine Abate. Media preoccupation with her father's supposed unsavory past, rather than her exemplary record of 20 years of outstanding public service followed Abate's appointment to a major law enforcement position in the nation's largest city. When Italian American leaders like Governor Mario Cuomo criticized the *New York Times* for participating in insinuation, notwithstanding Abate's unblemished 20-year record, the paper attempted to justify its coverage by placing Abate on the defensive: "The issue here, apart from the real or imagined sins of the father, is the candor of the daughter."[15] The supposition was that she deliberately held back her father's alleged disreputable past. City newspapers, along with television reports, focused on a 1976 New Jersey newspaper account in which her father was said to have spoken of having mob ties.[16] Her denial of any knowledge about this past led to charges of prevarication and accordingly raised questions about her credibility in such a sensitive position. Even while they used loaded and judgmental terms, critics like Mike McAlary denied they were denigrating Abate: "You are not smearing a public official when you report that she grew up under the same roof as an underboss . . . There is convincing evidence that he grew up riding shotgun for Al Capone . . . Did Ms. Abate know about her father's secret life and fail to disclose it? Was she ever asked to do a favor over an Atlantic City wedding cake or baptismal font? We're not talking about the sins of the father being visited upon a daughter. We're now investigating what may well be a daughter's sins of omission." [17] Other reporters (including Murray Kempton) were more discreet, but they, too, criticized Abate for misrepresentation in denying she knew about her father's criminal past.

Italian American organizations, including the Commission for Social Justice (CSJ), denounced the affair as inequitable and unjust. "We believe each person should be judged only by his/her own actions and not alleged actions of any relative."[18] Support also was found in Jim Dwyer's *Newsday* column, which excoriated the *New York Times*: "Having abandoned its own preachings, our national newspaper of record has turned to the Book of Exodus, whose wrathful God visits the iniquities of the father upon the children. Except that the newspaper never got around to spelling out the father's iniquities, said iniquities appearing to be guilt by association."[19] The smear campaign notwithstanding, Abate was able to retain her position. One can only speculate that this was due to the steadfast support of Italian American organizations like the Order Sons of Italy and the backing of various New York City and state officials. While federal, state, and city law-enforcement officials maintain that ordinarily their agencies do not investigate backgrounds of people seeking positions, there are exceptions. This case leads one to wonder whether exceptions escalate when Italian Americans are involved.

Excessive scrutiny of Italian Americans seeking to be employed or seeking to win contracts in New Jersey's casino industry is a current practice that appears to be discriminatory. In 1979, Congressman Andrew Maguire voiced objection to a statement by officials from the Department of Housing and Urban Development (HUD) that all those with Italian surnames seeking contracts would be automatically investigated to avoid subsidizing projects that are "backed by individuals associated with organized crime." When confronted with Maguire's objection, HUD officials claimed they were joking. It was not a joking matter, however, to individuals with Italian surnames seeking contracts in this industry, to learn that almost automatically their backgrounds, at least three generations back, were investigated more extensively than those without such surnames.[20] Perhaps more than we realize, criminality enters the prevailing mindset. So, for example, in 2000, Jon Corzine, who was then a candidate for the United States senate and is presently governor of New Jersey, and who ironically may have a partial Italian background himself, made disparaging remarks about Italians—remarks that were meant perhaps in jest but were nevertheless regarded as so insulting that he apologized.[21] There are also other occasional incidents that show a lingering prejudice in society.

For example, in May 2003 a village trustee of Port Jefferson, Long island used an ethnic slur in reference to a local Italian American restaurant proprietor that so outraged the business owner that he demanded an apology.[22] Whether an apology was made is not known, but what the episode exposed was the persistence of an attitude—hopefully one that is diminishing but nonetheless, still near the surface.

There has much debate over whether *The Sopranos* or the more recent animated movie *Shark Tale* denigrate Italian Americans. Normally one is reluctant to comment on television shows and movies not personally viewed; however, a final remark on the current scene may be in order. First, it would probably require additional time and study before empirical evidence of the purported damaging impact of *The Sopranos* is established. Having said that, it is disturbing to note the previously mentioned Zogby Poll that found most respondents tend to associate crime with Italians. The poll asked teenagers what sort of film and television roles a person of a given ethnic background would be most likely to portray; Italian Americans were expected to play crime bosses, gang members, and restaurant workers. Indeed, they were the most heavily stereotyped group in the survey: 44 percent linked Italian Americans with crime, whereas the next most frequent association—Arab Americans with terrorists—was just 34 percent. With regard to *Shark Tale*, a number of educators and responsible people who have viewed it are adamant in concluding that the animated film only serves to strengthen negative and harmful images and thereby reinforces stereotypes about Italian Americans. That this is aimed at children renders it perhaps even more alarming. In that sense, it appears to parallel the post-*Godfather* climate that found such widespread acceptance of the thesis of a natural inclination toward crime within the ethnic group that the image actually found its way in court cases.

Even granting that this survey of recent anti-Italian discrimination is not exhaustive, sufficient data has surfaced to indicate that the prejudice is still there. While the grossest, bluntest, and most desensitized examples of yesteryear happily have been relegated to the dustbin of history, the more sophisticated, astute, and elusive types of discrimination remain on the scene to varying degrees. Anti-discrimination laws, greater sensitivity, and proper education have all helped to diminish discrimination of course; however, it would be foolish in the extreme to believe that bigotry is over. Without succumbing to paranoia, it seems prudent to be aware of its pernicious presence and detrimental possibilities.

Notes

1. Salvatore J. LaGumina, *Wop! A Documentary History of Anti-Italian Discrimination* (1973; Toronto: Guernica, 1999).
2. Edward Alsworth Ross, "Racial Consequences of Immigration," *Century Magazine* 87 (February 1914): 617, 619.
3. On Ross, see also Chapter 4 earlier.
4. Noel F. Busch, "Joe DiMaggio," *Life*, May 1, 1939: 63–69.
5. Pete Hamill, *Why Sinatra Matters* (Boston: Little, Brown, 1999), 38.
6. Lawrence DiStasi, ed., *Una storia segreta: The Secret History of Italian American Evacuation and Internment During World War II* (Berkeley, CA: Heyday Books, 2001), 73–74.

7. Louis Adamic, *What's Your Name?* (New York: Harper, 1942), xii.
8. *New York Times*, October 9, 1993.
9. *New York Post*, May 26, 1993.
10. *Newsday* (May 26, 1993).
11. *New York Post*, June 1, 1993.
12. State of New Jersey, Department of Law and Public Safety, Division of Gaming Enforcement, December 3, 1990 (Commission for Social Justice Archives).
13. Supreme Court of the State of New York Brief in Application of *Leon D. DeMatteis Construction Corporation v. David N. Dinkins*, Index No. 7500/92, October 7, 1992.
14. Order of Supreme Court, Appellate Division, February 25, 1993, *DeMatteis v. Dinkins*.
15. "Sins of the Father," *New York Times*, April 23, 1992.
16. *New York Daily News*, August 25, 1992.
17. *New York Post*, April 24, 1992.
18. Letter from Vincent Romano, Chairman of the CSJ, to the *New York Times*, April 27, 1992.
19. *Newsday*, April 24, 1992.
20. *New York Times*, February 15, 1979.
21. *New York Times*, March 29, 2000.
22. *Newsday*, May 5, 2003.

10

"Good Enough"

An Italian American Memoir

Joanne Detore-Nakamura

"Play the piece for your father. Your mother can't appreciate it!"
That's what my German American piano teacher told me about the
Beethoven piece that I was practicing. Although both my parents were both Ital-
ian American, my Dad was "half-American," a mixture of German, Scottish, and
English, while my mother was Italian and Sicilian, an apparently more lethal
combination.

"Those kinds of Italians," said my piano teacher, "have no ear for music."

I never argued; I was too naïve and too polite. I simply took my piano book
and left with a bad lesson resonating in my head for many years after. It was just
another piece of evidence that "my people" were inferior and so must I be.

That's how self-loathing begins, with small, seemingly unrelated incidents cul-
minating over time. I wouldn't fully recover from the piano teacher's comment or
comments like it until I was a doctoral student many years later.

The kind of Italian you were mattered in my tiny working-class town of Frankfort, New York, a predominately Italian American town, although I remember that
Sicilians were considered Italians on a lower peg. Skin color was also important.
Being too dark was a problem for some Italians as I found out at a baptism celebration for my godmother's first child when I was probably eight or nine years
old. It was hot and my godmother's small, third floor apartment was crowded with
people. There was no air conditioning, food for an army of people, and hands fly-
ing this way and that, punctuating lively anecdotes told in half English and half
Italian. There was talk about dialects, about being *calabrese*, *napolitano*, or Sicilian, and whether your dialect was "the real" Italian or something less. And then
there was talk about skin color. A distant cousin or relative of my godmother's
drew comments from some of the women there. She was dark-skinned, with long,
beautiful curly, coarse hair the color of ebony piano keys. She wore a white, halter

sundress that set off the deep espresso color of her skin. In a mix of Italian and American, I heard someone whisper, "Ai! She's like a *Negra!*" said a distant cousin.

"She has to stay out of the sun!" another woman warned.

"What's a matter with her mother?" said another woman, with her hands pinched, rocking back and forth.

"Mama mia!" They added, like a chorus.

Too dark, I thought, was there such a thing? I had the opposite problem.

When I was in grammar school, my darker skinned classmates nicknamed me "mayonnaise face," "ghost," and "Casper." I was teased, taunted, and tormented for being too white and too smart, two ideas closely linked together in my community, and I was made to pay for being both. Although I was about 75 percent Italian-Sicilian with some English and German from my father's mother's side, I did not have the lovely olive skin tone of my mother or any of my Italian American classmates. I had translucent white skin like an Elizabethan, blue veins visibly streaming up the undersides of my arms. My mother often took me to the doctor's for alleged anemia.

"She's just light-skinned Mrs. Detore," the doctor would say. "There's nothing wrong with her."

Without a medical solution, my mother decided to tackle the problem herself. Every summer my mother ordered me out into the sun.

"Get out there and get some sun on your face. You look sick," she'd tell me, pushing me out the back screen door into the hot sunlight.

As a young girl, those who weren't Italian American were referred to as "Medagons," with an indignant twist of the right hand. German, Polish, Irish, English—any "white" ethnicity—was all lumped into the "Medagon" category. We, as Italians, were superior too everyone, at least that was the line that I heard while growing up. We were better housekeepers, gardeners, cooks, and workers. We had common sense when "they" had nothing but book smarts, good for nothing.

Yet, underlying all this talk of superiority was an undercurrent of inferiority that ran much deeper and much nearer to the truth of every Italian American in my small town of Frankfort, New York. There was an unspoken belief that we were not as smart as or good as the Americans who were our teachers, our bosses, our senators, and our presidents. They were Americano and middle or upper class. They bought into the party line of oppression and internalized every nasty stereotypical idea of Italians. It was easy to believe.

Following the village's pattern of migration, one can easily understand how the entire town could suffer from group-esteem problems. The town was German American first, then Irish American and finally Italian American. Each new wave of immigrants oppressed the next so that the Italian Americans, who were the last to arrive, bore the brunt of the discrimination. In addition to this type of oppression stemming from being an "out-group" or other, psychologists and educators began to institutionalize the "stigmatization" of Italian-Americans, according to Elizabeth Messina, who writes,

in January 1923, psychologist Dr. Arthur Sweeney's book, *Mental Tests for Immigrants*, was made part of the appendix to the hearings of the House Committee on

Immigration and Naturalization. Testifying before the House Committee on Immigration and Naturalization, Sweeney characterized "Latin" [Italian] immigrants as "imbeciles" who possessed primitive brain structures "scarcely superior to that of the ox, . . . who think with their spinal cord rather than the brain." He, too, urged Congress to "apply the new weapons of science [intelligence tests] to protect ourselves against the degenerate horde."[1]

In addition to influencing the political agenda, psychologists also influenced the way in which Italian American children were treated in the educational system. Messina found that "In 1920, Katharine Murdoch, an instructor in psychology at the Columbia University School of Social Work, wrote confidently in an academic journal, *School and Society*, that *Italian children* were *more retarded* [being average for one's grade level] in their intellectual development than were 'Negroes or Jews.'"[2] These prevailing attitudes within the broader culture would have a profound effect on the group self-esteem of the Italian American people within the village of Frankfort, New York, and its surrounding area, Utica.

The stigmatization began with the ghettoizing of Italian Americans. The Italians, like my grandfather's family, lived below the train tracks on the wrong side of town. Most of the children didn't attend school past fifth or sixth grade in my grandfather's time. This was due to a combination of factors including the fact that many children worked at an early age to bring in money for the family. Not many Italian Americans in my grandfather's time went to college, if at all, but there were many educated non-Italians in the town at the time, comprising the workforce of professional and skilled labor. In fact, Harold Smiddy, the Vice President of General Electric,[3] would marry one of Frankfort's most famous citizens, Lois Mixer Smiddy, whose family was one of the original settlers of the town, and lived in Frankfort as a summer retreat. Virtually no one in Frankfort knew that Smiddy was such a wealthy or well-connected businessman, including my own family. The Smiddys, who lived across the street from us, were among my most important early influences. Mr. Smiddy, whom I called "Smiddy," was like a grandfather to me and my constant companion each summer from roughly 1969 to 1977. He was one of the first Anglos who had no prejudice whatsoever and taught me to be tolerant. At the same time, Mrs. Smiddy, who had less patience for children than Smiddy, taught me how to needlepoint.[4]

I also lived next door to one of the early teachers in the Frankfort school system, Mrs. Mildred Lonis, who told me that it was a challenge to teach the Italian American children, not because they were not intelligent, but because their parents could not be convinced of the necessity or value of education. This anti-intellectualism came from a mostly peasant immigrant group who valued manual labor over intellectual pursuit. They felt that there was something suspect about people who knew too much from books. It was more honorable to work with one's hands. Compounding this attitude was a hierarchical power structure that insisted that one cannot be better than one's parents, yet the drive to achieve the American Dream was also competing with this notion. Finally, securing a good position with a reputable company was often very difficult for Italian Americans due to the prejudice that existed at the time.

Sitting in the living room and listening to my grandfather playing cards with his friends, I would hear stories of the "Medagons" (Americans) and their rejection of our people.

"Yeah, 'member that Phil?" said my grandfather's friend as he pitched his "tree" of clubs onto the pile of cards.

"Oh, yeah Charlie, I r'member. Same 'ting happened to my bro'der-in-law. He went to the light [Electric] company to get a job too. Had a big sign, 'No 'Talians need apply.'"

"Yeah, like we were trash. Them sons of bitches!"

I didn't understand it then, but that was why the majority of our village consisted of blue-collar workers. I didn't know anyone who wore a suit to work, except maybe the guy next door to my grandmother's house and everyone said it was just to impress his wife who was a math teacher. The fathers from the television shows like *Father Knows Best*, and *Leave it to Beaver*, were totally alien to me. My dad never wore a suit, didn't even own one until the leisure suit came into vogue. Then he bought a nice canary yellow suit that he wore for special occasions like baptisms or Holy Communions. He, like most men on my street, wore jeans to work. Men, like my grandfather, worked in factories, if they were lucky, doing line work or on construction digging ditches or driving trucks. It was hard, dirty work that left them spent by the end of the day or by the beginning of the morning, if they had the night shift. I listened as they complained about unfair treatment from the "Medagon" bosses and boasted of besting the system in some subtle way like taking five more minutes to get a smoke during lunch or of bragging about being able to run the factory better than the boss who had a degree but no common sense.

A strong sense of unity was also a part of the fabric of the village, which encouraged collectivist behavior as well as isolation. In his essay "Fascism and Italian-American Identity, A Case Study: Utica, New York," Philip Bean quotes one immigrant who described what life was like for Italian Americans in the 1880s: "It was healthier for us [i.e. Italian immigrants] to stick together on account of the Irish . . . In those days we had plenty of fist fights with the Irish or the Germans who used to call us 'dagos.'"[5] With the threat of violence from the outside, communities grew more insular and even prohibited members from dating, marrying or associating with non-Italians or Medagons.

The stigmatization of the Italian Americans can still be felt today if one simply looks at the numbers. According to a Frankfort historical website, in 1865 there were 3,087 people living in Frankfort, which then boasted "four churches, two hotels, a woolen factory, a grist mill, a saw mill, a distillery, a match factory, several carriage shops and the usual number of mechanic shops of various kinds."[6] As recent as the 2000 census, figures indicate that there are now 2,537 people, 43 percent of whom are unemployed; 48 percent or 1,239 are of Italian heritage; and only 6.9 percent of the total population has a bachelor's degree.[7] The manufacturing sector located in Utica and in surrounding areas has either closed, like Univac in the 1970s, or laid off many employees, making it difficult for workers with only high school diplomas to find well-paying jobs.

Now the condition of Frankfort's Main Street is emblematic of the town's contraction and isolation. What once was an attractive, bustling thoroughfare is now an eyesore with buildings in various states of disrepair and abandoned lots with loose gravel and out of commission trucks.[8] There are lovely homes in the outer lying, rural areas, though, as if signifying the flight from the town proper. Many of the residents like Gary Grates, who have obtained degrees from Utica College of Syracuse University, my alma mater, leave the town because there are simply few jobs for educated residents. Grates, President and Global Managing Director of Edelman Change and Employee Engagement, "the largest independent public relations firm in the world and the third largest overall" according to their website, is perhaps the most successful native of Frankfort. Grates hasn't lived in Frankfort since he graduated from Utica College in 1981. He has, however, established scholarships in the names of his parents and remains active with the Utica College Raymond Simon Institute of Public Relations.

Success stories like Grates's are hard to come by in the village, where the citizens seem to push out the very people who could help to rescue the town from its plight, perhaps stemming from that collective stigmatization that is ingrained within the community's psyche. When my dad began to take courses at the local community college, some people in our community were suspicious or even jealous. My father spent 11 years to get his 2-year degree, taking night courses while working full-time. My dad took a job for New York State's Department of Transportation when he was 17 years old. He worked his way up from surveyor to civil engineering technician, enduring below freezing weather in the winter and boiling heat and tar during the summer months. I watched him study for his classes and his exams after an exhausting day of work. I saw the pride in my mother's eyes when she spoke about my dad getting his college degree. Some semesters there wasn't any money for tuition, so the dream was deferred. If the job went into overtime, my dad would have to withdraw from a class because we desperately needed the extra money. However, my dad's success at getting that associate's degree was no surprise for my mother. She always believed in his intellectual ability and unfortunately doubted her own although she was certainly just as bright as he was. However, Dad was half "Medagon," and my mother and possibly all of her family attributed my father's brains to that half, the smarter half, the American half when in fact, it was the Italian half that had a legacy for intelligence.

It was that Anglo half with which I strove to align myself. After years of being taunted by my peers, I felt like I didn't belong in this village. I wanted to get out desperately. I knew from an early age that the only way out was through a college education. My parents encouraged me. They knew that there was power in education and weren't afraid for me to wield it. The nuns at the Catholic school seemed to notice my intelligence (or was it my skin color) too and fostered it to a point, always assigning the most difficult books only to me. When other students were given books with titles like *Fudge's Incredible Foibles*, I was given books like *The Lord of the Flies*. I wanted to be like the nuns who were all "Medagon" with light skin and light eyes, who spoke perfect English. With speech therapy and English lessons, they corrected my plural "yous" and my inability to pronounce "th." They helped me diagram my sentences and elevate my language. I was becoming one of them. I was becoming somebody.

When I got to high school after graduating valedictorian from my grammar school, I went on to the expensive private high school in the city of Utica,[9] a more diverse and more urban area. My father worked two jobs and my mother worked part-time to pay for the tuition, which was an incredible struggle for them. At the high school, I wasn't called names like "ghost" or "mayonnaise face." There were plenty of people my color or lighter. There were guys and girls from literally everywhere, although admittedly it was predominantly white. There were lots of Italian American kids—some at the top of the academic ladder like me, and others who were at points all along the way, but their parents were doctors, lawyers, or business owners. The Polish boy, on whom I had my first serious crush, was not the "dumb Pollock" of my grandfather's jokes. He was a smart guy, with a larger vocabulary than me, whose father was a dentist and whose mother was a nurse. I felt comfortable with my ethnicity during that time, knowing that I could become anything that I wanted because Italian Americans were just as capable as anyone else.

This idea changed, though, when I had to transfer to a public school due to financial strains on the family budget. My parents enrolled me in Ilion High School, the only school close by with a gifted students' program. As a girl from Frankfort, I was a "spaghetti bender," and I was going to the land of "cake eaters." There were few Italian Americans at the time[10] and one African American boy, whom everyone knew. Despite the small number of different students, everyone seemed to get along well. The students were very friendly to me, and I quickly made lifelong friends. Again, I thought that I was fitting in.

That was until I got my first steady boyfriend. He was Irish American from an upper middle class family. I didn't give it a second thought, although Frankfort had a long history of feuding between the Irish and Italians in the town.

When the Italians and Sicilians came to Frankfort with the first wave of immigrants in the early 1900s, the Irish bulked. Although they shared Catholicism, the Irish wouldn't allow the new immigrants to worship in their church, Sts. Peter and Paul. They eventually compromised, allowing the Italian immigrants to worship in the church—basement that is. Unhappy with this discrimination, the Italians built a church of their own, St. Mary of Mt. Carmel—a larger, more ornate, and more beautiful gothic structure just a few blocks down the street from the Irish church. As the Italians started to cross the railroad tracks into the avenues, the Irish started to move in droves to the next town over, as did the Germans and the English. My piano teacher, one of the last German American holdouts on our street, had once been overheard complaining to her English neighbors that her two daughters had no one suitable to play with any longer. There were only those greasy Italians left in the neighborhood and they always smelled of sausage and garlic. Later, she had no trouble accepting money from these recent immigrants longing to give their child the gift of music and culture.

I was a young teen, though, and not fully aware of the schism between the Irish and the Italians. My new Irish American boyfriend's family was so different from mine. His father had a four-year college degree from a prestigious Ivy League school and his mother had gone to an Ivy League women's college for two years before leaving to marry. His family discussed politics and world events at the dinner table while mine discussed my Uncle Frank's gallbladder operation or my Cousin Joey's latest pretty girlfriend or any number of food-related topics. His family wore clothes and shoes made by L. L. Bean, Izod, Aigner, and Bass. My family shopped at Sears. His family ate things like asparagus and boiled meats, listened to classical music at dinner and "retired" to the family room for a nightcap of martinis. I'd never even seen a martini before except on television. My family only drank wine on special holidays and it was often Mateus or something from a box. We had beer like Genesee but only if we had company. The boy's folks drank an entire pitcher of martinis before the night was finished. We still had the bottle of Mateus from Easter sitting in the fridge. It would be vinegar before we sampled it again.

It was after one of these martini pitcher evenings that it became clear to me that the boy's parents hated me. I probably should have realized this sooner. The fact that they never spoke to me at length or had sometimes refused to ride in the same car as me should have been a major clue, but I was clueless and naive. Then the sledgehammer came down that I couldn't ignore.

I can still remember the scene in the kitchen of the boy's home that Thanksgiving. I had just finished washing all the dishes from the family's dinner—ten people's plates and silverware from three courses and dessert. The boy's mother and sister had gone to see a cello concert and left me with all the dishes like a maid, something that my own mother would never have done to me. I had just finished drying the large roaster pan when the father told me that he wanted to speak with me alone. The boy and I had been dating for a year and this was the first time that the father wanted an audience with me alone.

"I just can't let this go on any longer," the father began.

I stood there dumbfounded and simply listened, holding the wet dishtowel in my hands wringing it, wondering what he was getting at.

"I have a duty to my country and to my God to stop you from seeing my son," he said slurring his speech a bit from too many martinis, perhaps unaware that he was perpetuating a stereotype of his own.

I was rendered mute as I listened to what played out like some scene from a bad movie.

"I know about you people," he shook his finger at me and continued. "I was over there, in Italy, during the war. All of your men are hoodlums, mobsters and all of your women are whores," he said intently staring at me, pointing his finger near my face, "You are nothing but an Italian whore! You'll amount to nothing, nothing I tell you. You'll end up pregnant and quitting school, one of those teenaged-mothers on welfare, and I can't let my son go down with you, my dear. I have a duty to save my son. I never want to see you again in this house or near my son. Do you understand me?" he yelled with his nose red and the veins in his neck ready to burst through the skin.

I couldn't respond. I stood stock-still, like I had been struck dumb. Then I felt tears welling up in my eyes, but I didn't want him to think that he'd beaten me so I ran outside without a coat in the freezing November air. I ran and ran down the street, aimless, tears soaking my face.

That day changed my life forever. Rather than see the boy's family for what they were, bigots, I saw myself as damaged. That day all the past transgressions suffered by my grandfather, his friends, my mother and now me collided into one defining moment—I would be nothing because I was Italian and working-class. From that day onward, I started to hate being Italian, to hate me. I tried to change my ethnicity and my class. I didn't even realize I was doing it. I started loathing Italian spices —wouldn't touch oregano, basil, parsley, or garlic. I stopped going to the Italian festivals our town would have like the St. Francis *festa* with fried dough, sausage and peppers, tomato pie (not pizza), Italian cookies, and more American fare like hot dogs and beer. The smell of sausage began to sicken me. I started dressing differently in my Izod polo shirts and Sebago boat shoes. I tried to become more Anglo. Years later, I would find out that the writer Helen Barolini also "re-appropriated her ethnic identity after dissociating herself from anything Italian whether Mussolini or doing shopping 'in grocery stores that smelled of strong cheese and salamis.'"[11] At the time, it didn't occur to me to stop seeing the boy. Instead, I tried to be everything his parents wanted me to be until I lost myself like shattered glass, split into tiny pieces some too small to ever be recovered, or so I thought.

I don't think I became whole again until I was in graduate school. I started rediscovering my heritage and myself when I was far away from home at Southern Illinois University where I was getting my PhD in English. I tried to get a hold of everything Italian American. That's when I read the book that changed my life forever—Helen Barolini's collection, *The Dream Book*. I will be forever thankful that Barolini didn't publish the book under her pseudonym, Barbara Barr.[12]

Angela Rubin, one of the humanities librarians at Southern Illinois and an Italian-American who took an interest in me, gave me the book. I was working as a research assistant for the library and taking a summer class entitled "Higher Education Administration and Women," a part of my women's studies minor. My interest in Italian American studies and working-class studies awakened in tandem. For me, my inferiority complex was always a matter of both being Italian-American and from the working class. I chose to write a seminar paper about my experience in academia as a working-class, first generation college graduate. That class and that summer represented some of the most profound personal explorations of my life when I discovered who I was and why I have never felt like I fit in. Despite years of struggling, I sometimes feel like a pretender and perhaps a part of me always will.

It was that summer that Angela Rubin fed me books and bibliographies of Italian-American literature and I devoured them eagerly. She was the first person who showed me that there was Italian American literature other than Puzo's *Godfather*, the book that cemented the Madonna-Whore and Gangster-Priest image of Italians in most people's minds. Angela told me that I should read *The Dream Book*, but neither of us could know the impact it would have on me.[13] When I opened its pages, I realized that I was reading about me for the first time. Within its pages, I read about my mother, my extended family, my community, and me. Essays written by Italian American women, academics, intelligent women who wrote of the very same type of experiences that I had had made me realize that everyone needed to read literature written by and about people like them.

In a culture in which women are expected to give up jobs in lieu of child-rearing, investing money into women's educations is often regarded as a bad business decision. In my working-class neighborhood in Frankfort, New York where I grew up, education beyond the bachelor's degree is looked upon as highly unnecessary, especially for women. When my neighbor learned that I was pursuing my PhD at Southern Illinois University, he told a friend of mine that it was "just a waste" after all I'd just "get married and pop out baby after baby and never use that big degree." In Helen Barolini's introduction to *The Dream Book*, she describes the attitudes toward education of many Italian immigrants, including my great-grandmother, who was illiterate in both her native Italian and in English:

> The ingrained suspicion of education was expressed in the saying, "Fesso chi fa il figlio meglio di lui"—it's a stupid man who makes his son better than he is. In America schools were not always regarded as the road to a better future; more often they were seen as a threat to the family because they stressed assimilation into American ways. Reading was ridiculed as too private, too unproductive, too exclusive an enjoyment—free time should be spent with the family group. Learning gave one ideas, made one different; all the family wanted as cohesion.[14]

As much as my parents yearned for me to do well in school, they never quite understood what it took to get to that point. Neither parent read in our house, and the only reading matter that I remember at home was *Popular Mechanics* and *Better Homes and Gardens*. My love of reading was considered very odd indeed. I remember my mother chastising me for reading and not joining in with the family television viewing.

Ironically, within the past ten years, my mother became an avid reader and got hooked on reading. She's already plowed through Jane Austen and Barbara Pym and for the first time, understands my passion for reading. Still, I remember feeling alone and separate from my extended family growing up, knowing that they always regarded me rather curiously. This attitude, that education separates one from one's working-class culture, was also expressed by the women that researcher Wendy Luttrell studied. Among working-class women returning to college, Luttrell noted that while "white working class women seek school knowledge to empower themselves" their newfound education usually leads to "separation or divorce."[15] Women who continue on in higher education risk disapproval and often emotional ostracism from family and community.

Because my community of Italian Americans was also more likely to be from the working class, the discrimination was even more pronounced. For many working-class youths, the dream of upward mobility through education is never realized. Researchers Carl A. Grant and Christine E. Sleeter studied 24 lower-middle-class junior high students from different racial backgrounds over a seven-year period. The study revealed that although most of the students began with dreams of higher education, by the time they graduated from high school almost none planned to attend college: "While in junior high, thirteen of the twenty-four students said they definitely planned to attend college. Only one said definitely no college; the rest (10) were undecided."[16] Yet "only three of the thirteen who said they definitely had college plans were heading for a four year college, and one dropped out his freshman year."[17] What happened during the interim of those seven years was a combination of the values and attitudes held by parents and even by guidance counselors in the schools.

According to the information obtained by Grant and Sleeter, working-class students received little information and push from guidance counselors to take more demanding classes needed to enter college. The student who did take demanding classes did so at the request and advice of "friends and family who had been to college and knew what preparation was needed."[18] Students who did not have access to college graduates were at the mercy of guidance counselors who took little interest in the direction of these students' career choices. The researchers suggested that guidance counselors often thought that students from working-class backgrounds would have a lower success rate in college and therefore did not recommend a higher education as an option unless the students suggested it themselves.[19] A study by Allan C. Ornstein and Daniel U. Levine confirms that "many teachers in working-class schools conclude that many of their students are incapable of learning" and that teachers often expect "little from such students and sometimes wind up praising below-grade and meaningless work," which fosters an attitude of "low-achievement."[20] Thus, many students from the working class are already predestined to enter blue-collar fields by virtue of educators' prejudices.

In addition, students from working-class background do not enter college because the processes are so alien to them. For instance, in Grant and Sleeter's study, students often cited a lack of money that prevented them from beginning college. Students from working-class backgrounds did not know that loans or scholarships were available to help finance their education because no one had talked with them about it.[21] Filling out student financial aid forms as well as applications to college is often a very confusing process for people unfamiliar with it.

Although I was in the top 5 percent of my high school class, I applied to the only school I knew offered a scholarship for people from the Mohawk Valley region that were in the 10 percent of their class, Mohawk Valley Community College. My guidance counselor never suggested anything else. Even though I was the regional winner of "The Outstanding Young New Yorker" essay contest, a competent musician who competed in area all-state, the literary editor of our yearbook, a participant in a host of extracurricular activities, including president of the honor society, I never received recruiting literature from any colleges. What is more, I never knew that people would continue to judge me for the quality of the institutions that I attended, even with a PhD. Although I knew that the Ivy League schools existed, I never applied to them because I knew that I could not afford the tuition. I doubted that they would have let a working-class kid like me into their doors. So I plodded on to the community college and felt no shame.

As a first generation college student, my parents encouraged me to do well; however, that's not the way it was for generations before me. My great-grandmother was illiterate and encouraged my grandmother to quit school by the eighth grade. My grandfather quit in sixth grade to help take care of his brothers and mother when his father died. Education wasn't valued. My great-grandmother first worked as a laundress and later in a sewing mill while my grandmother was expected to help with the chores and with the babysitting of her two younger brothers. Prior to this arrangement, my great-grandmother placed her three children in a federally or state-run daycare designed to enable women to work while the men were away at war but later stopped working when one of her children died from pneumonia. Later, when my grandmother had children and my mother expressed a desire to become a teacher and go away to college, my great-grandmother (who lived with her daughter by then) and my grandmother literally screamed, beat their fists, and otherwise threw a temper tantrum, threatening that they would both see an early death if my mother left. Of course, my mother's family was extremely poor because my grandfather had only seasonal work then and probably couldn't have afforded the tuition anyway, but my mother decided to forego education and worked as a salesperson and later as a bank teller. My mother held a series of part-time positions throughout her life—a salesclerk, receptionist, cashier, and later a teacher's aide. She was a wonderful teacher's aide and would have made a great teacher if she had believed in herself even a little bit.

After community college, I transferred to the local private college, a division of Syracuse University, to begin a degree in journalism and public relations. I hadn't actually known what public relations were at the time, but I loved to write and had been the editor of our community college newspaper. I chose Utica College because it was within commuting distance and they offered me a scholarship. There were many students from the working class who attended Utica College and I always felt at home there. My professors seemed to recognize that I had a talent for writing and nominated me for a prestigious Gannett Journalism Scholarship, which I won. However, none of them suggested that I enter graduate school.

After spending several years in public relations, I decided to attend graduate school and eventually finished my PhD. I went on the market when I was A.B.D. (all but dissertation), and ended up getting several interviews from which I was offered a choice between two positions—one at a small, four-year liberal arts college in Georgia and one at a large community college in Florida. The position at the college in Georgia was very appealing but the community was very racist. I was engaged to a Japanese American and I was Italian American. I was told by the proprietor of the bed and breakfast, "There just weren't many of *them* here—no 'Eye-talians' and no 'JaPANese.'" I decided to take the community college position, which was in the same town where my sister worked as a hospital pharmacist and was more multicultural.

After achieving tenure and rank as a full professor and serving as department chair, I left the community college for the four-year university, where I work today. Ironically, I work at a university whose student population is rather affluent. When I first arrived eight years ago, I had asked my classes how many students were from the first generation in their homes to attend college, and only one hand went up. When I said that I was from a family in which I was the first to have a four-year college degree, the students seemed to evaluate me differently. That has changed now. A few years ago, our university founded a First Generation Club, which allowed other first generation faculty and staff to come out of the closet. With scholarships, we have many more first generation students in our classes and have a welcoming environment.

I don't know if I will ever feel truly comfortable at a board meeting but I'm getting there. Sometimes I am afraid that my roots will show like an old slip peeking out under my knock-off couture dress. As I make my way up the social ladder, I hang in there for my children so that they can climb even higher than I have and will have an easier time. The difference is that I know some of the obstacles now and have worn away a path that's much easier to negotiate.

My parents raised two children who finished their doctorates, but they still don't often understand why I work so hard or so much for what they consider a low salary given my education, unlike my sister who is a clinical pharmacist. I'm sure the people of Frankfort don't understand either. There are certainly wealthier people in town without even a college degree. I suppose after all the degrees, the awards, the publications, I am still that little girl at the piano or in the kitchen. If I just keep working harder and longer than anyone else, maybe, just maybe, I will finally be good enough to be accepted.

Notes

1. Elizabeth G. Messina, "Psychological Perspectives on the Stigmatization of Italian Americans in the American Media," in *Saints and Rogues: Conflicts and Convergence in Psychotherapy*, ed. E. Mark Stern and Robert B. Marchesani (Binghamton, NY: Haworth Press, 2004), 87–121; especially page 99. See also Chapter 4 earlier.
2. Messina, "Psychological Perspectives," 99.
3. Smiddy is the creator of the "Management By Objective Theory," which he used successfully to restructure all of General Electric. For some cursory comments on Smiddy's relationship to Frankfort, see Melvin Zimet and Ronald G. Greenwood, *The Evolving Science of Management: The Collected Papers of Harold Smiddy and Papers by Others in His Honor* (New York: Amacom, 1979), 6.
4. In her later years, Mrs. Smiddy donated over $3 million to Ithaca College to create the Harold and Lois Smiddy School of Business, but, so far as I know, she did not donate any of her estate to her hometown of Frankfort, which according to Smiddy, she never really liked.
5. Philip A. Bean, "Fascism and Italian-American Identity, A Case Study: Utica, New York," *Journal of Ethnic Studies* 17, no. 2 (1989): 101–19; particularly page 101.
6. Laura Perkins, "The Town of Frankfort: Herkimer County, NY," *The US Gen Web Project*, http://www.rootsweb.com/~nyherkim/frankfort.html.
7. See U.S. Census Bureau's DP-2 Profile of Selected Social Characteristics: 2000, http://factfinder.census.gov (accessed May 24, 2005).
8. See the following website for pictures of Frankfort: http://frankfortny.tripod.com. Included on this site is a link to an unfortunate creative work stereotyping Frankfortites and Italian Americans, featuring characters with names like "Frankie Fingers" and "The Pizza Girl," entitled the CNYM Project (http://cnym.tripod.com/pics.html), which apparently went "on hiatus in 2003."
9. Utica is the birthplace of Italian Americans like Frank Lentricchia, world-renowned scholar, literary theorist, and graduate of my alma mater, Utica College, and of course of Mouseketeer, Annette Funicello. The grandmother of the writer Helen Barolini, whom Barolini visited often, lived in Utica.
10. See the 2000 U.S. census, according to which Ilion now has a population of 8,637 with ethnicities that are 22.2 percent German, 20.6 percent Irish, 13.2 percent English, and 12.2 percent Italian. Ilion also has higher educational attainment in comparison to Frankfort, with 25.5 percent earning college degrees (Associate's and Bachelor's) in comparison to Frankfort's 13.1 percent. Ilion's Main Street is also recently renovated.

A higher education level means more educated people in power in the local government and the results are telling. In 2001, Ilion was able to apply for and received a federal funding grant, provided by the Governor's Office for Small Cities (GOSC), which included $750,000 for a comprehensive downtown revitalization project in the Village of Ilion.

11. Stefano Luconi, "Becoming Italian in the US: Through the Lens of Life Narratives," *MELUS: The Society for the Study of the Multi-Ethnic Literature of the United States* 29, no. 3–4 (Fall–Winter 2004): 160.

12. Helen Barolini, "Making My Bones," *The Massachusetts Review* 42, no. 1 (Spring 2001): 51–62; especially page 57.

13. See the poem dedicated to Helen Barolini by Joanne Detore-Nakamura, "Dreams," in *Sweet Lemons: Writing with a Sicilian Accent*, ed. Venera Fazio and Delia De Santis (Mineola, NY: Legas, 2004), 263; printed here in the appendix.

14. Helen Barolini, ed., *The Dream Book: An Anthology of Writing by Italian American Women* (New York: Schocken Books, 1985), 8. Syracuse University Press published an expanded second edition in 2000.

15. Wendy Luttrell, "Working-Class Women's Ways of Knowing: Effect of Gender, Race, and Class," *Sociology of Education* 62 (January 1989): 39–46; see especially page 42.

16. Carl A. Grant and Christine E. Sleeter, "Race, Class and Gender and Abandoned Dreams," *Teacher's College Record* 90, no. 1 (Fall 1988): 19–40; especially page 23.

17. Ibid.

18. Ibid., 25.

19. Ibid., 26–27.

20. Allan C. Ornstein and Daniel U. Levine, "Class, Race, and Achievement," *The Education Digest* 55 (May 1990): 11–14; citation on page 11.

21. Grant and Sleeter, "Race, Class and Gender," 29.

Appendix to Chapter 10

Dreams

(For Helen Barolini)

Today I read about myself—
flesh and blood
in black and white,
living and breathing
between and among the pages
of a dream book.
The stories of Nana, Mama,
Putanas and Madonnas,
the separateness, the otherness,
united in a stream
of consciousness,
of narrative voices,
united in the silence
broken.
There they were, the others
I never knew
hidden by Anglo surnames and
nose-jobs. Hidden away
in ivory towers
too impossible to scale.
But Helen you threw down
your hair,
and I climbed up
and into
the ivory tower filled with
other dreamers.
Together we walked
hand in hand
across the bridge
into the world
outside the margins,
narrowing the space
between impossibility
and reality.

11

Stereotypes Sell, But We're Not For Sale

Gina Valle

Stereotypes sell, but we're not for sale! That is exactly what Carmelina Crupi, an Italian American now living in Canada, told Jack David of ECW Press when she declined being a part of a book they were expected to publish.

For several years I had been collecting stories from Canadian women of Italian descent, similar to the stories that are showcased in my first book *Our Grandmothers, Ourselves: Reflections of Canadian Women*, where I attempted to capture the immigrant and first generation Canadian experience through the power of narrative.

In 2003, I submitted the final manuscript for my second book to a Canadian publisher who was interested in publishing "the work." Once a contract was signed and we were on our way, the publisher introduced the title and book cover. More than half of the contributors found the title and book cover to be offensive as it depicted Italian women in a derogatory manner. In essence, we did not want to be represented as buffoon-like, loud and stupid. We strongly felt that we were being stereotyped, with a title of *Mamma Mia! Good Italian Girls Talk Back*. We voiced our concern and opposition to the proposed title and the related issue of the book cover. They were as follows:

1. The title is inherently disrespectful of women as it infantilizes them.

    Our stories depict the struggle to engage in the duality of two cultures, and although some of the stories revolve around childhood themes and dilemmas, we are writing our narratives as women, not "girls."

2. The title and cover are clichéd, stereotypical, and unrepresentative of our stories.

    The title and book cover promoted the existing stereotype of the loud, inarticulate (and by implication, unintelligent) Italian. In writing our stories, our attempt was to transcend this stereotype (of which we have been the object), whereas the proposed title and book cover reinforced it. Furthermore, there was a profound "disconnect" between the content and the title and cover.

3. The title conveys a lack of respect for the older generation, which is an integral part of the Italian culture.

    The title conveys a lack of respect for our culture and the older members of our families who sacrificed a great deal and, we believe, raised us to the best of their ability, given the resources they had and the circumstances they faced when they first arrived as immigrants. Overall, our intent for the book was to express gratitude to our families, whereas the title, with the dismissive adolescent overtones such as "Girls Talk Back", expresses just the opposite.

In our view, there were other suitable titles and book covers that we believed to be more culturally representative, original, and better suited to the content of the book. We encouraged the publisher to consider viable alternatives. In February 2004, I indicated in an internal email to the contributors that I would withdraw my story and introduction if I could not reach a compromise with ECW on altering the proposed title and book cover. In March 2004, ECW and I parted ways. I was no longer the editor of the book and within a week a new editor was found. She had been a contributor of my collection. Seven other contributors from my original collection signed on with ECW and each wrote two stories for the book. ECW's in-house editor and the new editor searched for more writers and in May 2004 the book was released with the *Mamma Mia* title and cover.

Why Stereotype?

For almost two decades I have worked extensively with ethnocultural communities in areas of literacy, first language acquisition, multicultural curriculum design, inner city school initiatives, and immigrant women's projects. As such, I have learned about, and witnessed the debilitating effects that stereotypes can have on individuals. The contributors, and many people in the Italian community at large, believe that the title and book cover depict Italian women as stereotypical hotheaded "girls" whose contributions to cultural literature are suspect. In my book, intelligent women authors shared their collective experience with a view to dispel the very myths and stereotypes perpetuated by the present title and book cover.

When I am stereotyped as a member of an ethnocultural community, it limits my ability to lead a full life. Stereotyping and labeling concentrate on specific deficits, offering a single lens that can distort reality. Stereotypes create expectancies and constrain our individual behavior. In the end, it takes less effort to pigeonhole people to predetermined biases than to attempt to understand the real person. If we did not live in such a multicultural environment, we could respond in predictable ways and dismiss the contributors' concerns as "It's just a silly book cover and title," "It's just senseless marketing," and "It's just one book." But I would argue otherwise: it is because we live in a multicultural country that we need to find practical ways in which to ensure that all citizens and all members of ethnocultural communities are able to live full lives, free of restrictive stereotypes. An effective way in which to ensure that citizens, no matter their origins, can participate in all aspects of their lives is to be vigilant of stereotyping when it occurs.

ECW Press stated that they did not anticipate the Italian community constituting their primary readership, and as such were using stereotyping to market and sell this book to non-Italians. This was the justification that was given for using stereotypes. Italian Canadians and Italian Americans make up a large, representative community that has contributed vastly to the development of culture in North America for centuries. We are educated, informed, and interested in our heritage and are active participants in numerous cultural, educational, and political systems. I found the situation quite troubling, that after centuries of Italian immigration to North America, I, the contributors in my book, and members of the Italian community at large, are still waging the same battles engaged in by our parents and grandparents to restore respect and public opinion for our culture.

Lessons Learned Thus Far

- Although 18 of the 20 contributors disliked the title and cover design and clearly told me so, for those who eventually went with ECW they did so in order to be published.
- ECW let it be known within the Italian Canadian and Italian American community that they were waiting for a controversy to unfold with the hopes that it would fuel sales. I received numerous requests from the media to respond. I declined.
- Legal counsel encouraged me to let the book speak for itself and if ethnocultural stereotyping was an issue, then it would be raised in its own right. After much reflection, and with all due respect for my legal counsel, I declined taking her advice. I did not have faith in mainstream reviewers to address this point of stereotyping. Whether stereotyping is subtle or blatant, each incidence has an accumulative effect with the potential to be damaging in the long run. As expected, the reviewers barely discussed the buffoon on the book cover or any part of the derogatory title.
- Protection of one's intellectual creative property is quite limiting, as I found out in my battles with ECW. The process of protecting ones ideas is lengthy, frustrating, and costly.
- The Italian American community was proactive on the issue of stereotyping and took a more supportive stand in my defense (by writing letters) than the Italian Canadian community. My Italian American counterparts have Hollywood to contend with and so I can understand why they felt it necessary to take a stand against stereotyping because of their repeated experiences with it over the years. In Canada, we have fewer incidences to draw from and have absorbed derogatory Italian American images much like the rest of the world has through television and Hollywood movies. Nevertheless, I would

have wanted to witness Italian Canadians make a stronger denouncement of ECW's behavior toward our community.

A Bureaucratic Process Worth Noting

Each year, publishers in Canada receive a significant amount of funding from two federal government sources: The Canada Council for the Arts and the Book Publishing Industry Development Program (BPIDP), and ECW Press is no exception, receiving substantial grants from both. Thus, I turned to my federal member of parliament for some answers on funding guidelines for these government agencies. I requested clarification from my member of parliament regarding measures that are in place within these government funding bodies (which are indirectly financed by taxpayers) to ensure that the projects they fund are free of ethnocultural, racial, or gender stereotyping.

The Canada Council for the Arts responded by outlining how the peer assessment committees work. They also stated that they felt that it was not appropriate for the council to interfere in decisions made by publishers regarding titles and cover design, and to do so would be censorship, which the council and Canadian society in general does not condone. They also assured me that the 2005 peer assessment committee would have an opportunity to evaluate ECW's 2004 publishing program and any resulting grant would be based on their recommendations. Several weeks later when I spoke to a council staff member about the peer assessment file, I was informed that the committee would not be presented the 2004 file, which now had letters from Canadians and Americans regarding this very issue of stereotyping and ECW's arrogance to our concerns, *unless the assessors asked to see the file.* I asked if most committees requested to see the previous years file and the answer was no.

The Book Publishing Industry Development Program (BPIDP) provided a generic, bureaucratic response indicating that the title and book cover design was "not sufficiently derogatory as to render the book or its publisher in contravention of the above guideline. Accordingly, it would be inappropriate for the Department of Canadian Heritage to intervene in this matter."

My response to both federal funding bodies was as follows: ECW Press was unstoppable. Despite the repeated requests of over half of the contributors, the former editor (me), members of the Italian Canadian and Italian American communities, the Association of Italian Canadian Writers, ECW proceeded to publish the book, put it on bookshelves, market it across the country, and profit from the publicly supported publishing grants they receive.

I strongly believe that ECW's actions are setting a *regressive precedent.* The Italian community in North America is one of the largest, and if their concerns are treated with such indifference, then surely other ethnocultural communities will be treated in much the same way when they come forward and voice their concerns about not wishing to be represented in a derogatory, stereotypical manner, as was the case with ECW.

I therefore then recommended the following: when the funding bodies release *public* funds to publishers, there should be a binding clause attached to the funding that demands that the publisher, at the very least, agrees to cultural, racial, and gender sensitivity and, at the very most, agrees to provide an avenue of appeal to the author that would go directly to the funding body for adjudication. In light of the fact that the funders are keepers of *publicly funded* grants, it would be in their best interest to appear to be working in a *transparent* and *accountable* manner, which taxpayers are increasingly demanding from their federal agencies. I further welcomed insights from the Council's Equity Coordinator whose mandate is to address issues related to cultural diversity.

As bureaucracy would have it, I received yet another bland response. I was reminded once again that to exercise control over a publisher's editorial decisions is antithetical to the principle of freedom of expression espoused by Canadian society, and although the book was available in bookstores across the country and being launched in different cities, the council suggested that I continue to discuss the matter with ECW Press. That advice seemed rather futile at that point. I was also assured that next year's peer assessment committee would have an opportunity to evaluate ECW's 2004 publishing program and resulting grants would be based on its recommendations. Somehow, I do not believe that I was being told the full truth.

Final Comments

I have spent quite a bit of time trying to grasp the optics of the situation; who were the power brokers; why it had transpired the way it did between the publisher, the funders, and the Italian community at large; why ECW's behavior was permissible with someone else's creative work; why the funders were repeatedly resorting to the argument of freedom of speech, and so on. The Canada Council for the Arts confirmed to me that they had never seen a situation such as this, where writers voiced their concerns, the publisher discarded the concerns, and chose to publish "the work" anyway with a handful of original ideas and contributors. Consequently, I hired legal counsel to safeguard my original ideas and ensure that they could not be used by ECW and the new editor. We were able to delay the printing of the book by ten business days, in which time ECW was obliged to alter the introduction, an author's section, references, and so on since it became obvious that much of what was in the book was my creative work.

After attending the conference on anti-Italian discrimination at Seton Hall in December 2004, I once again wrote the Council and the BPIDP requesting to meet with them and discuss seeing changes to the funding criteria and process, presenting arguments regarding the fundamental principle of freedom of expression within a multicultural context, requesting proof that the 2005 assessors will see the Canadian and American letters that were submitted regarding ECW's 2004 comportment, and addressing issues of accountability from publicly funded organizations. I received form letter responses.

I am the first to acknowledge that change unfolds at a glacial pace, and so patience and perseverance is important here. The incident that I found myself in was a microcosm of the *Shark Tale* and *Growing up Gotti* debacles we witnessed in 2004. Some say that we have only ourselves to blame as a community to have tolerated so much for so long. Why did ECW really not care about what most of us had to say? The answer is complex but manageable to deconstruct. Oftentimes, my parents had no choice but to walk away and accept what was handed to them in their new homeland, but I am not voiceless and we, as a community, have choices and strong voices we can turn to for leadership. In times such as these, I also turn to my parents and the advice they calmly give me, time and time again: *Pazienza. Pazienza. Pazienza.* (And say a few *Ave Marias* while you're at it.)

12

Shark Tale—"*Puzza da Cap'*"

An Attempt at Ethnic Activism

Jerome Krase

"*Puzza da cap,*'" an old Calabrian saying, was explained to me some years ago by then New York State Assemblyman and now New York Supreme Court Justice Frank Barbaro. "The fish stinks from the head," is a comment about the hierarchy of societal corruption and it is an apt title for this essay on *Shark Tale*. As a visual sociologist and semiotician, I thought I had seen it all when it came to images of Italians in America. Then the animated film *Shark Tale* happened and a new vista opened up on the subject: ichthyology. As I have argued in a number of essays and studies, still and moving images are central to the idea of ethnic discrimination in that they are crucial to how large complex groups like Italian Americans are often inaccurately and negatively displayed.[1] Therefore, I was not surprised when, in September of 2004, I received a telephone call from Alexandra V. Preate, the chief executive officer of Political Capital LLC, a public relations firm that had been engaged to develop a campaign critical of the film, its actors, producers, and its distribution company DreamWorks. It seems that my response to a web discussion of the potentially damaging effect of *Shark Tale*, especially on young Italian Americans, had hit a nerve and had then, without my knowledge, been widely distributed. In my measured remarks I had reminded readers that such children's stories as *The Story of Little Black Sambo* had been excised from children's literature, as were the "n" words from *Huckleberry Finn*. Someone at the firm had picked up the message and asked me to consult with them, and of course I agreed to do what I could. It is interesting to note that I realized in my conversations with them that the fact that I did not have an "Italian name" was seen as a positive factor.

I have been a paid and unpaid consultant to civil rights and community organizations for what now seems like ages. Over the decades, I have researched, written, and taught in the related fields of sociology and education. I also specialize in multicultural issues, so within a few hours of searching, I found hundreds of reports that argued against the use of negative ethnic, racial, and other stereotypes in children's media. I also saw that there was more to *Shark Tale* and its relentless promotion than meets the eye. The movie set box office records for the first two weeks of the month of October 2004, and the studio spent more than $70 million in production, plus $145 million for promotion.[2] Clearly DreamWorks was using the film to enhance its Initial Public Offering. They expected to land a whale of a catch at the expense of 16 million people who trace their roots to Italy.

There was much in the way of irony in the promotion of *Shark Tale*. The first was that its scheduled release coincided with the start of Italian Heritage and Culture Month (October). In the lead, I noticed many different forms of promotion, such as the deluge of *Shark Tale* clips on children's television. In an otherwise well-intentioned nationwide program, "Newspapers in Education," that the *New York Daily News* was running, two "lessons" were timed with the film's release that instructed teachers how to use *Shark Tale* in their classes. One was for "character education" and the other for natural science. The lessons cited "educational experts" affiliated with the New York City Board of Education as consultants. Scholastic Books simultaneously published *Shark Tale* cartoon novels for use in primary grade classrooms. Scholastic has an exemplary reputation in educational publishing. In both the "Newspapers in Education" as well as the "Scholastic Book" productions, funding came from DreamWorks.

A simple search on any academic electronic archive resource will find mountains of research showing how dangerous ethnic, racial, and religious stereotyping is to young minds. I will report here on one of the many electronically archived resources that should have blown *Shark Tale* out of the water. The buzzword among education experts in America today is "multiculturalism." According to Rose Reissman, in *The Evolving Multicultural Classroom*, "[Multicultural education] must hold at its core the principle of eradicating racial/cultural/religious stereotypes."[3] *Shark Tale* was carefully designed to reinforce and exploit them for profit. Since the film was produced to appeal to young children, we would assume that DreamWorks' alleged educational experts were familiar with the "United States National Standards for Civics and Government." They provide the "Basic Values and Principles of American Democracy for Kindergarten to Grade 4," and some are abbreviated for this paper.[4]

Students should be able to explain the importance of the fundamental values and principles of American democracy: individual rights to life, liberty, property, and the pursuit of happiness, the public or common good, justice, equality of opportunity, diversity, truth, and patriotism. Regarding *Shark Tale*, it is the benefits of diversity which are most important. Diversity has contributed to the vitality and creativity of the United States by increasing the range of viewpoints, ideas, customs, and choices available to each individual in almost every aspect of life. Understanding the benefits of as well as costs of diversity can reduce conflicts and discrimination. Diversity helps people appreciate cultural traditions and practices other than their own. Students should learn about others' customs, beliefs, history, problems, hopes, and dreams. Students in kindergarten through fourth grade learn how can people work together to promote the values and principles of American democracy. Students must learn that in order to protect their own rights, they must be responsible for supporting the rights of others, even those with whom they may disagree or dislike. They also must not discriminate unfairly against others because of their race, ethnicity, language, gender, or religious beliefs.

It is obvious that if the Center for Civic Education were to give an example of how not to educate children about diversity in America it would be to have them watch *Shark Tale*!

On September 27, 2004, I completed my analysis and penned "An Offer to Children that Parents should Refuse"—a press release that circulated internationally (see Appendix: Document 1). I also sent an email circular entitled "Professional Advice and Assistance Concerning *Shark Tale*" to the legion of scholars and scholarly organizations of which I am affiliated (see Document 3). It asked for advice as to how academics, scholars, parents, grandparents, and especially educational professionals might be able to effect some change so that parents are made aware of the need for caution. In response to the publication of the message and the press release, I received many messages of support.

The Story Behind the Story

My own involvement in the *Shark Tale* affair was late and modest. I rely on the accounts of two of the principal activists, Bill Dal Cerro and Dona De Sanctis, for much of its history.[5] On August 24, 2003, Bill Dal Cerro, Vice President of the Italic Institute, discovered that DreamWorks was producing a child's version of *The Sopranos* at that time called *Sharkslayer*. Voiceovers by producer-director Martin Scorsese, actor Robert De Niro, and an HBO stable of mobsters were a major selling point. The casting in *Shark Tale* and the easily recognizable story line have little to do with juvenile tastes but with adult ones. DreamWorks clearly decided to frame this animation as a *Sopranos-Godfather-Goodfellas* masterwork in animation in order to entice and entertain those who must take children to movie theaters and sit with them.

After some serious discussion about the first amendment and artistic expression issues, the Italic Institute sent certified letters to partners Steven Spielberg and Jeffrey Katzenberg (with a "cc" to Jack Valenti of the Motion Picture Association) on September 10, 2003. It was a simple request: "de-Italianize" the characters. They felt that since the film was still in production, and had a year to go before its release, that this was not unreasonable. The Anti-Defamation League (ADL) (formerly the Anti-Defamation League of B'nai B'rith) was also contacted, but in both cases there was no response. On November 8, a protest rally was held on Long Island with students from the Italic Institute's Aurora Youth Program. Concurrently, a *Shark Tale* file was created on the institute's website to register and coordinate protest activities. Then, on November 17, a nationwide appeal was made to Italian American organizations to join the fight against DreamWorks. It was clear that the community needed to mobilize all its resources.

During the month of December 2003, it was decided to create an organization known as CARRES, the Coalition Against Racial, Religious and Ethnic Stereotypes, whose formation was announced publicly in January 2004. It was composed of the three leading national Italian American organizations—the Commission for Social Justice (CSJ) of the Order Sons of Italy in America, the National Italian American Foundation (NIAF), and UNICO National—together with the New York-based Columbus Citizens Foundation and the Italic Institute of America. The group also included other Italian American organizations, the Arab American Institute, the Polish American Congress, and the National Conference for Community and Justice. CARRES's first official act was a written appeal to Steven Spielberg of DreamWorks.

After being rebuffed by DreamWorks, each of the five founding organizations of CARRES (the CSJ of the Sons of Italy, NIAF, UNICO National, the Columbus Citizens Foundation, and the Italic Institute of America) pledged $10,000 to fund a public relations campaign aimed at the national media, which, until this point, had all but ignored the issue. From January to October 2004, CARRES organized letter-writing campaigns, sent out press releases protesting the film and met with politicians. Italian American elected officials and those with large Italian American constituencies were major targets. As a result, Congressman John Mica (Republican-Florida), the cochairman of the Italian American Caucus in Congress, met with CARRES facilitator and NIAF Trustee Steven Aiello and NIAF's Political Liaison John Marino. He said he would call for a caucus meeting, but it didn't happen. Beginning in October 2003, 19 members of the Italian American Caucus were contacted but only one, Representative Bill Pascrell (Democrat-New Jersey), responded with a letter to Spielberg on January 9, 2004. One year later, in October 2004, Representative Rosa DeLauro (Democrat-Connecticut) also lent her support. The vast majority of the Italian American Congressional Caucus declined to participate or even respond. Adding to the deafening silence was the absence of a vigorous response from Italian American celebrities and other prominent members of the national community such as Mario Cuomo, Lee Iacocca, Jay Leno, and Alfonse D'Amato, among others. CARRES also unsuccessfully lobbied the Motion Picture Association of America, led by Jack Valenti, to give *Shark Tale* a PG-13 or R rating. The final rating was "PG. Parental guidance suggested." This included the advice that "Some material may not be suitable for children. Some mild language and crude humor."

CARRES also launched a boycott of the film—and of Burger King, Coca-Cola, Krispy Kreme, and General Mills, all of them companies that were promoting the film via their child-oriented products (see Appendix 3). OSIA National President Joseph Sciame and other CARRES leaders appealed directly to Italian Prime Minister Silvio Berlusconi to prevent the awarding of the honorary citizenship that the Republic of Italy was planning to give *Shark Tale* star Robert De Niro during the movie's premiere in Venice September 2004. The National Italian American Foundation that had honored De Niro in 2002 published a letter to him expressing its "extreme disappointment and feelings of betrayal" over his role in this film (Appendix 4). Here there was some success, as the honor was delayed (with great publicity), although De Niro later received Italian citizenship more than a year after the release of *Shark Tale*.

In May 2004, at The Tribeca Film Festival in New York, Robert De Niro and Jeffrey Katzenberg held a preview of *Shark Tale* for parents and children, and a protest was staged. Incredibly, the New York State Economic Development Corporation (EDC) had awarded the festival a $200,000 grant. It was incredible, because the chairman of the EDC was also the chairman of the Columbus Citizens Foundation, which was a member of CARRES. Representatives of CARRES attended and saw for themselves that the movie was filled with harmful negative ethnic stereotypes. Columbus Citizens Foundation President Lawrence Auriana issued a number of press releases, followed by a press conference in which where he denounced Steven Spielberg for hypocrisy (see Appendix 5). The press conference was poorly attended, and national television media continued to ignore the *Shark Tale* controversy.

The marketing of the animated film *Shark Tale* expanded into reading material for young children. Scholastic Books published the script of *Shark Tale*, in juvenile novel form, and marketed it to school systems complete with its Italian-named characters. In New York City, there was a successful protest led by Councilman Tony Avella in the spring of 2005 at City Hall against the use of the Scholastic Books in NYC classrooms. Avella demanded that Scholastic Books respond to a letter of complaint that had been sent by John Mancini, the chairman of the Italic Institute. The Italic Institute contacted these marketing firms but none would admit the obvious that their *Shark Tale* film and reading products were inappropriate for children. Newscaster Katie Couric, at the time of NBC's *Today Show*, did a voiceover in the animation and promoted the film on her national television program. NBC also ignored the appearance of Ms. Couric's questionable ethics and, at a later point, the Italic Institute decided to file a complaint with the FCC.

Assessments

The *Shark Tale* campaign did not change the names of the gangsters. It neither convinced the MPAA to give *Shark Tale* an "R" or even a "PG-13" rating, nor did it gain the support of major ethnic and other civil rights groups such as the NAACP and the Jewish Anti-Defamation League. Most disappointingly, few celebrities and prominent Italian Americans joined the fray. *Shark Tale* made a pile of money, more than $200 million dollars, and DreamWorks' IPO was successful.[6]

Few issues have ever presented themselves as a clear-cut example of ethnic bias in the media as with *Shark Tale*, directed at the youngest and most impressionable of audiences. It was also clearly outside the protection of the first amendment. One has no constitutional right to defame an ethnic group. Although Hollywood demonstrated some weaknesses, even greater vulnerabilities were exposed within the Italian American community. Wide gulfs were found between organizations, individuals, and between the government of Italy and the Italian American community.

During the CARRES campaigns, Dona De Sanctis was the principal media spokesperson. Although noting its many failures and disappointments, she wrote about some of the positive effects of the efforts of CARRES. The campaign sent a powerful message that *Shark Tale* crossed the line by passing mafia stereotypes to children too young to distinguish fact from fiction. CARRES influenced the MPAA to consider ethnic as well as racial and religious stereotyping in its rating criteria. CARRES also reached reporters here and abroad, and when the film opened, most of the critics took into consideration the film's stereotyping of Italian Americans. Below are excerpts of some of the reviews. In all cases, reviewers noted the ethnic and racial biases but there were differing takes on the movie's offensiveness and potential damage to children. Thus Howard Halle, in *Time Out New York*, wrote,

> *Shark Tale* appears to be a veritable cavalcade of stereotypes, parading not only wise guys, but black street characters, like two Rastafarian jellyfish named Ernie and Bernie, voiced by Doug E. Doug and Ziggy Marley. (Their tentacles are dreadlocks. Get it?). There's even a Jew: a sand shark named Don Feinberg.
>
> But one person's stereotyping is another person's diversity. According to Andy Spahn, head of corporate affairs for DreamWorks, "*Shark Tale* is a family appropriate film featuring a wide range of cultural backgrounds."[7]

Michael Wilmington wrote in the *Chicago Tribune*:

> *Shark Tale* also shows how the old Sicilian Mafia has become such a universal cultural pop artifact and point of reference that it can go cuddly and cutesy rather than criminal and bloody. Who would have thought that the director of *Mean Streets* and *Goodfellas*, and the guy who starred in those films and *The Godfather 2*, would wind [up] doing voices for comical cartoon fishes in an underwater parody of their crime masterpieces?[8]

In *Newsday New York*, under the amusing headline, "'Straight to sushi': Pun-laden *Shark Tale* gets caught up in day-old typecasting," John Anderson wrote,

> If *Shark Tale* is anti-Italian, then it is probably anti-black, anti-Jewish, anti-gay and anti-fish. Frankly, the underwater mob characters voiced by Robert De Niro and Martin Scorsese seem more New York than they do anything else. So maybe it's simply anti-urban. But the question has been raised, not just because this animated comedy features De Niro and Scorsese as gangster fish, but because DreamWorks managed to add potential insult to potential insult by opening it on Oct.1, the first day of Italian American Heritage Month. What's certain is that there's nothing in *Shark Tale* that's newly damaging to Italians. Or any other ethnic group. Which is actually symptomatic of the movie's freshness problem.[9]

A. O. Scott, in the *New York Times*, described the ethnic characters this way: "There are cheerful quasi-ethnic stereotypes—jellyfish Rastafarians, shark Mafiosi, aquatic ghetto kids with cans of spray paint—that are technically insulated against offensiveness because, well, they're all fish."[10]

Possibly the most notable outcome of the campaign was that it moved the critics to pay attention to instances of ethnic stereotyping that might otherwise have passed unnoticed—as has often happened in the past.

Summarizing the activist campaign against *Shark Tale*, Dona De Sanctis took note of the mixed results; however, she concluded "the most important achievement of CARRES and its struggle with Shark Tale is the fact that this is an historic alliance. For the first time in our history, the major national Italian American organizations with support from smaller state and community groups, banded together to fight the issue of stereotyping." My own conclusion is less optimistic. Expressions of bias, especially negative stereotypes, against Italian Americans continues to be an acceptable practice in the American mass media, notwithstanding expert opinion as to its damaging effects, especially on children. A new and expanded effort is required to convince people, especially Italian Americans in "the business," that this is no longer acceptable. How to do this is the biggest problem, and the greatest challenge.

Notes

1. Jerome Krase, "Between Columbus and Cuomo: The Italian Experience in America," *Italian American Review* 6, no. 1 (Spring–Summer 1997): 29–44. See also Krase and Ray Hutchinson, eds., *Race and Ethnicity in New York City*, Research in Urban Sociology 7 (Greenwich, CT: JAI Press, 2004); Krase, "The Inner City/Teaching about Seeing," in *Visual Sociology: Teaching with Film/Video, Photographs and Visual Media*, ed. Dianna Papademas, 5th ed. (Washington, DC: American Sociological Association, 2002), 112–16; Krase and Frank Sorentino, ed., *The Review of Italian American Studies* (Lanham, MD: Lexington Books, 2000); Krase, "Brooklyn's Blacks, Italians, and Jews: The Anatomy of Interethnic Conflict," in *Origins and Transitions*, ed. Mario A. Toscano (Naples: Ipermedium, 1996), 167–83; Krase, "Bensonhurst, Brooklyn: Italian American Victimizers and Victims," *Voices in Italian Americana* 5, no. 2 (Fall 1994): 43–53; Krase and Judith N. Desena, eds., *Italian Americans in a Multicultural Society*, Filibrary Series 7 (Stony Brook, NY: Forum Italicum, 1994); Krase, "Afro American Student Reaction to Italian American Culture," in *Italian Americans and their Public and Private Life*, ed. Frank J. Cavaioli, Angela Danzi, and Salvatore J. LaGumina (Staten Island, NY: AIHA, 1994): 125–36; Krase and Tibbi Duboys, "Education and Sociology Are About People," *Liberal Education* 78, no. 3 (May-June 1992): 14–17.
2. Dona De Sanctis, "*Shark Tale* Wrap Up: Was it Worth it?" *Italian America* 10, no. 1 (Winter 2005): 12–13; Lorenza Munoz, "DreamWorks Swings to Profit: 'Shrek 2' and 'Shark Tale' Help the Studio Earn $192 Million in the Fourth Quarter," *Los Angeles Times*, March 18, 2005, http://articles.latimes.com/2005/mar/18/business/fi-dream18.
3. Rose Reissman, "The Evolving Multicultural Classroom," available at http://www.ascd.org/publications/books/194173/chapters/Definitions-of-Multicultural-Education.aspx.
4. The Center for Civic Education, "National Standards for Civics and Government" (1994), available at http://www.civiced.org/k4toc.htm.
5. De Sanctis, "*Shark Tale* Wrap Up: Was it Worth it?" 12–13; Bill Dal Cerro, "*Shark Tale*: For the Record," *Italic Way* 33 (2005): 29–31.
6. Bloomberg News, "DreamWorks Animation Posts Profit on 'Shrek 2' DVD Sales," *New York Times*, March 18, 2005, http://www.nytimes.com/2005/03/18/business/media/18dreamworks.html?_r=1&ref=jeffrey_katzenberg.
7. Howard Halle, "MOB DEEP," *Time Out New York* (March 25–April 1, 2004).
8. Michael Wilmington, "*Shark Tale*: The computer-animated film combines overdone Mafia comedy with stale bromides," *Chicago Tribune*, September 29, 2004, (as reprinted on Metromix.com), http://www.chicagotribune.com/entertainment/movies/mmx–040929–movies-review-mw-shark,0,1696269.story.

9. John Anderson, "Straight to Sushi," *Newsday New York*, October 1, 2004.
10. A. O. Scott, "*Shark Tale*: Fish With Stars' Voices in a Pop-Culture Sea," *New York Times*, October 1, 2004, http://movies.nytimes.com/2004/10/01/movies/01SHAR.html.

Appendix to Chapter 12

Document 1. Krase press release, September 27, 2004.

"An Offer to Children that Parents should Refuse," by Jerry Krase

I haven't seen *Shark Tales* [*sic*] yet but I have read the *Shark Tale Movie Novel*, published by Scholastic Inc., as well as uncomfortably viewing numerous television commercials and print advertisements promoting it as a "family comedy." The fact that such children's fare is being distributed by produced by DreamWorks which is led by Steven Spielberg is difficult to understand. The least one can expect from a media industry giant such as Dream Works, and especially Steven Spielberg, whose powerful *Schindler's List* brought the reality of anti-Semitism home to a new generation, is respect for American diversity.

In their defense those who created and "starred" in the animation claim that using negative stereotypes of Italian and African Americans is harmless child's play. To excuse bigotry as entertainment is not merely disingenuous but frightening. The idea that ethnic, racial, and gender stereotyping in children's media is of little consequence is contradicted not only by common sense but mountains of scientific evidence. There is a long record of published research on the negative effects of negative stereotyping on children whose groups are stereotyped. From the classic studies on African American children of Kenneth Clark which moved a nation toward equity in education to more recent studies of young girls, the disabled, and new immigrant groups there is a consistent finding that negative stereotyping in media for youngsters is harmful both immediately and in the future. A simple search will find that, "A study of Asian-American schoolchildren has found that negative stereotypes can diminish a child's academic performance. On the other hand, positive stereotypes may spur better performance." This was published in the journal *Psychological Science*. What is probably the leader in efforts to correcting and preventing bias, the Anti-Defamation League, on their website argues that: "If young children are repeatedly exposed to biased representations through words and pictures, there is a danger that such distortions will become a part of their thinking, especially if reinforced by societal biases."

As an academic I am not one to propose censorship of this film but this kind of insensitive and discriminatory activity reveals a major weakness in our open and multicultural society. Portrayals of this sort to children have lasting effects and form the basis for future discrimination. In a democratic society we rely on the honesty and goodwill of leaders in the media to choose well and to use caution especially when dealing with children. Although to an adult such characterizations might indeed be humorous and ultimately harmless, for our children they could be devastating, especially when not corrected in early childhood and grade school curricula. Educators of all stripes should make their voices heard in this debate so that we can sensitize media creators and producers to the harm as well as the good they can perform. *Shark Tales* could be told and be even more amusing without the ethnic reference. Children might even learn about the varying behaviors of different species of fish rather than the stereotypical behavior of ethnic groups.

Most of us are appalled at how Jews are depicted early in the education of Middle Eastern children. In the United States, Arab Americans have been added to the list of common negative African American, Asian and Latino stereotypes. Continuing the media tradition of Italian American mafia stereotypes is not a palliative for these biases. Fables, cartoons, and fairy tales like this one can and should be de-ethnicized. Also, being sensitive to the complaints of a long list of others does not excuse one from even playfully portraying Italian Americans to young people even as redeemable vicious criminal monsters. Having spent most of my professional life working on issues of equity in our diverse communities I am neither surprised nor amused at the allegedly comic portrayal in a highly promoted children's animated film of damaging ethnic characters. I would think that community leaders, as well as social scientists and educators would join me in calling for a greater awareness of troubling biases reflected in children's media and more responsible actions on the part of leaders in the industry.

Document 2. Krase letter to the editor of the New York Times.
(The letter was not published in the newspaper).

Letters to the Editor
October 1, 2004
New York Times
Fax No. 212 556 3622
To the Editor:

I was surprised to read in A. O. Scott's review of *Shark Tale* ("Fish With Stars' Voices in a Pop-Culture Sea," October 1, 2004) about "cheerful quasi-ethnic stereotypes . . . that are technically insulated against offensiveness because, well, they're all fish." The fact is that for young children they are real characters, and they are made more real by negative ethnic and racial stereotypes. For instance, and in particular, the frighteningly ignorant and violent sharks have Italian last names or first names commonly heard in Italian-American communities (Luca, Frankie) and speak in a stereotypical lower class Italian vernacular. Promoting negative ethnic and racial stereotypes can make children wary of strangers who share the surface characteristics of media stereotypes. There is also nothing cheerful about inserting into the beautiful minds of children the idea that people who have Italian names, or use colloquial speech are also organized criminals. The other ethnic, racial, and gender stereotypes in the film are equally disturbing. As a social scientist who has spent a considerable amount of my professional life dealing with the consequences of bigotry I am amazed that someone writing for the *New York Times* would dismiss negative ethnic stereotyping in a children's feature as either "cheerful" or harmless.

PS: As one of 16 million other Americans who can trace his roots to Italy, I also find the employment of negative Italian stereotypes personally offensive and not at all amusing.

Jerome Krase, Ph.D.
Professor Emeritus
Brooklyn College
The City University of New York

Document 3. Krase email circular of September 29, 2004

*Subject***:** *Professional Advice and Assistance concerning Shark Tale (9/29/2004).*

Friends: As someone who subscribed to HBO in order to see *Sopranos*, it might seem odd that I am writing you concerning *Shark Tale* which uses ethnic stereotypes in an animated film for children. As you will see in the piece below my concern is that negative ethnic stereotyping in children's media is *ipso facto* dangerous and ought to be avoided at all costs. I am asking for advice as to how we as academics, scholars, parents, grand-parents, and especially educational professionals might be able to effect some change so that parents are made aware of the need for caution, and that in future ethnic references of this sort are not employed to simply sell something to children. As you know major films like this one are coordinated marketing campaigns for selling everything from food to toys. One of the most absurd (and offensive) aspects of the debate over the film was that the name of one of the "bad" characters was changed to an "obviously Jew-ish" one (I think it is now Don Feinberg) so that Italian organizations would be less offended. I also do not wish to be used by the promoters of the film to create more pub-licity for it as is this is also part of their marketing strategy. Any help and advice would be welcome. Jerry

Document 4. Statement by Lawrence Auriana, Columbus Citizens Foundation, September 14, 2004. [Source: Columbus Citizens Foundation].

Statement Regarding Ethnic Stereotyping in Movie for Kids: Spielberg's DreamWorks SKG'S Shark Tale
Tuesday September 14, 11:30 am ET
NEW YORK, Sept. 14 /PRNewswire/—The following is a statement by Lawrence Auri-
ana, President, Columbus Citizens Foundation:

Good morning. I am Lawrence Auriana, president of the Columbus Citizens Founda-tion, a non-profit organization that celebrates Italian-American culture.

Two days ago, I attended a showing of *Shark Tale* at the Toronto International Film Festival.

The animated film, by DreamWorks SKG, is unprecedented in recent children's mov-ies in its use of ethnic stereotypes to characterize villains.

In other recent movies for kids, the bad guys are identified by personality traits alone. They are greedy. They are power-hungry. They are arrogant. They are violent.

In *Shark Tale*, bad guys are identified also by ethnicity. They have Italian and Italian-American names, such as Don Lino, Luca, Giuseppe and Gino, and by their use of Ital-ian-American phrases of speech and slang, such as "capeesh," "consigliere," "maronne," and "agita." They praise violence as a virtue, they kidnap, they extort and they intimi-date. They are creatures of rage and revenge.

The movie introduces young minds to the idea that people with Italian names—like millions of Americans across the country—are gangsters. *Shark Tale* creates in its audiences an association between gangsters and Italian-Americans that will become imprinted in the developing minds of children.

DreamWorks is looking to profit from the mafia genre while inappropriately target-ing children. *Shark Tale* in large part is a parody of mafia films that are created for adult audiences. DreamWorks reinforces the connection to the mafia by using the voices of actors and directors who have repeatedly depicted mob characters, including Robert De Niro, Martin Scorsese and cast members from *The Sopranos*. But gang life and the mafia are not suitable in movies for children, however much DreamWorks may want to appeal to parents in an effort to increase the film's revenues.

It is startling that this film comes from Steven Spielberg's DreamWorks SKG. Mr. Spielberg has been a passionately outspoken opponent of stereotyping and discrimination.

In a *New York Times* article published on March 9, 2004, Mr. Spielberg was quoted, "We are in a race against time for the conscious mind of young people" and need to teach them "the dangers of stereotyping, the dangers of discrimination, the dangers of racial and religious hatred and vengeful rage." In testimony before the Senate Judiciary Committee in July 1994, Mr. Spielberg said, "People learn to hate."

Despite his enlightened statements about stereotyping, Spielberg has allowed Dream-Works to create the first children's film in many years that promotes bias. In interviews and speeches, Mr. Spielberg has talked about the pain he suffered as a child because of prejudice. In part because of DreamWorks's portrayal of gangsters in *Shark Tale*, in both the movie and the related books now available across the country, thousands of Italian-American boys and girls will feel a similar pain. They will be asked if their families are in the mafia. They will be looked at differently from their peers. They will be isolated. They will be stereotyped. Doesn't Mr. Spielberg feel their pain?

Shark Tale teaches young minds to associate Italian-Americans with violence and vengefulness. Mr. Spielberg's concerns about stereotyping are noble, but in supporting DreamWorks in its creation of this film and the related children's books, his actions contradict his words. On this issue, he is being hypocritical.

Negative stereotyping along lines of race, religion and ethnicity is unacceptable in America today, as are bias, prejudice and discrimination. We ask that Mr. Spielberg and DreamWorks make changes in *Shark Tale* prior to its release in the United States by doing the following:

- Removing Italian names from characters
- Eliminating Italian and Italian-American phrases and slang
- Removing physical gestures and customs found in Italian and Italian-American culture
- Removing from bookstores DreamWorks' *Shark Tale* titles

The Columbus Citizens Foundation celebrates Italian-American heritage. The Foundation supports cultural and educational programs, including grants and scholarships for elementary school, high school and college students. In 2003, the Foundation awarded over $2 million in scholarships and donated $1 million to help complete construction of the New Millennium High School, near the site of Ground Zero in lower Manhattan. It also donated $300,000 to the Fallen Heroes Fund, which benefits the families of servicemen and servicewomen slain in Afghanistan and Iraq.

The Columbus Citizens Foundation also produces New York City's Columbus Day Parade, which was first held in 1929. In 2002, the Foundation declined to allow cast members of *The Sopranos* to participate in the parade.

The Columbus Citizens Foundation is a member of the National Coalition Against Racial, Religious and Ethnic Stereotyping (CARRES), which since January 2004 has asked DreamWorks SKG to remove Italian-American names, mannerisms and speech from the film. The membership of CARRES includes the Order Sons of Italy in America, the National Italian American Foundation, UNICO National and the Italic Institute of America.

Document 5. CARRES press release, September 24, 2004.

National Coaltion against Racial, Religious and Ethnic Stereotyping. Italian American Coalition Alerts Parents to Shark Tale Violence and Stereotyping.
CALLS FOR NATIONAL BOYCOTT OF MARKETING PARTNERS

Washington—September 24, 2004—The Coalition Against Racial, Religious and Ethnic Stereotyping (CARRES) today alerted parents to the violence and ethnic stereotyping in DreamWorks' soon- to-be-released animated children's movie, *Shark Tale,* and called for a national boycott of all products that promote the film and its characters.

The movie is about a fish named Oscar, who gets involved with gangster sharks and killer whales. The gangster-fish have Italian names and are voiced by Robert De Niro, Martin Scorsese and actors from *The Sopranos.* It premieres nationally Oct. 1, the first day of Italian American heritage month.

Shark Tale is a production of DreamWorks SKG, owned by Steven Spielberg, Jeffrey Katzenberg and David Geffen. To promote it, DreamWorks formed partnerships with some of the nation's largest corporations, including Coca-Cola and Burger King.

Since January CARRES has petitioned DreamWorks to change the names of the gangster characters and remove Italian expressions from the dialogue. It also has written to the movie's corporate sponsors asking them not to promote the film.

"Since our requests fell on deaf ears, we are calling for a boycott of Coca-Cola, Burger King, Krispy Kreme, General Mills, Hasbro Toys and Activision, the movie's principal marketing partners," says CARRES spokesperson Dona De Sanctis.

It is the first time that the major Italian American organizations have called for a national boycott to protest the defamation of people of Italian heritage.

Italian Americans represent the fifth largest ethnic group in the United States, numbering 16 million according to the U.S. Census Bureau.

CARRES is composed of more than 25 ethnic organizations, including all the major national Italian American organizations:

- The Order Sons of Italy in America (OSIA)
- UNICO National
- The National Italian American Foundation (NIAF)
- The Columbus Citizens Foundation
- The Italic Institute of America

"*Shark Tale* is a kid's version of *Goodfellas,*" says CARRES member John Mancini, chairman of the Italic Institute. "We are profoundly disappointed in Steven Spielberg who chooses to negatively influence children this way."

"*Shark Tale* will be translated into many languages and reproduced on DVDs," says OSIA National President Joseph Sciame. "The characters will be in video games, on cereal boxes and fast-food meals all over the world."

Referring to the movie's corporate partners, UNICO National President Michael Mariniello notes, "How could these otherwise socially responsible corporations, whose businesses are sustained by American families of every racial and ethnic background, be a party to such a reactionary movie based on ethnic caricatures? It literally takes America back to the 1940s."

Lawrence Auriana, president of the Columbus Citizens Foundation, targeted Spielberg's role. "Despite his enlightened statements about stereotyping, Spielberg has allowed DreamWorks to produce the first children's movie in at least 25 years that promotes bias. By supporting this movie, Spielberg is being hypocritical." Auriana's foundation, which organizes New York City's annual Columbus Day Parade, banned members of the cast of *The Sopranos* from marching in the 2002 parade.

U.S Congressman, Bill Pascrell Jr. (D-NJ) contacted DreamWorks on Jan. 9 and again on Sept. 8, requesting a review copy of the film before its Oct. 1 national premiere. "I am concerned that the character images of this film do not meet a wholesome standard and will instill societal prejudices in our children," he wrote.

For additional information and interviews, contact:

- Dona De Sanctis,
  CARRES spokesperson, 202/547 3833
- Rosario Iaconis, president,
  Italic Institute of America, 516/488 7400
- Emanuele Alfano, spokesman,
  UNICO National, 973/429 2818
- Larry Auriana, president,
  Columbus Citizens Foundation, 212/922 0123

Document 6. NIAF Press Release on Resolution concerning Robert De Niro, October 28, 2004.

Source: National Italian American Foundation.

National Italian American Foundation Unanimously Votes to Oppose Honorary Italian Citizenship Award to Robert De Niro and to Denounce the Film *Shark Tale*
Thursday October 28, 10:38 am ET

NIAF Sends an Open Letter to Robert De Niro Condemning His Involvement With DreamWorks Animation SKG's *Shark Tale*
WASHINGTON, Oct. 28, 2004
Introduced by the NIAF Board of Directors
Laid on Table 10/14/2004

RESOLUTION: THE POSITION OF THE NATIONAL ITALIAN AMERICAN FOUNDATION ON THE DREAMWORKS FILM *SHARK TALE*

- Whereas, *Shark Tale*, an animated film by DreamWorks SKG and Dream-Works Animation SKG, continues a sordid history of negative stereotyping of Italian Americans and other ethnic groups; and
- Whereas, *Shark Tale* is being targeted and marketed to young children who are our most vulnerable population; and
- Whereas, numerous research, including the Miller/ADL and Zogby studies clearly demonstrate the damage negative ethnic stereotyping has on children; and
- Whereas, Steven Spielberg has shown himself to be hypocritical and insensitive regarding his use of ethnic, religious, and racial stereotyping has on children; and
- RESOLVED, the National Italian American Foundation unanimously condemns *Shark Tale*, DreamWorks Animation SKG and DreamWorks SKG, and its founders on promoting ethnic bigotry and defamation.

Document 7: Letter from NIAF to Robert De Niro, October 27, 2004.

Source: National Italian American Foundation.

October 27, 2004
Mr. Robert De Niro
Stan Rosenfield Public Relations
2029 Century Park East, 1240
Los Angeles, CA 90067
Dear Mr. De Niro:

On behalf of the National Italian American Foundation, we are writing to you to express our extreme disappointment and feelings of betrayal relating to your role in Dream-Works SKG and DreamWorks Animation SKG's animated children's film, *Shark Tale*. After honoring you with the coveted NIAF award, we cannot understand why you could neither comprehend nor accept the negative effect of this film on children.

We appreciate the entertainment value of satire but find it entirely inappropriate to confuse satire with negative stereotyping, especially when the work is in an animated film that is both targeted and marketed to children. Numerous studies, including both the Miller/ADL and Zogby, have concluded that negative stereotyping targeted at young children has a long-lasting damaging effect. DreamWorks Animation SKG's contention that *Shark Tale* "pokes fun at a number of film genres" and does not solely stereotype Italian Americans but other ethnic and racial groups, does not justify marketing the film to children. We condemn negative stereotyping and prejudice in any form.

Finally, your insulting and intemperate comments in response to criticism of your involvement with *Shark Tale* by the Italian American community are entirely inappropriate, insensitive, and disrespectful. For a man of your professional stature we would have expected a more reasoned and civil discourse. For all of these reasons, we are advising the Government of the Republic of Italy to not extend to you the privilege of honorary citizenship.

Sincerely,
Hon. Frank J. Guarini
Chairman
Contact: Steve Aiello
Hill and Knowlton
(212) 885 0340
saiello@hillandknowlton.com

13

If Defamation Is Serious, Why Don't Italian American Organizations Take It Seriously?

LindaAnn Loschiavo

You have not converted a man because you have silenced him.

—John Lord Morley (1838–1923), *On Compromise.*

Publicists and politicians know this: to be effective in public life, nothing is more important than defining yourself before the opposition does, and one way to do so is with the words you choose—the message that is being sent. What messages have Italian Americans been sending? What is our public image—and is it at odds with reality? If it *is*, how can the Italian American leadership help alter public opinion?

Perceptions of Italian Americans can be defined (1) by mass entertainment and the media and also (2) by the stories of our own people: self-expression sculpted into narratives that are then financially supported and promoted by our nonprofits. Other ethnic groups have successfully manipulated public opinion because they have defined themselves by writing their own testaments, texts that have then been generously underwritten and efficiently publicized by their nonprofit organizations. This is the reason you do not see a lot of plays on or off Broadway devoted to "Murder by the MEYER LANKSKY Mob"—or plays that depict Irish Americans getting drunk and violent at "Patrick and Pegeen O'Reilly's Wedding"—even though you do see many plays and films and television shows devoted to the Tony 'n Tina franchise, Italian mobsters, goombahs, and cafones. The real issue is not gangster imagery, of course, but the lack of any alternatives except for WHINE-making.

An examination of the five major Italian American nonprofit associations indicates, unfortunately, that they offer little or no support for these crucial "alternatives," alternatives that have been funded for decades by the savvier ethnic nonprofits.

My insight is based on a major (*unfunded*) study of my own that explored 1,000+ nonprofit American-based organizations run by these five ethnic and racial groups:

- Italian Americans (the fifth largest ethnic group in the United States, making up 5.6 percent of the population)
- Jewish Americans (who are 2 percent of the U.S. population)
- Irish Americans (who are 10.8 percent of our population)
- Hispanic Americans (12.5 percent)
- African Americans (who make up 12.9 percent)

How do the Italian American groups compare to other ethnic nonprofits when it comes to valuing bylines, authors, historians, playwrights, or storytellers? Only one major Italian American nonprofit, the National Italian American Foundation (NIAF), has a mission that specifically mentions "support for books dealing with Italian history."

In comparison, numerous Jewish groups, for instance, do fund and support students and writers who concentrate on Jewish history. One group that supports Jewish history raises funds that amount to an annual income of $59,338,736. Another group that supports Jewish history has an annual income from fundraising of $5,304,303. These are but two of numerous examples of how the other ethnic groups encourage, build, and emphasize a drive for "an interest in history," along with cheerleading and funding achievement from the student level on up.

Here are other eye-opening examples:

- Though Italian Americans are 5.6 percent of the U.S. population, we have NO nonprofit groups based in the United States that are dedicated to specifically funding authors and printing our authors' books, fiction or nonfiction. ALL the other groups do.
- Though Italian Americans are 5.6 percent of the US population, we have NO groups dedicated to specifically funding or encouraging dramatists. ALL the other groups do.
- We have NO theaters that exist to stage Italian American plays. ALL of the other four groups have eight (or more) well-funded theaters apiece to stage plays and sponsor theatrical achievement within their ethnic community. Perhaps this will change. A few years ago *Sopranos* castmate Michael Imperioli founded Studio Dante, a small New York City theater with quite an irregular performance schedule and one constant: each production featured at least one actor from *The Sopranos*.
- Italian American dramatists seldom win major playwriting awards. All the other groups that do sponsor and fund dramatists and theater help their writers to win major awards.
- From 1901 to 1999 Italian American writers won FEWER THAN A DOZEN major literary awards.
- None of our Italian American groups post statements on "Self Assessment," indications that they do not assess how well their programs and goals function

to empower the membership or advance this ethnic community. Most of the other major groups spend money and time on "Self Assessment" studies.
- Many Italian American groups have mission statements focused on filiopietism instead of on support for homegrown authors and scholars.

Italian American associations, lacking both an awareness of the present and a feeling of responsibility for the future, love to blame the media (that is, writers) and Hollywood (writers and certain Italian American "wise guy" actors) for their negative portrayals of people who claim Italian heritage. These old toothless tigers stick to the laziest form of activism—letter writing—confusing intent with behavior, activity with productivity, hindsight with foresight. Meanwhile, they are losing membership and their homegrown writers (lacking support) are losing opportunities to win the awards that would bring acclaim to the entire community.

Instead of blaming the media, Italian American organizations should learn how other groups cultivate a positive public image.

Irish American Nonprofits

Progressive Irish Americans understand that writers need exposure and a stage and, in turn, that the community at large benefits when their own writers are in the spotlight. Since 1920, the names of Irish American writers have been cheered at literary award ceremonies in this country: Eugene O'Neill earned a Pulitzer for *Beyond the Horizon* (1920) and also a Nobel Prize for literature (1936). O'Neill (1888–1953) continues to be a role model and a symbol of success because his estate offers a prestigious annual playwriting prize in his name. Following in his footsteps, the prolific Irish American writer John Guare (born 1938 in Manhattan) won an Obie Award for his play *Muzeeka* (1968); *House of Blue Leaves* won both an Obie (1970) and a New York Drama Critics Circle Award (1970–71); *Six Degrees of Separation* (1990) scooped several awards; and Guare has also received a Tony Award along with several Tony nominations. Another versatile Irish American writer John Patrick Shanley (born 1950 in the Bronx) won an Oscar for his popular screenplay, *Moonstruck* (1987), and his newest plays can attract John Turturro and other stars. The moral of the story is that O'Neill, an excellent role model, inspired numerous disciples.

In her poem "Spenser's Ireland," Marianne Moore pondered Irish stubbornness. To see stubbornness and innovation in action, consider the International IMPAC Dublin Literary Award, the largest prize in the world for a single literary work. Mayor Gay Mitchell of Dublin was unhappy with his country's association with poverty and violence in Northern Ireland, so even though Dublin is in the South, he sought good publicity in the form of a book prize and an American angel to bankroll it. The result is that James B. Irwin, Sr., a Bronx-born businessman, finances the wow-powered prize: 100,000 euros ($130,000 U.S.). "We may have put a bit of reality into prizes in the literary world," admitted Irwin. "Since authors cannot survive on a $100 reward, this honor is intended to allow the winners to focus on their next work." While most book awards are judged from submissions by publishers, IMPAC takes nominations from large public libraries around the world, which result in a list of 125 titles. Since it was first awarded in 1996 with a prize of 100,000 Irish pounds (then $160,000 U.S.), the IMPAC prize has been bestowed on nine previously unknown writers, none of them American. IMPAC had another impact: England's Booker Prize and Whitbread Award both upped their purses. The moral is that good public relations comes from writing checks to endow prizes, not by writing complaint letters.

Another way to burnish a group's reputation and fuel the creation of literary capital is by establishing a nonprofit theater and nonprofits that focus on aiding emerging and established dramatists. Over a dozen Irish American nonprofits are devoted to funding, encouraging, and producing Irish and Irish American drama. In addition, there are two Manhattan showcases for plays: the Irish Repertory Theater, founded in 1988, which owns its own building (at 132 West 22nd Street) and boasts an annual revenue of $1,476,301; and also the Irish Arts Center (An Claidheamh Soluis), founded in 1972, which owns its home (at 553 West 51st Street), where they stage plays, and provide free workshops in the Gaelic language, Irish music, and drama year-round, and also plan to show Irish films. Meanwhile, Irish American filmmakers are nurtured and promoted by Terence Mulligan, who heads Film Fleadh Foundation in Manhattan.

Polishing the reputation of dramatists who claim Irish birth or heritage is an enormously successful chain launched in the 1990s by seven siblings from the Guilfoyle family, who hail from Kilkenny, Ireland: The Playwright Tavern & Restaurant. Operating in Manhattan (three locations), near Yale University in New Haven (three more locations), and in Miami (one location), The Playwright is decorated with photos and artifacts that feature Irish and Irish American VIPs of the playhouse: O'Neill, George Bernard Shaw, Oscar Wilde, Samuel Beckett, Brian Friel, Terrence McNally, along with Broadway legends such as Neil Simon and Arthur Miller. Richard Guilfoyle has no objection to adding an Italian American dramatist to his equal opportunity wall, and as soon as one of us wins our first Tony or Obie, a frame is waiting. His promise acted on me like an amphetamine of hope.

Jewish American Nonprofits

The Jewish people are a minority in this country: 2 percent of our population. They make their presence known because it is so obvious how much they revere books and learning, and they quickly comprehend that writers need exposure and a stage and, in turn, that the community at large benefits when their own writers are on a pedestal. Since 1925, the names of Jewish American wordsmiths have been cheered at literary award ceremonies in this country when Edna Ferber became the seventh novelist to pocket a Pulitzer for *So Big*. Four years later, in 1929, playwright Elmer L. Rice (born Elmer Leopold Reizenstein in Manhattan, 1892–1967) won a Pulitzer for *Street Scene*, a compassionate drama of tenement life in New York, which was revived by Kurt Weill in an operatic version in 1947. Ferber and Rice were good role models and Jewish names have dominated prizes in literature ever since the 1920s.

Try to name a major Jewish playwright, and a staggering number of giants rush to mind: Miller, Hellman, Mamet, Odets, Rice, Hecht, Chayevsky, Simon, and others, who first stamped the American theater with a uniquely "Jewish consciousness." There are also the new traditionalists: Wendy Wasserstein, Marsha Mason, Donald Margulies, and others. Then there is the group that has identified itself as gay: Paula Vogel, Martin Sherman, Larry Kramer, Moisés Kaufman, Jon Robin Baitz, Harvey Fierstein, Tony Kushner, and others. Since 1877, the tradition of Jewish theater has been supported, developed, and funded by nonprofits such as New Jersey's United Jewish Centers of Metro-west. Currently, more than three dozen Jewish groups coast-to-coast extend their resources to the next Arthur Miller. Dramatists can count on generosity from nonprofits such as the midtown Manhattan based National Foundation for Jewish Culture, who commissioned 66 plays exploring the Jewish experience that were produced by professional theater companies recently. The same group supported 38 filmmakers with more than $1 million dollars to produce stirring, thought-provoking, and award-winning documentaries that have reached audiences in the millions; they also awarded many prizes and grants to emerging writers of Jewish fiction. Successful composer Stephen Sondheim began a nonprofit in 1981, Young Playwrights, to nurture writers under 18 to develop their talent and be paired with mentors. His celebrity attracts mega-watt funding.

Another way to burnish a group's reputation and fuel the creation of literary capital is by establishing a nonprofit theater as a way of building an audience and creating visibility for emerging and established dramatists. Founded over 128 years ago, the 92nd Street "Y" offers theatrical performances at its Tisch Center for the Arts, the new home of the Jewish Repertory Theater (after its company manager was killed in the 9/11 disaster, and the group lost its Time Square location). Since World War I, the Folksbiene Yiddish Theater has been featuring older classics to theater-lovers. The upstart Jewish Theater of New York (founded by a young Israeli, Tuvia Tenenbom) makes its voice heard for six months in Manhattan, then has its shows tour. Other states also have well-established Jewish theaters even as their acting companies keep an eye on Broadway. Moral: When there is an embarrassment of riches to extend to authors, the community at large is less likely to be embarrassed by movies and plays mostly depicting Meyer Lansky types and Jewish gangsters.

This talent for writing and winning has enriched this group as well as the American culture around it. Perhaps this is why Jewish nonprofit groups have a reputation for rewarding bookish types with endowments and opportunities. For example, in 1888 the Jewish Publication Society of America (JPS) was founded in Philadelphia. Now, 116 years of continuous operation later, and they are still publishing 12–15 titles annually by Jewish authors and retaining a prodigious backlist of 1,000 titles. Thus their assets total $4,148,012 and their annual revenue is $1,873,218. Though JPS is the oldest nonprofit publisher of Judaica, there is friendly competition to attract authors among several presses. Jewish college students also get a chance to work their words for money via The Elie Wiesel Prize in Ethics Essay Contest. This annual competition funded by the Nobelist and his wife offers a first prize of $5,000 and other awards.

If the Italian American leadership would take a page out of American Jewry's book, they would find a time-tested recipe for four-star image-making, spelled out line by line and worth copying. In 1947, The Jewish Book Council was established to promote the reading of books on all aspects of Jewish thought and culture. As well as Jewish Book Week (an annual festival that includes contributors from across the globe), the council administers the *TLS*-Porjes Prize for Hebrew-English Translation and a Primary Schools Poetry Competition and provides an extensive online archive of Jewish writers from around the world. You might not realize when Jewish Book WEEK is held because numerous Jewish book clubs actively promote and encourage writing and reading year-round. In 1949, the National Jewish Book Awards were established by the Jewish Book Council. These prizes are presented in several categories to North American and Israeli authors to honor excellence, either for one book or for a lifetime of achievement. It is the oldest American awards program in the field of Jewish literature and is recognized as the most prestigious. Among the notable literary winners are Howard Fast, Chaim Grade, Bernard Malamud, Cynthia Ozick, Chaim Potok, Philip Roth, and I. B. Singer. Researchers and historians can also win a prize for scholarship. Each winner receives a cash award and a citation. The publisher of the award-winning book also receives a citation. These presentations are made at the National Jewish Book Awards ceremony in New York City in the fall of each year during National Jewish Book MONTH. In 1998, the Koret Foundation, in cooperation with the National Foundation for Jewish Culture, established the annual Koret Jewish Book Awards to heighten the visibility of the best new Jewish books and their authors. Eligible for consideration are recently published books on any aspect of Jewish life in many categories and cover titles that were published in or translated into English. Moral: The more the focus is on the books, the less the subject is merely the crooks.

Hispanic American Nonprofits

It is obvious that Hispanic Americans are aware that writers need exposure and a stage and, in turn, that the community at large benefits when their own writers are sunned in a spotlight. Since 1904, Latino literati have been applauded at American award ceremonies: José Echegaray y Eizaguirre (1832–1916) earned a Nobel Prize for drama (1904) and other authors who wrote in Spanish followed his path in the decades ahead. But the first comet who blazed past New York's literary lights and held his own in English was Miguel Piñero, a 25-year-old Puerto Rican–born New Yorker, serving a jail sentence for robbery in 1972, who wrote with his soul on its knees. Two years later, Piñero (1946–1988) was catapulted to four-star fame with the staging of his first play, *Short Eyes*, a graphic portrayal of life, love, and death among prison inmates. *Short Eyes* ran away with the New York Drama Critics Circle Award and was made into a film. A poet, actor, and playwright, Piñero helped establish the Nuyorican Poets Cafe in an East Village storefront in 1973; seven years later, the group bought their building on East 3rd Street, helping to drive away crime by attracting performance poets and other late-night literary enterprises. Meanwhile, Piñero's influence as a pioneering voice for Latino artistic expression ran parallel to his unrepentant relish for narcotics, impulsive crime, transgressive sex, and other forms of self-destruction. Before he died, he created a cult following. Inspired by Piñero's literary successes, a young Cuban American, Nilo Cruz, told a PBS audience in July 2003, "He made me realize it's important to document our stories." Cruz persisted and won several awards and fellowships, including two NEA/ TCG (National Endowment for the Arts / Theatre Communications Group) Theatre Residency grants, a Kennedy Center Fund for New American Plays award, and a Rockefeller Foundation grant. Last year, Cruz got the gold ring: a Pulitzer Prize for drama.

Most of Piñero's followers viewed writing not as a solitary activity but as an entrance into the wonder-world of entertainment. Poetry readings turned into flashy "poetry slams." Slams became footage for MTV. And staginess demanded an ever larger stage. As one more way to burnish a group's collective reputation and fuel the creation of literary capital, neighborhood theater groups were established to magnify visibility for emerging and established dramatists. In the United States, there are more than four dozen nonprofits dedicated to Hispanic drama. In addition, there are several New York City playhouses that offer comedies, dramas, and musicals: the well-funded 35-year-old Spanish Repertory Theater (138 E. 27th Street); El Barrio's cavernous Julia de Burgos Cultural Center, which houses The Puerto Rican Traveling Theater Company; the Thalia Spanish Theater in Sunnyside, Queens; and the superb space on Theater Row known as INTAR (International Arts Relations). Moral: Give them a page, and they'll want a stage—and, fortunately, the NEA keeps baptizing Latino nonprofits with Benjamins.

Miguel Piñero wannabes, however, are rarely content to have their plays produced with a limited run, not when they long for a movie deal. Films are an unmatched medium for appealing to an audience in the millions but, unfortunately, the most visible genre for Hispanics consists of police or detective dramas, where they are invariably cast as low-life scum. Meet Frank Alvarez, 29, who ditched his East Los Angeles gang five years ago to play gangsters instead—for the standard union day rate of $675—and gets roles regularly because of his links to Suspect Entertainment. Seven years ago, Suspect Entertainment was founded by Manuel G. Jimenez, 31, a bald ex-convict who hot-wired cars as a teen before advancing to armed robbery and who now trains and employs 30 actors, most with Mexican roots. *Sí, sí, sí,* the idea of ex-homies peddling the mobster lifestyle may sound alarms for those who feel that Chicano villains, like Latina maids, are already disproportionately represented on screen. But wait. Suspect Entertainment, sparked by bigger ideas, is trying to shed the stereotyping. Suspect just produced an indie film, *Party Animal*, as a move to diversify beyond crime flicks. Moral: More money, more moral solutions.

Nonprofit publishing is wooing Hispanics via exclusive imprints. In Chicago, for instance, Swan Isle Press has been producing bilingual collections by poets Raul Barrientos, Olivia Maciel, and others. And the nation's largest, most respected Hispanic outfit, Arte Publico Press, attached to the University of Houston, continues to celebrate Hispanic culture by printing contemporary and recovered literature for adults and children. Moral: Loisaida today, laurel leaves tomorrow.*

---

* *Loisaida* is the Nuyorican expression for "Lower East Side."

Under our nose is an outstanding current example of how the Italian American leadership fails where the Hispanic American community succeeds. An Italian American writer, Leon J. Radomile, wrote and self-published two similar titles: *Heritage Italian-American Style* (followed by a bilingual second edition) and *Heritage Hispanic-American Style* (followed by *Patrimonio hispanoamericano*, a bilingual edition in November 2003). *Heritage Italian-American Style* was awarded "Best Fact Book" for 2003 by the Bay Area Independent Publishers Association. *Heritage Hispanic-American Style* won the Latino Book Award (*Premio al Libro Latino*) in the nonfiction category, sharing the honor with a title by Isabel Allende at the annual Latino Book and Family Festival (the largest Latino consumer expo in the United States). Honoring worldwide Latino writing in Spanish and English is also the mission of the Latino Literary Hall of Fame and the Latino Book Summit at BookExpo America. In contrast, no accolades were presented to *Heritage Italian-American Style* by the Italian American nonprofits, indicating how much less they do than the Latinos when it comes to honoring ethnic identity, history, and authors.

Another example is *Killer Smile* by Lisa Scottoline (New York: HarperCollins, 2004), with a plot marinated in a *ragù* of Italian enemy aliens, was atypically a very poor seller for the former litigator. *Killer Smile* entered the bestseller list ranked at No. 14 and "vanished two weeks later," according to the *New York Times*. In contrast, Scottoline's latest legal thriller, *Devil's Corner*, entered the *New York Times* hardcover fiction list at No. 9 and has sold better. More often than not, the Italian American community does not buy books from its authors because their nonprofits have not set a good example of how to demonstrate support.

African American Nonprofits

Black American groups have also shown their enlightenment. They have become aware that writers need opportunities and a stage and, in turn, that the community at large benefits when their own writers are applauded and lauded. Since 1959, Broadway audiences have welcomed authors of color when *A Raisin in the Sun* by Lorraine Hansberry (1930–1965) became the first play written by a black woman to be produced on The Great White Way. At 29, Hansberry was the youngest winner of the New York Drama Critics Circle Award and the first black writer to receive this award. Starring Sidney Poitier, the play ran for 530 performances. While students held "sit-ins" in Greensboro, North Carolina, Hansberry penned the screenplay for the film version, produced in 1961 by Columbia Pictures; it won a special Cannes Film Festival Award. More plays followed, along with Lorraine Hansberry's autobiographical memoir, *To Be Young, Gifted, and Black*, a bitterly ironic title. Her use of the term "black" was a conscious rejection of the terms "Negro" and "colored" (a genteel term in 1959 for African Americans). Sadly, cancer cut her down at age 35. Fortunately, she out-distanced the answer to these lines by Langston Hughes in his poem "Dream Deferred": "What happens to a dream deferred? / Does it dry up / Like a raisin in the sun? Or fester like a sore / And then run?" Her name lives on and, meanwhile, black prize-winners were already embracing dreams and wresting open all the sacred doors: Gwendolyn Brooks (1917–2000) won a Pulitzer for poetry (1950); Ralph Ellison (1914–1994) won a National Book Award for his first novel, *The Invisible Man* (1952); LeRoi Jones (born 1934) won an Obie for his play *Dutchman* (1964); Charles Gordone (1925–1995) won a Pulitzer for drama (1970); August Wilson (born 1945) won a Tony Award (1985), a Drama Desk Award (1986) and a Pulitzer for drama (1986) among other honors.

To enhance a group's reputation and mint some new literary capital, non-profit theater groups are necessary for emerging and established dramatists. In the United States, there are more than three dozen nonprofits dedicated to black drama. An excellent Manhattan venue founded in 1963 is The American Place Theater, a nonprofit, off-Broadway theater that strives to showcase the plays of African Americans. It has received over 34 Obie Awards and 15 Audelco Awards for Excellence in Black Theater, as well as a special Obie award for its "uncompromising commitment to unconventional and daring plays." In 1965, playwright Douglas Turner Ward, producer-actor Robert Hooks, and theater manager Gerald Krone established the still vibrant Negro Ensemble Company. Additionally, the Hinton Battle Theater (on West 42nd Street) as well as a number of fine venues in large urban areas around the United States are giving black dramatists, directors, and actors an opportunity to excel and celebrate their culture.

Additionally, now more than ever, role models in the literary black community are establishing nonprofit presses, literary magazines, and endowing prizes and competitions. According to the African American Literature Book Club, AALBC.com is the highest ranked, most frequently visited site dedicated to promoting blacks books and authors on the Internet, averaging over three million hits per month. Its competition includes Black Expressions Book Club, A Place Of Our Own (which promotes African American Literature and Events), the female-dominated Imani Book Club (founded 1999), and many others.

Literary laurels in this Afrocentric community take various forms. The Coretta Scott King Award is presented annually to an African American author and an African American illustrator for an outstandingly inspirational and educational contribution. And in November 1997, a dozen of the most influential black authors of the twentieth century were portrayed in a special series of stamps issued by the Inter-Governmental Philatelic Corporation; these stamps were distributed in the former Soviet Union, Asia, Africa, and South America. As the publishing industry grows, internal resources expand. In 2000, the African American Book Club Summit was founded. Working within this niche, TriCom Publicity. devotes itself to promoting the latest in African-American literature. Moral: Nothing's better than a role model to help a community take a new role: leadership.

Italian American Nonprofits

Italian American organizations have mission statements quite unlike the other four ethnic groups discussed. Whereas the Irish Americans, Jewish, Hispanic, and black nonprofits are focused on forward momentum and empowerment for individuals *within the group*, most of the Italian American mission statements show that our groups prefer, above all, to promote the culture of Italy or to do charitable works. One way Italian American groups promote the culture of Italy is via a great number of programs that teach Italian, reward teachers of Italian, promote trips to Italy, and focus on the achievements in the arts from Italians. While other ethnic groups take pride in their homeland, their focus and funding indicate that far more attention is placed on programs that advance talent. These other ethnic groups prove that "charity begins at home."

Italian American groups do things differently. For example, Order Sons of Italy in America (OSIA), an organization that is one hundred years old with a membership of 750,000, has this mission statement: "Supporting Educational and Charitable Programs." Following its mandate, OSIA donated $1,000,000 to the Alzheimer's Association, a generosity that does not seem to advance nor empower their membership. When it comes to authors, OSIA writes about certain books, plays, or films in their own publications to spread awareness; however, OSIA does not fund authors. Moreover, although the organization has had a National Book Club for more than 100 years, the book club does not buy and resell books but instead publishes a list of books that it recommends for purchase from booksellers.

Although most other ethnic nonprofits league with writers and foster drama as a way of paving the route to visible acclaim (in the form of Tony or Obie Awards, for example) and prestige that will reflect on the community at large, the Italian Americans have NO nonprofits specifically centered on theatrical development, not even one. Perhaps that explains our lack of awards in this area. The closest we come to a nonprofit that even *funds* theatrical projects is NIAF, which does make awards to playwrights and documentary makers. However, NIAF makes far more funding available to Italian American students and teachers of Italian than to authors.

UNICO National, with a membership in the thousands, does reward writers in the form of an annual Ella T. Grasso Literary Award Contest first prize of $1,500. On UNICO's website, it states: "In the past the Ella T. Grasso Award Contest has attracted a number of fine *amateur* writers. This year you are requested to make as many people aware of this award as possible; with your help and cooperation, we will be able to attract an outstanding group of writers." Aside from "help and cooperation," UNICO could woo good writers with a larger carrot. (In contrast, the Elie Wiesel Prize in Ethics Essay Contest awards a First Prize winner $5,000).

Tiro a Segno, founded in New York City in 1888, is an organization of 400 members dedicated to the preservation of Italian heritage and culture in the America. In 2000, Tiro a Segno increased their funding to establish a Visiting Faculty Fellowship in Italian-American Culture at New York University. This supports lectures primarily by college teachers who may or may not be professional writers.

Creating a corrective measure to end negative stereotyping in the media, a measure in which "funding" and "authors" are words that seem to shun each other's company, like bees too fastidious for honey-making, seems misguided. According to *Communication for Social Change*, a study commissioned by the Rockefeller Foundation, "the first stage in the process of social change is the recognition by the larger community (or a smaller subset of the community) that there is a problem that constrains their aspirations for the future, or has the potential to hurt the community or members of the community. This stage is so fundamental that it is unlikely that any process would be implemented *before there is a basic recognition of a problem*" (emphasis added). And the basic recognition of our lack of literary advancement problem can be seen in one key place: in our mission statements.

After researching mission statements and goals of Italian American nonprofits and then comparing ours with those of any ethnic group whose writers have won major literary awards, it becomes clear how other organizations stage-manage the success of writers and thus increase the esteem attached to the entire group. The good news is that there is so much room here for improvement.

Solutions

The following recommendations are presented NOT as an indictment but in the spirit of a "call to action."

1. Consider the example of two well-respected groups, one based in New York City and the other in Washington, DC. The revenue available to fund the programs and to fulfill the goals of New York's elite Columbus Citizens Foundation is considerable: over $4 million. This abundance gets chan-neled primarily into scholarships for students and for organizing the annual Columbus Day Parade in Manhattan. Their mission statement is this: "To promote Italian culture." The endowment of the Sons of Italy Foundation is over $1 million. Their mission statement is this: "To support educational and charitable programs." The mission statements for most of the Italian Ameri-can organizations in the United States are similarly modeled. Notice that there is nothing in a mission statement like that about supporting writers.

   In contrast, the organizations of many other ethnic groups—those with higher and lower endowments—often specify that their mission is for the advancement of culture through the arts, libraries (i.e., books), research, lectures, and writing. It's no wonder these groups have a hefty number of Pulitzer Prize and Tony Award winners among them.

   Taking this cue, a revised mission statement is the first step towards a positive change.

2. How can a nonprofit direct its support to emerging and established dra-matists, individuals who will portray their group onstage in a realistic (not demeaning nor stereotypical) way? Consider the example of seven modestly funded Irish American groups located in Chicago, Ohio, California, Colo-rado, Pennsylvania, and New York. Here's a typical mission statement: "To challenge, educate, and entertain audiences with quality, professional theatre at a reasonable price, focusing on Irish, English, and Classical." The objective of these groups is to provide an appreciation of Irish culture through the promotion of theater. To that end, these groups have supported the work of Tony Award winners Terrence McNally and Brian Friel, among others.

   In contrast, there is NO Italian American group in America with the word "theater" in either its mission or mandate. (Belmont Playhouse, once located at 2385 Arthur Avenue, Bronx, NY, had focussed on Italian American drama briefly, during the 1990s, but disbanded after April 2000.) Though there are Italian American groups whose name includes the word "*teatro*," invariably these refer to societies that support opera or music, not drama.

Taking this cue, an existing Italian American group should extend its scope in order to focus on playwrights and screenwriters or a new group must be formed.

3. Writing protest letters has its place in a system determined to correct social injustice. However, replacing offensive, violent, stereotypical mass entertainment—entertainment that reaches millions—with even better shows and films should also be a goal. The caring and of feeding of Italian American writers could be the remedy. However, people who write protest letters to condemn self-perpetuating mischief should heed the words of Albert Einstein, who defined insanity as doing the same thing over and over—while expecting different results.

4. Take the Italian American writers to heart and develop a coordinated cultural development strategy. For example, pioneer efforts that directly link the literary arts with business members in the group to foster economically beneficial environments for long-term growth. The vast majority of business intermediaries, while interested in working with the creative sector, have yet to make definitive moves in that direction.

5. Offer affordable and collaborative working environments for literary artists within other cultural organizations. For instance, if you know of a successful Italian American actress, pair the actress with some Italian American screenwriters.

6. Try to integrating the creative sector of Italian American poets and dramatists into residential and business communities. Innovate supportive strategies at the local level to make the connection between arts and culture and local economic development. Provide writers with targeted support.

7. Create a new funding stream, in conjunction with private funders, to support and seed efforts. Philanthropic funders can help through more joint programming and by targeting funds to collaborative efforts. For example, Deutsche Bank has initiated such a program through a just-released Request for Proposals for place-based strategies to unite cultural and economic development. JP Morgan Chase is integrating their development and arts grant-making as well. Any city can provide technical assistance and collaborative grants to economic organizations interested in working with cultural groups such as writers.

Heed the grapevine: Mass entertainment remains uninfluenced by feeble WHINE-makers. Cultivate your homegrown writers the way that other groups have been doing for decades and the image of the Italian American community will shine. In order to make a difference, we must focus on defining ourselves before the opposition does. By making changes now, we will be in a position to create a literary legacy in the twenty-first century. If we do succeed, then perhaps we will have that new literary legacy's prestige as a role model for the next generation.

14

Narrating Guido

Contested Meanings of an Italian American Youth Subculture

Donald Tricarico

L et me begin with an anecdote. Long before the media spectacle of 2009–2010 surrounding MTV's *Jersey Shore*, the police department of the small New Jersey shore town of South Belmar warily eyed the 2000 Labor Day weekend marking the last "fling" of the summer. An "internal police memo" identified a particular group for special scrutiny: "Let's end the summer by taking a 'bite' out of the remaining 'guidos' and have some fun while we are doing it." When news of the "memo," written by a police corporal with an Irish surname, was leaked to an Italian American antidefamation organization, the latter lodged a formal protest with the town government. The town's mayor, who had an Italian surname, maintained that the term "guido" did not refer to Italian Americans but to "people from the city," undoubtedly preferring the insult to fall on a group that was too amorphous to field an antidefamation constituency. The maneuver failed to satisfy an official of the Italian American organization because "Everyone in the United States knows that 'Guido' is 'an Italian slur.'" This, at least, was the definition of the situation that was registered on the organization's website.[1]

Now, let's complicate things. Many "stories" have been told about "Guido." Law enforcement agencies, elected officials, and antidefamation activists are not the only ones weighing in with narrative accounts that vie for the truth. Scholars of the Italian American experience similarly understand "Guido" as a category of prejudice. The erudite and authoritative catalogue of Italian American popular culture compiled by Pellegrino D'Acierno provides a formal definition of "guido" as a "pejorative" term that originates in "a dominant mass media stereotype projected onto Italian American men since the 1970s."[2]

"Guido" does seem to have become the new ethnic insult reserved for Italian Americans.[3] It has surpassed the classical epithets of "guinea," "dago," and "wop," pointing to a paradigm shift in ethnic prejudice. There is, however, an Italian American "story" that is not being told when Guido is reduced to a "story" that disparages Italian Americans—a story that, ironically, antidefamation and scholarly readings still corroborate.

This essay tells a "Guido" story. It is based on the point of view of young Italian Americans who *call themselves* "Guido." It proposes to see Guido, not as a category imposed from the outside to defame Italian Americans, but as a complex "transaction" inside and across the ethnic boundary.[4] It is my intention to (re)locate Guido in youth culture practice *within* a broader ethnic group experience.[5] I contend that Guido narrates the relationship of youth in New York City's Italian American neighborhoods to American popular culture, the city, and ethnicity at a particular historical juncture. Guido emerges out of the urban experience of Italian Americans in New York City and, like other "common cultures", can be traced to the "symbolic work" of youthful participants.[6] In particular, it *names* the "moment" in which American youth culture consumption, and by extension mainstream American culture, becomes strategically linked to Italian ethnicity.

The theoretical approach of this essay relies on a "constructionist" or "transactional" model of ethnicity. Its core assumptions relate ethnicity to strategic "choices" made to invoke ethnicity in "discursive" or "interactional" processes within larger structures of opportunities and constraints.[7] A constructionist model of ethnicity is combined with a cultural studies perspective on "contemporary youth subcultures." A classic statement is made by the Birmingham School, which has been modified in subsequent critical debates.[8] For the purposes of this essay, the literature on youth subcultures underscores the "agency" of "youth formations" in response to "structural conditions." In particular, youth subculture can be a "construction site" for ethnicity. As discussed in the text of this essay, ethnicity alters the dynamic of youth subculture by complicating the response to structural problems. Invoking ethnicity can be interpreted not as an "escape from class" in general but as an escape from the lower class position that informs a "negatively privileged ethnicity." Indeed, the new class signifiers associated with a prestigious consumption style is the basis for challenging ethnic stigma.

D'Acierno is on the verge of conceptualizing a youth subculture, since he recognizes a "style" that defines "Italian American men." His definition precludes "agency," however, since it implies that they are only ciphers of popular culture, perhaps including the very mass media images that disparage them and their ethnicity. D'Acierno's "guidos" are too passive to name themselves and to oppose stigmatization, although he is moot on whether they internalize this "pejorative" as an identity. In this story, "guido" has significance for the "construction" of Italian American ethnicity *only* as a new stereotype.

In this story, Guido originates in the "agency" of young people exploiting the accessible resources of popular culture and ethnicity. Their symbolic work is understandable not only as "youth culture practice," but also as *ethnic practice*. That is, it deploys popular culture to formulate new cultural signifiers that subvert ethnic stereotypes of Italian Americans while it uses ethnicity to organize a youth culture scene. I interpret Guido as a collective challenge to ethnic stigma and argue that the disparagement of Guido grew out of local youth culture practice, although the distinction between Guido as a *subcultural category* and an *ethnic category* is blurred. Guido emerges as a category of ethnic prejudice within this scenario. It also feeds into a conversation about the status of Italian Americans in New York City. The larger significance of this story may be found in a "struggle for recognition and respect" that shapes the assimilation of subordinate ethnic groups in American society.[9] This chapter makes the case that it is a matter of intellectual integrity to own the story of Guido within the Italian American experience and that a true story is a more prudent method to defuse negative stereotypes.

Guido as Youth Subculture

A "youth subculture" is a group whose practices "revolve around the symbolic meaning of stylized presentations of self and around the symbolic meanings those performances have."[10] Meanings originate in the popular culture, especially in the mass media, but are translated and rearranged to suit a youth agenda.[11] Guido is a youth subculture in this basic sense that it names a category of youth defined by "style."[12] A signature style is assembled from commodities and leisure activities appropriated from the commercial popular culture.

The "symbolic work" of style-based youth subcultures communicates a shared identity that is immediately meaningful in terms of the selection and arrangement of cultural elements.

> Instead of wearing baggy and oversized clothes, Guidos make sure their clothes are tight. Straight legs are very common. They go perfect with their Skecher boots. Shirts have to be tight to show off their muscles and tattoos. You still need a gold chain to go with your outfit. New accessories have been added. Now it is almost mandatory to have one of the newest cell phones attached to your belt. [John, 2001]*

There is a conscious awareness of sharing a style-based identification with other youth that places them in a "youth category." Shared style implicitly establishes difference in relation to youth others. Collective identity and difference are "produced" in a peer group dynamic.

> My friends and I pretty much have the same hairstyle. All the girls wear it straight and shoulder-length. All the guys wear it short and gel on top. If one were to wear it differently we have to make sure our friends would "approve." We wear pretty much the same type of jewelry; things like gold crosses, pretty rings, and bracelets our boy-friends gave to us. Before I started hanging out with this group all I listened to was rap and reggae. Now all I listen to is freestyle and club music. When we drive around in our cars, that is all that we play and when we go to clubs that is all that we hear. Most people say that freestyle is all Italians listen to. I have to say that for the most part, that is true. [Corrine, 18]

Ethnic youth subcultures also appropriate ethnicity to "work for them."[13] As the above testimonies suggest, being "Italian" is primarily referenced to styles like

---

* Informants have been given pseudonyms.

"tattoos" and "club music" that are not referenced to a traditional heritage but a youth culture "symbol bank."[14] Ethnicity is invoked to validate insider authenticity. It gives coherence to a collective style profile that expresses a position in contemporary youth culture. It filters new styles poached from other subcultures or appropriated from the broader "symbol bank" of mainstream popular culture:

> In recent years, body piercing has become a staple in an Italian teen's style. These piercings include tongue rings, eyebrow rings, and belly rings. Guidos still wear gold crosses and Christ heads, but now tend to have earrings in both ears. [Jennifer, 2004]

Despite appropriations from commercial style markets and global media like television and the Internet, there is a typical subcultural conceit that "Guidos make their own style." [John, 2001] This "production" of a style ensemble or "bricolage"[15] of diverse cultural elements is meaningful in the making of a youth category because it is named in reference to Italian ethnicity. When certain "stylized presentations" that symbolically represent Italian ethnicity surface, Guido is at least implicitly possible. It is deliberately performed or "stylized" by second and third generation youth within local urban scenes. While styles are fluid, core fashions like gold crosses, warm-up suits, and tank-tops facilitate the consciousness of a youth "style tradition"[16] that can pass as, or be confounded with, a "traditional style."[17]

In Guido, Italian American ethnicity is symbolically represented by style to symbolize a local youth category. Guido makes the relationship among Italian ethnicity and youth style precise—a way of being Italian referenced to an ensemble of cultural signifiers, to certain commodities and ritual activities and images. To this extent, ethnicity also draws boundaries intended to include some and exclude others. It establishes parameters for stylized performances most notably clubbing as the quintessential Guido social ritual, in particular as the stage for style performance and the competition for sexual partners.

Identity transactions occur across boundaries. Guido has been corroborated by significant youth others who are able to make subtle distinctions in style. A 20-year-old offered this characterization in the spring of 2001:

> Guidos can easily be recognized in a crowd. No matter what the occasion a Guido is dressed like he is going to a club, or on his way to work out at the gym. Tight muscle tee shirts are a wardrobe staple. These shirts can be worn with sweatpants and Nikes or with a "shark skin suit" and dress loafers. An oversized gold chain and a diamond stud earring are accessories that complete the look. [Michael, 20]

Guido has intermittently been "named" in the mainstream mass media, a critical event in the formation of youth subcultures.[18] A 1997 *New York Times* article framed Guido in the context of local style-based youth culture: cruising cars that "peel off for Francis Lewis Boulevard," "bellbottoms and platform shoes," and "tight shirts."[19] Themes of youth culture fun and pleasure paper over the narratives in the public discourse that label Guido as threats to the civil contract. Indeed, Guido was first named in the "moral panic" in response to a 1989 "racial killing" in Bensonhurst, the city's largest Italian American neighborhood. These meanings echo in subsequent reports of street violence in the city involving a young male with an Italian-sounding name and an "Italian American 'look.'"[20] The Jersey shore "police memo" reiterates the themes of deviance and moral panic.[21]

The Guido "Moment": The Structural Basis of Italian American Youth Style

If youth subcultures originate in a historical "moment,"[22] Guido appears to have crystallized in the 1970s when the dance music genre of "disco" attained popularity. The 1977 film *Saturday Night Fever* is read by both Guido style leaders and rank and file as an origin myth, although the partly fictional Rik Cohn essay in *New York Magazine* on which it was based suggests that a vernacular urban dance subculture was already in place. Still, the appearance of a film about young working class Italian Americans in Brooklyn was particularly fortuitous for pop culture authenticity. Disco afforded a comprehensive subcultural style complete with a signature "look," a sound, and an urban scene that has continued into the present. And it provided media culture validation of the city's Italian American youth's special calling to disco; the Guido name, reflecting a collective consciousness of this youth culture position, would crystallize later (see below). The film is an origin myth for the Guido subculture; iconic images of "Tony Manero" (John Travolta) dancing in a white suit symbolizes a subcultural connection, for example, when displayed on the webpage of local dance music impresario DJ "Brooklyn's Own Joe Causi." This historical moment legitimates Guido authenticity. Thus, the web pagebiography for "DJ Mike C" of an Internet radio station dedicated to "spread the [dance music] vibe on a global scale" mines the golden age for personal credibility:

> I learned to spin back in the late 80s. Self-proclaimed "guidos" in my hometown of Brooklyn taught me everything I needed to know. [Personal email communication, 2000]

This seminal period is reverenced in the nostalgia for classic disco on dance radio and on public television and in live shows directed at Italian Americans and others who have aged out of youth culture.

As a youth culture "moment," disco facilitated greater movement away from "greaser" as the dominant style for youth in Italian American neighborhoods. This is significant because "greaser," a label that has distinguished Mexican Americans in the southwest, signified a "negatively privileged ethnicity" with a "dominated" ethnic culture.[23] Greaser is also a "taste culture" tainted by a lower class status. Greaser produced a significant pop culture moment in Doo Wop, which registers a significant contribution from Italian Americans especially in New York City and Philadelphia. However, disco was accompanied by a more intensive and broadbased commitment to stylized consumption. It entailed a deeper foray into a popular entertainment culture with markedly fewer restrictions on commodified fun and pleasure. The outer limits of hedonistic club culture consumption were represented by the new Manhattan discos in the 1970s like Studio 54.

The emergence of contemporary style-based youth subcultures is predicated on requisite discretionary income and consumption; sufficient leisure is also a factor, a development bound up with delayed marriage and employment.[24] Working class youth in Italian American neighborhoods into the 1960s had limited discretionary income for youth cultural consumption; Italian American youth culture in the West End of Boston in the late 1950s was truncated by the onset of adulthood in the late teens.[25] The material conditions for a full-blown Italian American youth subculture crystallized in lower middle class and blue-collar Italian American communities in the outlying boroughs. To this extent, Guido is hardly a "lower class" consumption pattern.[26]

A central orientation to commodity consumption provides a sharp contrast with greaser. According to a self-identified "Guido" from Queens named Mike, "To be a true Guido means that you are able to afford the Guido lifestyle, which includes the expensive clothes, cars, and nights." Nightclubs have emerged as "cathedrals" in a "landscape of consumption," a development that took an ironic twist when the infamous Manhattan club Limelight opened in a renovated Episcopalian church.[27] Compared to previous eras, contemporary youth are "able to choose from a greater range of consumer goods and services and images," and the new "urban nightscapes" of consumption "offer abundant resources for experimentation and play."[28] Italian American youth subculture has incorporated such sites as tanning salons, gyms, pool halls, and beauty parlors where "the Guidettes get manicures, pedicures, and have their eyebrows waxed." Impressive financial expenditure has been built into dating relationships. Josephine's "boyfriend" and "future husband" has an income derived from "a family business":

> This allows him to buy me the material items such as diamonds and the latest clothing gear. Just the other day he bought me the entire Chanel snowsuit for when we go out in his 2001 four-wheeler, now that winter is here. [Josephine, 20]

While Josephine is actually claiming a high ranking style in the status hierarchy, Guido also symbolizes the "consumer desire" or "longing" for consumption if not its "visible practice."[29]

> Money is very important to Guidos and is seen as a high social status. If you don't have the money for the Guido lifestyle you have to pretend you do. [Michael, 19]

Italian American youth culture development into the 1960s was also stunted by ethnic family traditions. Guido also presupposes diminished familial and community traditions, leading to an erosion of "adult surveillance" necessary for more autonomous "youth formations."[30] Italian American youth were freer to consume popular culture, which has historically provided "a free space for the imagination—an area liberated from old restraints and repressions, a place where desire did not have to be justified and explained."[31] The pursuit of "immediate sense gratification" (i.e., "party"), especially within peer group contexts, is not easily reconciled with a traditional morality grounded in a scarcity economy; even when family values embrace core American consumer values, popular youth culture creates a "hedonistic" consumer.[32]

Youth like Josephine, who possessed a traditional side, managed to be "bifocal,"[33] by remaining "close" to the family and even participating in ethnic communal functions like the religious *feste* and immigrant society affairs. However, urban dance clubs are a dramatic break with ethnic family culture. They are places to "indulge in 'adult' activities of flirtation, sex, drink and drugs, and explore cultural forms" (like music and clothes) as the basis for "autonomous and distinct identities."[34] More than any other places, dance clubs "play out fictive scenarios of changed identities."[35] According to a self-described "club junky" named Maria,

> Many young adults go to clubs to escape reality; it provides them with a fantasyland. The extra loud music puts people in a place they love, a place where they can get away from family members, school, and the workplace. Clubs make you forget all your problems and dance the night away. [Maria, 19, 2004]

The club fantasy affords the dream of entering the celebrity entertainment culture. Maria adds that the clubs are places where patrons are "discovered" by talent scouts for their dancing and even singing, adding that Club DNA in Astoria, Queens, held a talent search modeled after the hit television program *American Idol*. It happens that Maria's fantasy was based on a Hollywood narrative: "Just like in the movie *Honey*, about a young girl who was spotted in a club dancing and then danced in music videos which was her dream." In the meantime, a "young girl" can pose as a "hottie," a flagrantly sexualized club-based persona. While females are typically cast by the male "gaze" as sex objects, it is a measure of changing sexual mores and the gender politics of club culture that females who "turn heads" and "break hearts" on the dance floor are now empowered to label males as "hotties."

Dance club culture also shifted youth culture identity beyond the provincial confines of the ethnic community; clubbing creates a consciousness and practice that is incompatible with the neighborhood bars and lounges, social clubs, Italian cafés, and other "third places" characterized by provincial forms of solidarity and "adult surveillance." A cosmopolitan dance club scene created conditions for the expansion of local peer groups, or "cliques," into a youth "category" thrown into relief by differences from youth others.[36] Club culture, in other words, facilitated a breakthrough to a more inclusive identity referenced to ethnicity and coded as "Guido", namely an Italian American position in club culture. It became the cultural focus of an Italian youth category: "You can't compare the club [Sound Factory] to anything! We [Italian Americans] tear up the dance floor." As the preeminent Guido narrative, clubbing became a template for the consumption of popular culture and "urban nightscapes": "Guidos dress like they're going to a club even when they're just hanging out." In effect, club culture style sublimated, if not replaced, the neighborhood as the frame of an urban Italian American ethnicity in the context of youth culture. "I have to say that [we] Italians love freestyle." Thanks to the club scene, it was possible to imagine a youth category based on ethnicity that spanned the five boroughs and extended into the suburban diaspora.

Mass Media Frames

Mass communications media comprise the "mediated center" of contemporary societies possessing the "socially sanctioned power of constructing reality."[37] It is not surprising that youth subcultures seek representation and media institutions are increasingly amenable. This is evidenced by the new MTV channels that target content to Indian Americans (Desis), Chinese Americans, and Korean Americans. While MTV was not available until recently, Italian American youth were able to find their reflection in a local dance music station. While mainstream mass media have been instrumental in labeling Guido deviant, "winning space" in the commercial entertainment and media culture provides unequivocal legitimacy in local youth style markets, validating their credentials for stylized youth culture fun and pleasure. Recognition by dance music radio puts them on a par with groups such as Blacks, Latinos, and gays that have formatively shaped local club culture.[38] Incorporation in the mass media culture has the effect of making groups known to the larger society within familiar cultural understandings. Mass media access has made it easier for Italian American youth to imagine community with Italian American media celebrities and personae as style leaders.

While *Saturday Night Fever* possesses mythical value, a local dance music station has mediated a Guido scene since the 1980s. The crash of disco and the ascendance of rap routed dance music station WKTU in the early 1990s. When it returned to the air in 1996 on the strength of a revivified dance music scene, with a publicity stunt in Times Square that invoked the mythic energy of *Saturday Night Fever*, it was anointed as "the Guido station" and "the official radio station of all Italians." WKTU's Guido connection was embodied in the personalities of "Goumba Johnny" Sialiano and "Brooklyn's Own" Joe Causi. Sialiano is a stand-up comedian with an Italian neighborhood accent, whose material is lifted from Italian American neighborhood culture, including an implicit knowledge of local Mafia culture. Causi grew up in Bensonhurst, the symbolic homeland of Guido, and vigorously cultivated a subcultural connection to dance music and the local club scene. On a Sunday evening radio show broadcast from Studio 54 featuring classic disco, Causi presented a cast of stylized Guido personas with such names as "The Supreme Cuginette," "Joey Balls," and "Carmanooch," whose comedy is rooted in the Italian American neighborhood culture, and whose song "The 12 Days of A Guido Christmas" is given seasonal play. Causi routinely code-switched into stylized insider phrases like "How ya doin'?", especially in the actual or "imagined" company of ethnic homeboys, and once expressed nostalgia mingled with resentment for a lapsed Italian Bensonhurst, which an influx of immigrants has made "like the friggin' United Nations."

WKTU mediates a wider connection to the commercial media and entertainment culture that is a defining feature of the "postmodern tribe."[39] WKTU presents a world of fun and pleasure that is highly commodified, creating wants and shaping a hedonistic taste culture for Italian American youth. There are commercial advertisements for products that are consumed to cultivate the "look" of a "hottie" like tanning, whitening strips for teeth, and weight control. Promotional contests feature destinations of youth cultural hedonism as prizes, including spring break in Cancún and a Caribbean resort aptly known as Hedonism. The station's Guido personalities drop the names of celebrities whose commodified media personas are consumed by fans on the air and during personal "appearances." The micro-culture of dance radio is validated by the "consumption space" of urban dance clubs with their expensive cover charges, drinks, and personal overhead (clothing, haircuts, jewelry, etc.). Of course, the music that is the soundtrack of this youth party is commodified as CDs and Internet downloads.

The Internet emerged as a mediated center for popular youth culture in the 1990s. Local Italian American youth appropriated the resources of Internet chat for their social rituals and stylized presentations. Henceforth known as ItalChat, a chat room scene surfaced in the late 1990s in (cyber)space sponsored by a com-mercial Internet service provider; as such, ItalChat is an artifact of the commercial popular culture and reflects a broader trend toward a youth culture practice on the Internet. However, ItalChat is predicated on the agency of subcultural Italian American youth who establish the interactive forum everyday in the name of Ital-ian American ethnicity. As a media space, it is accessible to youth from through-out the metropolitan area and beyond and seems largely driven by the desire to expand network capital for the cultivation of dating and sexual partners. ItalChat also facilitated identity experimentation in particular with gangsta Hip Hop, a style identified with a preeminent turf rival in urban black youth.

A radio niche and Internet chat provide a frame of reference for an Italian American youth category that is becoming increasingly dispersed, further subli-mating the local neighborhood as a subcultural frame. At the same time, because media spaces can be easily infiltrated, youth others are more likely to be included in the conversation. A niche on WKTU is particularly tenuous. As a commer-cial mass media outlet sensitive to the dynamic of market shares, WKTU has to cultivate the largest possible audience. Industry constraints perhaps explain the departure of Joe Causi for an upstart dance music station in 2004. There has been a growing commitment to a burgeoning Latino population in broadcast range with a historic ethnic connection to dance music styles like salsa, bachata, and meringue. However, there has not just been an erosion of Guido but an amal-gamation of Italian and Latin ethnicities. Goumba was part of a morning crew that was "anchored" by a Latino and also included a conspicuously Puerto Rican persona who deferred to "Goumba" as "Papi," reflecting an ethnic hierarchy that likely placates Guidos. The musical anthem for this ethnic blend given frequent play for a time was the Rosemary Clooney standard "Mambo Italiano" although the lyrics actually promoted the Latinization of Italian Americans: "Try an enchi-lada with your baccalà." Although Goumba is chauvinistic, he easily crosses the ethnic boundary especially for the sake of Guido libido, as when an attraction to African American singer Samantha Mumba led him to fantasize about a "Mumba/Goumba" union on the air. Goumba rapped to Latin beats and sprinkled some Spanish lyrics in his Guido anthem "Feds Threw a Party," which narrates the story of a prison term for tax fraud stemming from his involvement in a club owned by local Mafiosi. Goumba periodically invoked an ethnic boundary like when he chastised his Puerto Rican sidekick during the "2004 Meatball Contest" because "You don't call an Italian woman 'mami.'" However, Latin and Italian American personalities display a fraternization that mocks serious ethnic enmity. The very concept of ethnic difference appeared arbitrary when Goumba toyed with the notion that the professional baseball player Alfonso Soriano, who is a black Panamanian, was "Italian" because his name ends in a vowel, and because he was a star performer on the New York Yankees.

Stylization of Street Culture

Guido is historically defined by an aggressive masculinity.[40] Schneider links this motif to an economy of lower class masculine "honor" manifest in physical intimidation and the control of turf.[41] Elijah Anderson defines this oppositional urban youth subculture as a "code of the street" found in the lower class black inner city; interestingly, Anderson noted in passing that, owing to similar structural conditions, this street culture "can be observed in working class Italian . . . communities."[42] A "street experience of leisure" combining "fighting" and "male camaraderie"[43] continued to frame Italian American youth subculture through the 1990s. An especially valued trait is an inveterate bellicosity ("Don't f___ with a Guido!"). Street-based youth subcultures invest heavily in social capital to counter ubiquitous threats. This is expressed in codes that value having "lots of friends" who "watch each other's backs."

> I remember one time I was at a club and saw these Guidos I am kind of friends with. They were about to get into a fight in which they were outnumbered and destined to lose but went out fighting for each other. This is a very good way to be and I think more subcultures should take care of their own as they do. [David, 19]

Typically, having "your back covered" was not just a defensive strategy but a prompt to "start a beef."

Organized masculine aggression is prominently imprinted in the local Italian American youth style tradition; the "Big Bad Guidos" of the 1990s are descendants of the greaser "gang" known as "The Golden Guineas," who were based in the Fordham section of the Bronx and in Bensonhurst in the 1950s and 1960s. It is a noteworthy ethnic pattern that Italian American street culture has had a formative relationship with the local Mafia syndicates that monopolized organized crime activities and maintained order in the neighborhood to inhibit intervention by law enforcement authorities.[44] This likely inhibited the emergence of potent youth "street gangs" of the sort that have plagued inner city black neighborhoods. Local Mafia crews were able to neutralize young males who made a name for themselves in the street by intimidation, if not by recruitment into syndicate employment; tough Guidos could become Mafiosi, although Mafiosi were often Guidos.

A "streetwise" ethos remains focused on the commitment among young males to defend neighborhood turf especially from denigrated minorities. Although the "moral panic" in response to the highly publicized Howard Beach and Bensonhurst incidents had subsided, a tough street culture remained part of the fabric of more working class Italian American communities like the Ridgewood and Glendale areas of Queens in 2001:

> If they are really bored, they will drive around just to look for someone to beat up. Sometimes they would come back with a story of how they just jumped some black kid because it looked like he was up to no good. [Corrine, 18]

Turf-based masculine honor appears to be rife in the initial stages of transitional neighborhoods. In the summer of 2004, an Italian American youth who had moved to a town in nearby Nassau County was charged in a violent street attack of a Sikh man in Ozone Park. A "racial attack" in Howard Beach the following summer once again thrust Italian American youth subculture into the headlines. This episode echoed the 1986 incident not just as a "bias attack" but as "turf conflict." Nineteen years later, however, the principal Italian American "attacker" and the black "victim" had "a number of things in common": "Although neither had any steady work, both had a taste for luxury items, from the Prada shoes that Mr. Moore was carrying to the Rolex watch that Mr. Minucci was wearing."[45]

While aggressive masculinity is still in the picture, Guido stylizes lower class urban tendencies. Stylization has always acted on lower class American street culture. Anderson maintains that "the basic requirement" of the "code of the street" is "the display of a certain predisposition to violence," relying on "facial expressions, gait, and direct talk" as well as "clothes, grooming, and jewelry."[46] An apotheosis of stylized street culture masculinity has been achieved in "gangsta" Hip Hop, which has growing appeal for Guido.

The stylization of Italian American street culture has been predicated on social mobility. It correlates with the withering of the "mean streets" of the Italian American tenement slums in favor of more comfortable residential communities in the boroughs and the inner suburbs. The need to invest honor in neighborhood turf is diminished because there is private wealth in clothing, jewelry, automobiles, and houses. It is ironic that violent street episodes have occurred in neighborhoods, like Bensonhurst, with high rates of home ownership; Howard Beach in Queens has been described as middle class and suburban. However, these areas border lower class black communities, and their Italian American residents are once removed from defended neighborhoods in East New York and Canarsie. Italian American youth that have retained a street code repertoire may be experiencing limited educational mobility. The profile of the attacker in the 2005 Howard Beach episode suggests a response shaped by an organized crime affiliation.[47]

Stylization allows for the aesthetic manipulation of masculinity within the expressive culture, but on the surface (e.g., "a look") rather than physically acted out. The macho Guido attitude toward females is stylistically expressed in the "wife-beater" t-shirt, which is also known as a "guinea tee." For a 19-year-old college student who grew up on Long Island, Guido is a pose that "requires a Brooklyn accent with a lot of cursing, preferably in Italian." A muscular physique represents another prominent area of stylization. The accent here is on "looking ripped" as an aesthetically acceptable bodily representation ("look") rather than fighting. It is also embedded in the stylized consumption of workout culture. "Guido" can be distinguished from "greaser" by the greater opportunity to stylize masculine aggression via hedonistic consumption.[48] The contemporary Guido "look" makes traditional masculinity problematic in the form of "sculpted" eyebrows and shaved torsos initially identified with a gay club aesthetic.

A more stylized look works in the clubs, rather than in the streets, as "consumption spaces." Clubbing also undermines an aggressive masculine code as a venue that actively curbs fighting. Indeed, clubbing promotes the feminine in sharp contrast to street culture. Italian American females defined as "respectable" were insulated from the "mean streets" by ethnic family and religious culture. When they ventured there, they were "Guidettes," essentially decorous sex objects.[49] As an "urban nightscape," the club is safer for females than the street. Females are relatively privileged by club management because the sex ratio is skewed toward males. Their gender repertoire also fits more comfortably into the expressive culture of clubbing. For extra protection, young Italian American females have characteristically gone clubbing in groups of friends and relatives.

This has been necessary because dance clubs remain articulated with urban street culture. Violence can flare as youth with "street" sensibilities impulsively act out sundry "beefs." Organized crime rings have turned club venues into drug supermarkets; the frequency of overdoses has created a health crisis at Manhattan clubs.[50] Drug distribution has been franchised out by criminal syndicates including Italian American crime families. Chris Paciello, who once described himself as a "big Guido from New York," worked his way up the ladder by "shaking down drug dealers" in Manhattan clubs like Limelight before opening his own clubs in South Beach with the backing of the Bonnano crime family. Paciello graduated to the club scene from violent street crime in the Bath Beach and Bensonhurst sections of Brooklyn.[51] Paciello's legal surname is Ludwigsen but he felt that his Guido pose and vocational aspirations called for "a stage name" that was more authentic.[52]

Meanwhile, rank and file Guidos have cultivated Mafia poses including a jargon with expressions like "How ya doin'?" and "fugghedaboutit." Mass media images of the Italian American Mafia movies serve as guides for stylized ritual performances.

> Not only do they act like the Mafia but they try to appear like the Mafia as well. They talk with their hands, whisper to each other when they have to talk; they even kiss each other on the cheek. They obviously relate to all the Italian mob movies, such as *Goodfellas*, *The Godfather*, *Casino*, and many others. [Corrine, 18, 2001]

Mafia movie imagery has become a guide for a style of consumption. Michael, for example, maintained that young Italian American males like himself are "inspired by movies like *The Godfather*, *Goodfellas*, *Scarface*, *Casino*, and *A Bronx Tale* because they portray spending money, having nice cars, nice clothes, beautiful women lots of power and the good life." Another self-styled Guido from Queens referenced a scene from Mafia movie to describe a scene from his personal life-movie:

> We didn't have to wait in line as one of the guys had a connection that put him on the waiting list of the club. It was like we were Ray Liotta when he entered the Copacabana through the back door in *Goodfellas*. [Anthony, 20, 2001]

Such imagery also "sentimentalizes" and "distances" the male street culture traits of camaraderie and aggression within a Guido style pose.[53] A sign that Mafia movies have emerged as a major symbol bank is their appropriation for a ritual social activity.

> When my friends and I are really bored we usually watch a movie. Of course, it's a choice of *Goodfellas*, *The Godfather*, or *A Bronx Tale*. They were not my favorite movies until I started hanging out with these kids. When we first started to hang out, they would say a line from a movie. I never understood what they were talking about. Now that I've seen almost all the Italian Mafia movies, I can join with the quotes: "I'm gonna make him an offer he can't refuse!" [Corrine, 18, 2001].

Like gangstas who strive to "keep it real," however, Guidos claim a more authentic relationship to the Mafia.

> The Italian American youth does not only see these people in movies like *Goodfellas* and *A Bronx Tale*, but in front of their very eyes, living right in front of them. The average Italian American youth lives in a predominantly Italian American neighborhood where you are sure to see "gangsters" [Michael, 20, 2001].

Local Mafia figures are admired for their ability to command respect on the street and their consumption style. This is especially true of John Gotti, although probably because he became a media celebrity with unprecedented news coverage and an HBO movie. Youth with Mafia family connections have comprised a Guido elite based on powerful "connections" and financial power, allowing them to be both style leaders as well as tough guys. This was on display in a fracas between youth whose fathers were Mafia rivals that closed the Metropolis dance club in College Point, Queens, in 2001.[54]

Although John Gotti was "the dapper Don," the silk suits and the designer warm-up suits that he affected were not appropriate in club culture. Gotti's three grandsons, however, happen to be at the nexus of youth style and Mafia authenticity performed in a cable television reality show called *Growing Up Gotti*. While their grandfather cultivated a suave adult figure, the grandsons are on the cutting edge of a Guido style that is merging with Hip Hop. Gotti as gangsta suggests that the Mafia is bankrupt as a source of "cool" urban youth style and, perhaps, not streetwise enough to cope with the sensibilities of new urban actors. Ironically, Guido may be reinvigorating a Mafia myth by an association with gangsta which liberally "samples" Mafia myths to create personas like "Capone" and "[Irv] Gotti" and acquires a historical memory for a subgenre known as "don rap." The negotiation with gangsta was highlighted in a *Growing Up Gotti* episode featuring a black rapper from the Midwest who legally changed his name to "Gotti" in homage to the erstwhile "Don."[55] The rapper was a house guest at the big white mansion in Old Westbury, Long Island, in return for including the boys in a recording session for a song called "Vote Gotti for President." A "fictional" kinship was intimated in references to the three Gotti brothers as his "cousins," who, in turn, "treat[ed] Gotti like a brother," according to their mother. The brothers, who notoriously symbolize the Guido crossover to black youth culture, were now "talking about getting into the rap business themselves." However, mother Victoria kept the rapper at a distance and was especially stingy with Gotti family cultural capital.

WKTU's Italian American personalities also incorporate Mafia imagery into Guido style. This is especially true for "Goumba Johnny," who coyly intimates that being a "wiseguy" is more than a pose. The name "Goumba" is linked to the Mafia stereotype as a corruption of the Italian word "*compare*" or "godfather" which is meaningful in the Mafia model of social capital; an antidefamation complaint was filed against the Mayor of Yonkers when he referred to "back room goombas" as a characterization of urban political corruption. "Goomba" and "Guido" are used interchangeably in some circles and there has been a push by some Italian American youth to restate their position in the name of "Goomba" perhaps influenced by a how-to (be a "goomba") book written by an actor who plays a gangster in *The Sopranos*.[56] Goumba Johnny's Mafia credentials were aired in an autobiographical song that he recorded in 2001 called "Feds Threw A Party." The song presents Goumba as an Italian American businessman who is persecuted by the FBI and generalizes FBI persecution as an Italian American problem—the central motif in the antidefamation efforts of the Italian-American Civil Rights League in the late 1960s. However, Goumba cultivates Mafia "street credibility" by using Mafia argot and displaying Mafia social capital, for example, by allowing Victoria Gotti to create exposure for her new reality television program on which Goumba later appeared.

An Italian American who fashions a celebrity media persona around the Mafia constitutes a major problem for Italian American antidefamation organizations.[57] "Goomba" was no doubt behind the 2003 parody of the mandatory public service broadcast system that was called "Guido Alert" in which instructions were issued to Guidos to engage in "emergency" pop culture rituals like viewing *The Sopranos*. This caused the Italian American service organization UNICO National to complain to the station, which terminated the bit, although it issued no public comment on the matter.[58] Although offensive to Italian American elites, the production was likely the inside joke of a media personality with impeccable Guido credentials, a salute to his Guido roots and a constituency that he represents in the mainstream media culture.

Ethnicity and the Social Structure of Local Youth Culture Difference

New York City's dance club culture is highly variegated, containing a number of musical subscenes like "techno" and "house," which are related to constituencies defined by class, race, and sexual orientation. Manhattan clubs have been at the top of the club culture hierarchy, drawing a social "elite" that includes not only gay "club kids" but media celebrities and other VIPs who are rigorously separated from "the chaff." [59] An orientation to new forms of consumption centered on "the city" marks a signature "moment" for Italian American youth in the outer boroughs. Italian American youth used ethnicity to stake a position in the local club culture hierarchy distinguishing them from the "bridge and tunnel crowd" disdained by the elite.

In the local club scene, ethnicity is performed as style. Guido style features the prevalence of "house" and "freestyle" music, inflected by explicit ethnic markings like the song "L'Italiano" and other music by Angelo Venuto and his group "The Italians," and a presiding DJ with an "Italian" name and a local reputation. A "Guido club" is marked by the preponderance of youth in the style that symbolizes a particular subcultural performance ("Italians in the house!!!"). The prevalence of one style meant that others were ruled out. This typically had the effect of erecting a boundary against specific groups. Thus, a dress code proscribing "baggy pants" and "sneakers" discourages the "thug" or "gangsta" styles identified with ethnic youth in black and Latino neighborhoods: "Thugged Out Stays Out!" Being a Guido or a Guidette, then, is an identity performed in relation to other stylized youth culture identities in the city. The need for border work is intensified by the fluidity of contemporary youth styles. This is facilitated by the accessibility of mass media culture and by the accelerated mixing of diverse cultures in contemporary "urban nightscapes."[60] Ethnicity asserts a bounded identity and difference when styles change and cross boundaries. In the Astoria, Queens, dance club DNA, it is easy to mistake a "Guido" for a "Greedo," referring to the style pose of Greek Americans who are known to accessorize with an orthodox cross. The use of ethnicity creates a more urgent racial boundary with blacks and Latinos, who similarly define a youth culture in relation to the street and the dance club. Without emphasizing ethnicity, for example, Guidos might be mistaken for Latino/as in the clubs that feature "Latin Freestyle," a sound heavily influenced by Latin rhythms and popular among Latino/as in the city. In light of turf disputes with black youth, the most vexing border issue is how to consume Hip Hop now that it has become a dominant youth culture idiom. Asserting Italian ethnicity appears to be an attempt to have it both ways: to claim difference and draw a social boundary while appropriating elements of what has defined the other culturally.

Tensions are exacerbated as groups "jockey for power" in the competition for scarce youth culture capital.[61] This is evidenced in the struggle to keep control over styles that provisionally establish distinctive boundaries. Guidos are accused by gays of poaching their styles like body waxing, which may be linked to the bodybuilding aesthetic; the ongoing "gayification of Guido," reflecting the continued assimilation of gay influence in disco culture, perhaps explains a signature "homophobic" pose.[62] Guidos level similar accusations against rival others, especially the appropriation of Mafia imagery for "gangsta" Hip Hop. Perhaps more importantly, ethnic boundaries regulate competition for scarce youth culture rewards, most notably access to sexual partners. Club culture opened a style market to youth from diverse ethnic and class backgrounds abetted by commercialized mass media that disseminated information about dance club venues: "If you're looking for Italian girls come here," announces the Internet site for Club NYC.[63] However, youth constituencies, especially males, erect boundaries to restrict sexual competition, whether sorting themselves by style as a surrogate or code for ethnicity or, as the Club NYC blurb suggests, by blatant ethnic references. Ethnic boundaries are important in the eroticized atmosphere of dance clubs where inhibitions are lowered by the consumption of alcohol and drugs. Since ethnic boundaries are typically confounded with sexual boundaries, the appearance of rival others who might be "looking for Italian girls" could prove incendiary as in the 1989 Bensonhurst incident.[64]

Boundaries are enforced against Guidos, especially in Manhattan clubs. The Guido persona has been a poor fit for a club culture formed by "blended" sensibilities of "Blacks, Latinos, and gays."[65] Their chauvinism clashes with the "underground" global movements like the "rave scene" with its universalistic ethos of "Peace, Love, Unity, Respect." Violence has too often erupted from a hypermasculine pose that conflates sexuality and physical intimidation as suggested by this posting on the Club NYC message board (November 30, 2003): "Hott, sweaty, sexy shirtless, muscely [sic] Italians." Their collective agenda to "hit on" girls provokes other groups. While Guidettes will go clubbing "just to dance," Guidos "dance just to meet girls," and, notwithstanding the iconic significance of "Tony Manero," who was also a good fighter, they have earned a reputation as poor dancers. Their muscular look is read by club culture elites as intimidating rather than sensual. A former club industry security worker maintained that Guidos were "red flags" who were "prone to violence," and "kept on a short rope," primarily to assuage the concerns of gay clubbers [Charles, 2000]. The macho and homophobic Guido pose has historically been discrepant with the gay culture that shaped disco and the microculture of prominent Manhattan clubs. In the late 1990s, Guidos had become the cause for moral panic in the Manhattan club scene. This reverberated in a thread on the Club NYC website in 1998: "The club scene in NYC has gone down so fast. Why? In one word Guidos." The *Village Voice* columnist Trish Romano, assessing the 2003 closing of the Manhattan clubs Exit and Sound Factory, worried about "perhaps the most serious consequence of the closures: Guidos will suddenly descend en masse, ruining the few remaining 'cool' clubs."[66] Although macho aggression was a key piece of the problem, Manhattan club culture elites are expressing distaste for the way ethnicity and class intersect in the formation of an urban youth style. While contemporary youth subcultures fashion style to "escape" class,[67] Guidos are read in class terms by Manhattan club culture elites when lumped into "the bridge and tunnel crowd." Class inferiority is also conflated with ethnic stigma. At bottom, elite designations place Italian American youth outside the pale of club culture "cool." Club culture narratives have dovetailed with mainstream narratives of Italian American ethnic deviance in the city.[68]

Ethnic identity and difference in local youth culture is rooted in larger divisions in the city. To a large extent, these divisions are based on claims to scarce resources like housing and safe neighborhoods and prestigious consumer items like SUVs and iPods. Tensions with blacks continue to have notoriety in the public discourse, although intergroup tensions have a local flavor. There are skirmishes between young Italian Americans and recent Albanian immigrants in the Bronx that seems to be rooted in neighborhood succession. When asked about the relationship between Italians and Greeks in Astoria, a 20-year-old named Fabrizio began by sounding a note of harmony: "*Una faccia, una razza*" ("One face, one race"). However, this declaration of unity was immediately qualified:

We get along, but you have to watch out. Greeks are two-faced. They call you "guinea" and "wop" behind your back.

Fabrizio was even more wary of the Albanians, who "pretend they're Italian," but are uncomfortably exotic: "Have you ever seen the guys smoking those funny looking things?"—alluding to the water pipes available in the Muslim cafes in Astoria.

Ethnic niches in popular youth culture are tenuous, owing to the incessant crossover of styles and the inclusiveness of urban nightscapes. Local Italian American youth have historically oriented their subcultural identities to popular music genres dominated by blacks and Puerto Ricans. While Italian Americans may not have received their due as creative producers, "house" and "freestyle" as well as classic "disco" originated in black and Latino clubs in New York City.[69] However, Italian American youth have insisted on ethnic boundaries in regard to how this dance culture is to be "consumed." A similar scenario pertains to the appropriation of Hip Hop. Dance clubs promote social as well as musical "mixes," as suggested in a 2003 Clubplanet.com online review of a Manhattan club: "The women were incredible, lots of races, Spanish, Italian, black, white all the mixes were there and friendly [sic]."

Although club culture afforded an opportunity for ethnic mixing, it could also reinforce ethnic boundaries. It is telling that "Italian(s)" were represented as a social category juxtaposed to blacks, Latinos, *and* whites suggesting that they comprised a distinct "race."

Ethnicity and Subcultural Ideology

Youth subcultures fashion "ideologies" that "are a means by which youth imagine their own and other social groups, assert their distinctive character and affirm that they are not anonymous members of an undifferentiated mass."[70] As a youth subculture, Guidos staked a claim to prestige based on pop culture capital by having the "coolest" cars and other commodities.[71] However, this has been combined with a discourse of ethnic "distinction" that manufactures "a sense of social worth" in its own right.[72] This allows them to stake a claim to "cool" *because* they are "Italian."

Youth culture consumption is historically structured by ethnicity and other social divisions, especially class.[73] Guido emerges as a neighborhood style connecting Italian American youth to urban youth scenes throughout the city. The formation of a style-based youth subculture in the name of ethnicity entails substantial "symbolic work." Paul Willis maintains that this is possible and even necessary because "traditional resources" and "inherited meanings" have "lost their legitimacy for a good proportion of young people."[74] As suggested earlier, the symbolic representation of ethnicity as youth style presupposes the erosion of traditional ways of being Italian. However, youth are able to apply "symbolic resources and raw materials" to "produce meaning" adapted to a new set of circumstances.[75]

This symbolic work is evident in the choice of the name "Guido." While Guido is the product of several identity intersections, it most obviously refers to Italian ethnicity in an implicitly masculine way, and females are accorded a derivative identity as "Guidettes." Why Guido became an identity symbol invites speculation. D'Acierno traces its origin to either a common Italian male name, reflecting the masculinist character of the "display" or, to the preeminence of a car culture, citing the Italian word "*guidare*" which means "to drive."[76] A car culture is prototypically greaser, and Guido is predicated on a relationship to club culture that transcends working class greaser style. I favor the former position but because it is conspicuously "Italian." I argue that this quintessentially "Italian" name was chosen by Italian American youth in the same way that the name "Gino" designates the recent subcultural position of Italian Canadian youth in Toronto. The intent to create solidarity through Italian ancestry is perhaps more readily apparent in the terms "*cugin*", and more recently "goomba," which explicitly trade on kinship metaphors and which have been interchangeable with Guido. In looking to identify with a conspicuously Italian male, Italian American youth may also have sought to appropriate an aura of exotic stylishness rather than an Italian style. While this suggests the formative influence of recent arrivals, Guido has been overwhelmingly oriented to American popular culture; there is nothing comparable to the cultural nostalgia of second generation Indian youth for "bhangra" music.[77]

Further, far from internalizing a "pejorative" identity, the name Guido "talks back to" ethnic stigma. Identification with a "negatively privileged" ethnicity is an oppositional stance that enhances insider solidarity.[78] This involves a "symbolic reversal" that challenges ethnic epithets and other constructions of Italianness in mainstream culture. It may actually be a reversal of "pejorative" meanings internalized by Americanization. It is possible that Guido was put in circulation by more acculturated Italian Americans if not actually coined by them, reflecting a practice where recent immigrants who are "just off the boat" are assigned a lesser status as "greenhorns" and "greaseballs."[79] The unequivocal Italianness of Guido made it easier to establish difference.

A blatantly oppositional ethnicity can be read in current Guido poses. In ItalChat, which serves as a backstage arena for cultivating difference, the historic insults "guinea" and "wop" were incorporated in stylized identity narratives. While historical understanding seemed shallow, the matter was brought into the present when a "white boy" in the room complained about "greasy guinnys" who "come to my country America."[80] Harold Isaac points out that when ethnic insults become "badges of basic group identity" ethnic pride and power is enhanced because "inferior status and outsiderness" is confronted directly.[81] When appropriated by the stigmatized group, symbolic insults are used "banteringly, even affectionately, and sometimes, in a say-it-with-a-smile transference."[82] ItalChat youth played with these epithets in ways that mocked their very existence and the relations of power on which they were based:

> What up my woparones?
> The Ginzo is here!!!
> Bensonhurst . . . where a ginny can be a ginny.
> I am the ginniest ginny in this room.

"Guido" is historically freighted with the baggage of stigma that was revivified in the response of the mainstream media to the Bensonhurst "racial killing."[83] It is a name that, like "nigga," warrants a careful determination of insider status. It has acquired value as a "symbolic challenge", even surpassing "wop" and "guinea," and Italian American youth have claimed this nomenclature as an insider prerogative.

The word "Guido" is supposed to criticize Italians but some Italians actually like the fact that they are called "Guido." So really this word has many levels of affect. It all depends on what generation and how strong the person's pride is in the word "Guido." The word "Guido" applies to me and also to my friends. Because we did take that offensively we actually like it when we are considered "Guidos." It gives us what you would say is a rep. [Frank, 2004]

Symbolic challenges to ethnic stigma are bound up with the accumulation of sub-cultural capital. Groups routinely use popular culture to stake claims to "distinction."[84] Style-based youth subcultures accumulate and display youth "subcultural capital," cultural forms like music and clothes considered prestigious or "cool" within youth social spaces.[85] Guido represents a strategy by Italian American youth in the city to not only "win space," but also to achieve "distinction" in popular youth culture. This subcultural strategy exploits forms of ethnic capital. As already noted, ethnicity is appropriated to create a youth category with some style integrity and more or less bounded performance spaces. Guido also claims "distinction" based on ethnicity, a claim that "social power" is derived from Italian ancestry as well as popular youth styles. As such, Guido not only represents an ethnic claim to youth culture "distinction," but also a youth culture claim on ethnic "distinction." Where distinction was a matter of being Italian, the accumulation of ethnic capital became an agenda for impression management.

Promoting Italian ethnicity was a conspicuous agenda for a dance music radio station whose ostensible mission, according to its slogan, was to be "The Beat of New York." WKTU emerged as a prominent "construction site" for Italian pride. Joe Causi rhapsodizes about his Sicilian heritage, including the virtues of the island's olive oil. This musing often bends toward his other heritage, the disco scene: "The Sicilians are better. Sicily is a beautiful island full of music and culture. Where do you think I got this beat from?" "Goumba Johnny" Sialiano is insistently ethnic even promoting an invidious identification with Italian American ethnicity as in this caller interview:

> Goumba: "Hey kid, are you Italian? Big points if you're Italian!
> Kid: "Yea!"
> Goumba: "Always tell people you're Italian. Be proud that you're Italian!"

Goumba made Italian Americans aware of their importance for the city. He once coined the phrase "Staten Italy" to underscore the sizeable number of Italian Americans in Staten Island, implicitly establishing a turf relationship with an entire borough and prompting a new subcultural phrasing among callers: "I'm from Staten Italy, fuggedaboutit!" While his Italocentric worldview could be casual and extemporaneous, it could also be premeditated, as with the annual "Meatball Contest" celebrating Columbus Day with a trip to Italy as a prize. This fore-grounds an ethnic heritage in the form of a "quasi-folk culture" centered on the family rather than a classical culture managed by elites.[86] It also had to be fitted to American pop culture grammar and meanings, so that as soon as a 2004 final-ist credited her "Grandma Giovanna" for her meatball recipe there was a segue to the recording artist Prince's dance song "Party Like It's 1999." WKTU's radio personalities, then, are ethnic entrepreneurs as well as style arbiters, who use the vernacular language of pop culture to celebrate the ascendance of Italian Americans in a pop culture space.

While contact with popular culture often trivializes ethnicity, rank and file Guidos claim an authentic connection to an organic ethnic culture:

> A Guido's family is very important to him, and the same goes for a Guidette. A Guido is always protective of his family members. They always respect and stick up for their mothers and grandmothers, who they call "ma" and "nonna." They usually work for their father and plan to take over the family business if there is one. A Guido always watches over their sisters and never lets a guy go near them. Guidos usually live at home until they get married. [Silvio, 2002]

This may be an idealized interpretation, but it informs a commonly held belief in a core cultural difference that separates them from others. Moreover, while popular culture typically fuels rebellion against core parental values, no unmanageable tension is perceived with the traditional family system. Accentuating ethnicity may be an attempt to assure parents that they are able to hold on to ethnicity despite a commitment to "club culture" and stylized personal consumption in general. Thus, ethnic constraints on the dating scene are compatible with parental preference for ethnic endogamy. Although widely viewed as "spoiled," the persona of "the Italian American Princess" may be read as an attempt to reconcile "hedonistic consumption" with traditional family culture by being "Daddy's Little Girl" and giving the bill to "Papa":

> A Guidette looks for protection and financial support from their family. Guidettes are very close with their fathers. They are their father's favorite, which makes them Daddy's Little Girl. That's how the expression "Italian American Princess" came about. [Silvio, 2002][87]

The support for consumption is broadly consistent with an ideology of assimilation focused on the well-being of children and is legitimated by themes of familial nurturance. It is plausible that children are assigned the lead in matters of discretionary personal consumption to showcase the family's new class culture, as Italians who are successful Americans. The younger generation seems to be in a more privileged position to consume than traditional parents who are primarily defined by "production" norms (i.e., labor) and who have been brought up in a scarcity culture. Growing up in more affluent households, second and third youth have been socialized by the mass media to be entitled consumers.

The online chat room scene ItalChat offered a media space in which Italian ethnicity was deployed as the glue of an imagined community. Since Internet chat is a "writing culture," a discourse of ethnic distinction was rather transparent, literally spelled-out on the screen as text. Owing to the sparseness of visual cues and the relative anonymity of cyberspace, subcultural credentials were requested on demand and in writing:

Is everyone Italian in here?
If you're not Italian get out.

In this scenario, ethnicity was a prerequisite for subcultural authenticity and was accumulated as subcultural capital. In other words, having Italian ancestry was privileged in the same sense that freestyle music conferred distinction. Substantial effort was invested in creating stylized presentations of Italianness. One extemporaneous presentation revealed a competition for status:

100% Italian
100% here as well
100 Italian (born in Italy)
110% Italian
I am the Italianest [*sic*].

While it presented a boundary that excluded others, ethnicity was a scarce resource that determined insider prestige and rank. Mixed ancestry and American birth carried lower status value; while it may be a conventional usage in the lexicon of American ethnicity, it is noteworthy that youth identify as "Italian" rather than as "Italian American."

Italian ethnicity in ItalChat was constructed as something fixed and given not as a "social construct." In one version, Italian ethnicity was naturalized or biological: "The initiation to be Italian is to be born one." Another portrayed it as God-given and ineffable:

The best thing that God could have given me is being Italian.
Don't try to be Italian. It's a gift. And I'm blessed with it.

A verse that repeatedly surfaced in personal webpages conveyed a mystical sense of purity and solidarity based on biological uniqueness:

Italian Pride is in My Mind.
Italian Blood is My Kind.
My Italian pride I will not hide.
My Italian race I will never disgrace.
Italian Love is all around.
My fellow Italians never let me down.
Show your pride.

The construction of an essentialist, biological ethnicity was conveyed by the hijacking of the acronym FBI, which was made to signify "Full-Blooded Italian." This insider meaning is performed by the professional wrestling character "Little Guido," who styles himself as the leader of "Full Blooded Italians" and has appeared at wrestling shows with "Goumba Johnny." Considering that the FBI, not the mass media, was the major target of the Italian-American Civil Rights League, which recruited support from the city's Italian American neighborhoods in the late 1960s and early 1970s, the hijacking of this symbol of federal law enforcement authority had oppositional significance. It articulates a current of ethnic resentment that has lingered in the vernacular Italian American neighborhood culture after all these years. The safe space of ItalChat generated a "hidden transcript"[88] that crudely critiqued relations of power that have negatively privileged Italian ethnicity in this society.

A sentiment of "constructed primordialism"[89] created a distinction that was blatantly invidious:

> Everyone is equal but Italians are better.
> If you ain't Italian I'm sorry.
> If its [sic] not made in Italy it sucks.

An "essentialized" Italian ethnicity was a warning to jealous "wannabes" and "fake Italians." It also reversed the historical dilemma of an inferior ethnic ancestry. Italian ethnicity conveyed status while others were stigmatized by a "lack" of ethnic capital.[90]

Simon Frith attributes a preoccupation with distinction to a "transitional" and "marginal" social position that causes contemporary youth to "seek a sense of autonomy and status and self-esteem to balance against their time of insignificance. Hence the role of peer groups (something between the family and society) and their symbols of pride and self-assertion, membership and exclusion."[91] It can be argued, however, that these youth are responding to a society that has historically marginalized Italian Americans and stigmatized them for a "negatively privileged ethnicity."[92] This can explain why so much symbolic work is invested in creating ethnic distinction within youth culture practice.

The construction of an "essential" ascriptive ethnicity allows Italians to "traffic in their own honor"[93] and corner the market on "distinction." Italians were "special" even apart from consumption style and youth culture, while others were lacking, regardless of how stylish they were. This social logic is understandable as a symbolic calculus in Manhattan clubs where Guidos were stigmatized by elites for the wrong style and a dubious ethnicity. In "the struggle for recognition and respect," it was possible to fall back on ethnic capital as they valued it.

"Jockeying for Power" and Ethnic Prejudice

Rather than see Guido as a label imposed from the outside, I contend that it emerges from a negotiation about the meanings assigned to Italian American ethnicity. This perspective assigns "agency" to Italian American youth who rework their ethnicity in reference to leisure and consumption styles. This is a characteristic response in "the struggle for recognition and respect" on the part of minority immigrant populations in American society as a core assimilation strategy.[94] The Guido "struggle" has been immediately located in a competitive youth culture situation where groups "jockey for power."[95]

The competition for status based on scarce resources is invariably character-ized by opposition and conflict. There was an abiding concern in ItalChat with the status of their youth category in the hierarchy of local youth subcultures.

- Italians Rule!!!
- Italians Rock, the Rest Jock.

When a thread appeared on the Club NYC message board in 1998 that condemned the presence of Guido in Manhattan club culture, the response was quick and certain:

- We need more Guidos in the New York clubs!
- Guidos are back in style.

Youth subcultures typically disparage one another in the identity politics of securing a privileged style and the related competition for scarce rewards. Guido, however, is remarkable for the vilification it has received from other youth cul-tures. This has becomes more apparent with the rise of the Internet as a youth culture space, broadening the transaction of meaning in the process. Thus, an interactive "urban dictionary" allows a visitor to submit a "definition" of "guido" and to vote on the appropriateness of other submissions. According to the most widely accepted "definition," a "guido" "can be found nightly at mainstream dance clubs they read about online (S[ound] F[actory], Webster Hall, etc.) . . . Guido cars usually have a boomin' system through which cheesy music like freestyle, commer-cial club/trance and hip-hop (anything KTU plays) is loudly blasted." [96] The rather lengthy passage from which this is excerpted expresses antipathy for Guido on the level of youth culture style. It avoids ethnic disparagement and, in fact, points out that the Guido is "not necessarily of Italian descent." However, the moment youth stake a position in popular culture in the name of "Guido," the denigration of a youth subculture cannot easily be separated from the denigration of Italian ethnic-ity and the possibility that embedded ethnic prejudice is being activated. "A stupid Italian American who slicks back his hair with various amounts of goo, wears tight-fitting tank-tops, only does upper body workouts, blasts stupid nigger and club music from his car, wears gold chains outside of his shirt, and speaks like a f——g moron." [97] Venturing further in the direction of ethnic prejudice, a post on a local club industry message board linked the denigration of style to historic insults:

- 100% Italian w/ a Heavy Duty Ginzo attitude
- Black slick-backed hair w/lots of gel in it
- Lots of muscles, usually shown off wearing a tight shirt
- Starts fights on any fleeting moment
- Have a Cadillac or some Mafia style Ginny car
- Hang out on 86th St in Brooklyn. [98]

An extended treatise on the subject of "Guido" in a "punk" webzine invoked an historic ethnic slur to discredit a youth category that is perceived as hostile to alternative youth subcultures like "punk": "Define a guido. A Guido is one of the lowest forms of life currently co-inhabiting our planet . . . a young wop who rides atop whatever trend is hot, drives a cool car . . . beats up everyone and anyone that is in anyway out of the ordinary."[99] Antipathy for Guido often vacates the realm of youth culture competition altogether. A 1998 posting on the Club NYC website tapped into a theme of ambiguous "whiteness" to discredit Italian ethnicity: "All Italians from Sicily are part Black. Since the island was invaded and there [sic] women were raped by Africans thats [sic] why they are so dark. Get it?"[100]

It is even more remarkable that local broadcast radio participated in the denigration of Guido and Italian American ethnicity. Both instances occurred on local radio stations whose music is identified with other youth subcultures. In one, the morning drive-time personalities on Z100 FM radio in New York City (March 20, 2003) delineated a caricature of "Guido" that featured "tank tops," "a tan that comes in a can," and sexual impotence resulting from the use of "[ste]roids" for bodybuilding. An attempt to emasculate Guido is evident in the line, "Guidos in the club on the phone, they don't tell you that they live at home," a reference that also mocks an ethnic pattern of family cohesion. This jab at Guido may also have been aimed at the subcultural icon "Goumba Johnny" and the formidable competition of WKTU's morning show.

An egregiously biased comment was attributed to the classic rock station, WAXQ FM, during the morning "drive time" on June 26, 2002: "Italians are niggers that have lost their memories."[101] While this remark does not explicitly mention Guido, an implicit reference can be assumed given the station is a media outpost for a rival local youth culture. As already noted, the darkening of urban Italian American males was a motif in the deviance profile elaborated in response to the Bensonhurst incident and reflects a persistent undercurrent or hidden agenda in the popular culture that denies whiteness to Italian Americans. Questioning the whiteness of Italian Americans makes their ethnicity even more deviant. Without addressing a particular comment or source, the raised conversation about Italian American racial identity in the popular culture was joined on WKTU when Joe Causi embraced a nonwhite ethnicity. Noting the geographical proximity of southern Italians, especially Sicilians, to Africa, Causi summarily declared that "Sicilians are dark meat." He added that biological mixing was accompanied by cultural mixing that enhanced the group's musical inheritance and "rhythm." Causi has a vested interest in making an authentic claim to dance music culture. However, biological as well as cultural identification with Africa is problematic for an ethnic group claim to whiteness.

It is plausible that disparagement of Guido and Italian American ethnicity in the public discourse has been legitimated by the moral panic in direct response to the 1989 Bensonhurst incident. The highly publicized "racial killing" occasioned the entrance of the term "Guido" into the public discourse; the mainstream press attributed the killing of a Black teenager to young males identified with "Guido." While Guido, and ultimately the Italian American community, was framed as racist, this moral panic succeeded in lumping urban Italian American youth into a category headlined by dangerous black and Latino youth, implying that they could not be comprehended as "white" notwithstanding a "racial attack." The moral panic in the mainstream print media demonized "Guido" as a "folk devil" for episodes of "wilding"; these metaphors infamously stereotyped African American youth in "the Central Park jogger" case and recalled the menacing "dago" of yesteryear. Like ghetto youth, Guidos were a "menace to society"; indeed, Italian American Bensonhurst was portrayed as a "closed" and "insular" world. The narrative of an Italian American menace was situated in an ethnic group narrative. This featured a pronounced Mafia spin, reinforcing a prominent ethnic stereotype and establishing another parallel with "gangsta" black youth. Moral panic in the press made it easier to express enmity for Guidos, and for Italian Americans more generally, in the public discourse. A post-Bensonhurst "menace" motif was evident when a local politician criticized a Giuliani administration policy that targeted nonwhite neighborhoods for aggressive street policing: "What makes him think if he stopped every Italian kid in Gravesend, Coney Island, Ozone Park, and Bensonhurst, he wouldn't get a fair amount of gun possessions there?"[102]

While Guidos were framed as opposed to core values of a liberal society, not only in regard to racial equality but norms of civility, they also constituted a cultural and economic threat to constituencies reshaping the image of New York City as a global capitalist city in the late twentieth century. The urban danger represented by Italian American youth made it difficult for affluent cosmopolitan elites and tourists to safely consume ethnic culture. Guido references a style that is degraded both as American ethnic culture and as class culture. The achievement of "Little Italy" as legitimated by the New York City Planning Commission is that it reconciles Italian American ethnicity with a commercial economy based on the tourist "gaze." "Little Italy" makes it possible to consume "Italian" culture rather than Italian American culture, in no small part because the lower- and working-class Italian American population has been resettled to the outlying boroughs and suburbs. Perhaps even more unacceptable was that insularity and aggressive turf defense resisted easy incorporation of Italian American neighborhoods as "real estate" that can be consumed by urban elites ramifying out from Manhattan and gentrifying working-class neighborhoods in the outlying boroughs.[103]

However, alongside images of urban menace is the intimation of status panic. In particular, there are hints of resentment for a "rising class" culture.[104] Harsh criticism reserved for Guido styles betrays envy of the *nouveau riche* status of prominent subcultural youth and the Italian American community. This is evidenced in stereotypes of Guidos as "spoiled" by consumption. A youth antipathetic to Guido interpreted this in the context of the American immigrant narrative: "Their hardworking parents spoil them rotten because they grew up in poverty and now they live vicariously through their sons and daughters." It is also evidenced in the disparagement of arriviste taste in the media culture, an agenda in Hollywood films like *Married to the Mob* and *My Cousin Vinnie*. It is plausible that the marginalization of Guido at hip Manhattan clubs is fueled by the arrival of Italian Americans with a socially incorrect style. When Guido is overgeneralized as a "negatively privileged ethnicity," arriviste Italian Americans are put back in their place. Resentment for a higher consumption status is exacerbated by the perception of invidious status claims, like the social snobbery of "a Guido fraternity" on a state college campus:

They act toward others with prejudice, superiority, and a lack of respect. They think they are better than the rest. One of the lines they use to refer to people is "They aren't worthy." Instead of saying "They're not cool," they say "They're not worthy." I mean that in itself says how much they put other people down. [Daniel, 2003]

In this scenario, privileging Italian ethnicity becomes a banner for a privileged new class culture. Ethnic prejudice against Italian Americans may be a response in kind for negatively privileging others and their ethnicities.

The Guido Story: An Ethnic "Route" to the Mainstream

A true story must be faithful to what really happens. I have argued that the story of Guido must be situated in "youth culture practice" grounded in Italian American neighborhoods in New York City. Young Italian Americans invoke Guido as a group identity and assign meaning by referencing popular culture and ethnicity. It takes a position in youth style markets in the name of Italian ethnicity, especially at the local level. These claims have elicited a response from significant number of "Others" in youth culture and in the mass media, thereby transacting Guido across subcultural and ethnic boundaries.

The concluding section will examine the larger meaning of Guido for Italian American ethnicity, especially as it moves further into the mainstream. This begins with the recognition of ethnic youth subcultures as a hybrid "social formation."[105] Guido has been portrayed as a "youth formation" that uses ethnicity to symbolize identity and to articulate status claims. However, it may also be considered an "ethnic formation" within local youth culture; Guidos have effectively usurped the claim to Italian ethnicity for use in local youth-style markets. There is further blurring when "guido" evolves as an ethnic generalization and stereotype. Although a youth subculture, Guido does emerge out of social conditions that are general for an Italian American experience that has unfolded in New York City (and throughout much of the urban Northeast). Above all, it is a product of Italian American neighborhood culture, which is historically predicated on ethnic boundaries. At a particular historical "moment," Guido signals the relative shift in the orientation of dominant youth culture practice in Italian American neighborhoods from turf, the *sine qua non* of greaser, to style and new opportunities for hedonistic consumption in popular culture.

The consumption of goods and services and media images refocused the "struggle for recognition and respect" for Italian American youth culture practice.[106] Guido can easily be recognized as a strategy whereby subordinate ethnic groups "buy into" consumerism as a definitive measure of Americanization and the cornerstone of their "aspirations for happiness and community."[107] It is not surprising that, when the opportunity arrived, Italian American youth turned to commercial popular culture to construct an identity and lifestyles; in *contradis*-tinction to Italian American adults, they literally bought into youth style markets shaped by the mass media around commercial "cool."[108]

Stylish consumption and consumer desire are typically deployed by lower youth subcultures to "escape class." While Guido is clearly an "escape" from class, it has embraced ethnicity and even fetishized it as "subcultural capital." This is noteworthy because "escaping class" in American society has typically involved jettisoning the signature of lower-class ethnicity. Guido tries to solve this problem by embedding ethnicity in new class culture signifiers. To this extent, stylish Italian American youth may be the avant garde of a "rising class," asserting a claim on a new consumption status in the name of ethnicity. Guido offers a consumption guide for a "rising class" of Italian Americans as the featured component of a new ethnic script. Although a youth subculture, Guido reconstructs Italian American ethnicity; a "reworked" ethnicity is intended to "work for them" on both expressive and instrumental levels.[109]

As a structuring element of American popular culture, Guido has implications for the larger question of assimilation into mainstream American society. An attempt to reconcile Italian ethnicity with contemporary youth culture can be understood as partial or "segmented assimilation."[110] This is further refined by George Lipsitz's concept of "bifocality" that captures the "duality" of being "unable to exercise simple assimilation or complete separation."[111] The upshot is ambivalence and contradiction, with youth "at one and the same time calling attention to ethnic differences and demonstrating how they might be transcended."[112] In light of a preoccupation with creating distinction, I would argue that the negotiation of "ethnic difference" has to be seen as a function of a "struggle for recognition and respect." In other words, "choices" to assimilate popular culture and invoke ethnicity seem to be in the "service" of "social power."[113]

The concept of "bifocality" may be an oversimplification because it acknowledges only two cultures. In New York City, the creation of distinctive ethnic boundaries is not solely referenced to the "mainstream culture" but to other ethnic groups who are negotiating their own "bifocality" and influencing each other along the way. Perhaps a more sophisticated rendering is offered by the concept of "new ethnicities" as "a development of late modern societies" that "fuse aspects of the popular" with "an imagined traditional culture and the vernacular knowledges of the local urban/regional settings."[114] This concept has obvious value for a contemporary urban youth subculture like Guido, whose "symbolic work" is heavily oriented to the commercial mass media. However it is addressed to local concerns, in particular the moral panic that labeled Guido deviant in the mainstream media.

While the "new ethnicities" concept usefully points to a "fusion" or "hybrid" culture, the notion of "bifocality" makes it possible to analytically separate popular culture and ethnicity and to focus on their weighted and variable influences. Like other contemporary youth subcultures, Guido continues to mutate further in the direction of "a particular style of leisure-oriented consumption" focused on "things that give immediate pleasure and little lasting use."[115] The proximate reason for this is a powerful and heady surge of commercial popular culture that "trivializes" ethnicity with its penchant for "fictional narratives."[116]

Guido has increasingly acquired a commercial character. Consumers can now buy into Guido as a commercial style, which is an ironic turnabout since Guido is a franchise for consumption. The men's designer clothing brand Guido New

York fuses the subculture with the "commodity." Meanwhile, Guidos are attempting to market themselves before someone else does. An Internet site for Guidoland (www.guidoland.com) owned by "Yo Frankie Productions," merchandises Guido and, implicitly, Italian American ethnicity. In the interest of maximizing sales, it contends that "Being a Guido or a Guidette is less about ethnicity and more a way of life. Whether you're African-American, Irish, Jewish, Asian, Latino or any other ethnicity, you can be a Guido!"[117] The organization New Jersey Guido (www .njguido.com) sublimates Italian ethnicity within a youth culture ideology of hedonistic consumption: "Basically we want to show off the crazy ass New Jersey scene." A "party" identity can be consumed by clubbing and buying merchandise linked to the NJGuido website. The organization portrays an evolved form of Guido as a "sophisticated" urban life style defined by "youth, beauty and flash."[118] Although it offers a quasi-formal organization that suggests that a structured scene is still relevant, ethnicity is eschewed as a distinctive social or cultural boundary. A subcultural ideology invokes a muted ethnicity in the form of nostalgia for a closeknit Italian American family that has been replaced by a peer group "party" culture.

Ethnic nostalgia is better preserved in an "oldies" culture marketed by Guido radio personalities and comics. It is largely made available to cohorts of Italian Americans who have aged out of dance culture into parenthood and the middle class suburban diaspora. Guido was available in the nostalgic musing of "Brooklyn's Own Joe Causi" on the radio and in "oldies" performances by 1970s "disco divas." Guido nostalgia is merchandised by "Guido comics" known as "The Haya-Doin' Boys," whose website presents an insider parody that lists the markers of a local subculture in the 1980s titled "You Know You're a Guido If . . ." For example,

- You owned or drive a Mustang/IROC/Trans Am.
- You cried when Hot 97 turned to all rap.

That the very same items circulate under the heading "You Know You're Italian If . . ." suggests that a form of ethnic expression has emerged that is tailored to a particular youth culture experience. In all this commercialized nostalgia, it is hard to tell whether the "old days" are missed because subjects were younger or "more Italian."

The reality television show *Growing Up Gotti* has no time for historical memory other than to embellish the myth of its deceased patriarch, John Gotti. It juxtaposes the corrosion of traditional ethnic family culture to flagrant merchandising and hedonistic consumption. The Gotti boys do not explicitly present as Guido but this identity can be easily read in their "style" by other subcultural youth. An arriviste suburban affluence imparts still more elevated status signifiers to Guido (e.g., "Guido mansion", "Guido estate"). Still, there are meaningful links to Italian American neighborhood culture. This point was underscored when the protagonist in the 2005 Howard Beach "racial attack" was identified as a member of the young Gotti entourage who made an appearance on the television show.[119] The Gotti boys also endorse the selective adoption of gangsta style, an option that is less complicated in affluent and white Old Westbury than in the city. The show's website merchandises a youth style as a new urban hybrid in which classic Guido tries to stand up to FUBU and Rocawear. While it will not be as momentous as Hip Hop, which rankles with many youth, this Guido may find a small niche as an ethnic youth style like "Cholo," offering an alternative version of the "inner city vibe."[120] The Gotti boys are poised to become style leaders for more affluent Italian American adolescents who are "growing up" with them in suburban sections of Queens and Nassau County.

Pop culture commercialization of Guido and Italian ethnicity proceeds furthest outside ethnic neighborhood culture. Ethnicity and style have a greater urgency for youth "left behind" in neighborhoods that have become settlement areas for new immigrant groups; Guido recreates an authentic ethnic community through style that can be mobilized against an urban landscape that marginalizes them. Youth in these areas continue to instigate street violence that is directed at recent immigrants. It is possible to see "consumer desire" as compensation for blocked opportunities in working-class communities like Bensonhurst who find themselves increasingly surrounded by blacks, new immigrants, and urban elites who each pose different kinds of status problems. Guido may also be a "magical recovery" of ethnic solidarity for individuals who are left out of the suburban Italian American diaspora as well as new urban lifestyles shaped by global forces. A privileged ethnicity provides an escape from the class culture of gentrifying neighborhoods. The marginalization of these youth has precipitated a siege mentality that was generalized as an ethnic problem in ItalChat: "To be Italian is to be loved by some, hated by many, respected by all, and harmed by none." Ideologies of ethnic and turf honor may also be a backlash to mainstream moral panic, especially among disaffected males lacking the economic and cultural capital to adjust to the continued erosion of defended Italian American neighborhoods. It is noteworthy that this backlash is increasingly expressed by gangsta style, suggesting many Italian American youth may have vulnerability to "an oppositional culture associated with urban youth of color."[121] A stylized gangsta code, originally developed as the voice of ghetto black youth, lends an even angrier tone to Guido disaffection. A webpage biography in the world of ItalChat narrated an epic story of marginality and paranoia titled "Da True Life of a Guido," depicting a moral world in which there are "fellow Guidz" and "enimiez" are everywhere "Guidos always watch each others backz." The erosion of traditional ethnic culture is unable to buffer more "dangerous and problematic" aspects of "assimilation into urban youth culture" and "Americanization."[122] Stylized manifestations of a street code may be an expressive vehicle for the failure to realize consumer desire, coupled with the corrosion of ethnic communal traditions.

The absorption of gangsta accompanies a confused narrative of Italian American youth in the public discourse. In contrast to similar episodes in the late 1980s, media accounts of the 2005 "racial attack" in Howard Beach did not represent Italian American youth by their nationality but as "white." At the same time, the latest incident was performed against the backdrop of a massive style crossover; Italian American assailants made the same stylized gangsta presentations that affected by the three black youths involved. Tellingly, the physical assault was accompanied, and perhaps crowned, by style appropriation when the Italian American youth "pulled off" a pair of "Air Jordan sneakers" from the black youth after allegedly hitting him in the head with a bat.[123] The image of Nicholas Minucci, the chief protagonist, in the press reiterated themes of a street culture that was patently gangsta: "varnished luxury" combined with "unemployment" and a disposition to "violence."[124] While identified as "white" in press accounts, the style profile of Minucci and his associates further "darkened" them in the eyes of a mainstream audience. Still, familiar signifiers of urban Italian American deviance were near at hand in the report of Minucci's "friendship with the children of Victoria Gotti."[125] Reactions on blogs and message boards suggest that youth culture insiders immediately recognized a Guido thread in current style development. I would argue that the crossover to gangsta Hip Hop reinforces Guido's historic commitment to street culture masculinity and style, managing to preserve the position of blacks as consummate "others."[126]

The identity transactions that comprise Guido point to the ongoing "dialectical" construction of Italian American ethnicity. Guido is more a narrative of about "routes" than "roots," a narrative about "becoming." It is never a simple assimilation story when "pre-existing cultural forms" are put to "new uses."[127] A careful reading requires an appreciation for subject positions within the ethnic group created by intersections with social identities such as age, class, gender, and place. Although a category of prejudice, Guido opposes ethnic prejudice through youth culture agency, especially in the cultivation of a consumption style.

The 2000 South Belmar Labor Day incident was a brushfire that, in retrospect, anticipated the conflagration sparked by MTV's reality show *Jersey Shore*, which debuted in December 2009. The show validated Guido as a youth style compatible with MTV's brand of hedonism, which featured casual sexual relationships (i.e., hooking up). Although *Jersey Shore* is a particular representation of Guido, it has the weight of reality because it is constructed by an influential media outlet. Successful ratings reverberated in the popular culture, including other prestigious mass media outlets. The ensuing media spectacle has solidified Guido as a category of the media culture with immediate implications for commercialization. Media celebrity has yielded highly visible style leaders who can shore up performances of Guido.

Jersey Shore elicited a counternarrative from antidefamation organizations. Responses in the public discourse were often strident and became part of the media spectacle; in fact, a UNICO spokesperson was interviewed for an MTV "news program." The antidefamation discourse reiterated that Guido was an ethnic slur and therefore a category of media prejudice against Italian Americans. Challenges from Italian American scholars based on empirical evidence were dismissed as traitorous self-loathing.[128] A chronic inability to recognize Guido *as* Italian American culture became obscurantist as well as intellectually dishonest. An antidefamtion stance is predicated on an essentialist conceit that equates Italian ethnicity with an elite ideology. It denies ethnic agency to a narrative *rooted* in a lower class culture, namely the urban Italian American neighborhood, and *routed* toward arriviste consumption.[129]

The failure of antidefamation ideology to own Guido denies a story that Italian Americans should narrate about themselves as *a specifically Italian American story*. Refusing to own Guido is counterproductive as an antidefamation strategy because it allows the story to be told in ways that are framed by ethnic prejudice, even while it keeps the antidefamation agenda going. It also concedes the narrative to commercial interests like MTV. Ironically, the story of Guido becomes, by default, a story that insults Italian Americans.

Notes

1. www.italianamericanonevoice.org, accessed October 7, 2002. An earlier version of this essay "Youth Culture, Ethnic Choice, and the Identity Politics of Guido" by Donald Tricarico appeared in *VIA—Voices in Italian Americana* 18, no. 1 (2007).
2. Pellegrino D'Acierno, *The Italian American Heritage: A Companion to Literature and the Arts* (New York: Garland, 1999), 689.
3. Although an earlier film, *Spike of Bensonhurst*, hinted at the existence of a youth subculture, the "Guido" stereotype explicitly entered the mainstream mass media with the 1997 film released by Paramount (Viacom) titled *Kiss Me, Guido*. The film was made by Tony Vitale and purports to challenge the "stereotype" that derides "Guidos" as "stupid" and "unrefined" Italian Americans. (See Bernard Weinraub, "In 'Guido,' No Mafia, No Guns and No Guys With Money," *New York Times*, July 17, 1997). Vitale "owns" Guido personally, claiming that he was himself a "Guido" as "a teenager" in the Bronx. However, the character of "Guido" in the film is not situated in the urban ethnic culture and, unlike *Spike*, there is not the slightest hint of an urban youth subculture. The film may have unwittingly solidified a stereotypical portrait, especially for audiences without direct experience of Italian American life in New York City. The emergence of a negative ethnic stereotype may explain why the "Guido" name was expunged from the title of a spin-off CBS television sitcom in 2001 called *Some of My Best Friends*.
4. Joane Nagel, "Constructing Ethnicity: Creating and Recreating Ethnic Identity and Culture," in *Majority and Minority: The Dynamics of Race and Ethnicity in American Life*, ed. Norman R. Yetman, 6th ed. (New York: Allyn and Bacon, 1999), 57–71.
5. An initial ethnography of mine in the late 1980s mapped Guido as an Italian American youth subculture in New York City. See Donald Tricarico, "Guido: Fashioning an Italian American Youth Subculture," *Journal of Ethnic Studies* 19, no. 1 (1991): 41–66.
6. Paul Willis, *Common Culture: Symbolic Work at Play in the Everyday Cultures of the Young* (Boulder, CO: Westview, 1990).
7. Nagel, "Constructing Ethnicity"; Steven Cornell and Douglas Hartman, *Ethnicity and Race: Making Identities in a Changing World* (Thousand Oaks, CA: Pine Forge, 1998).
8. Andy Bennett, *Popular Music and Youth Culture: Music, Identity and Place* (New York: Macmillan, 2000).
9. George Lipsitz, *Dangerous Crossroads: Popular Music, Postmodernism and the Focus of Place* (London: Verso, 1994), 121.
10. Gary Schwartz, *Beyond Conformity or Rebellion: Youth and Authority in America* (Chicago: University of Chicago Press, 1987), 16–18.
11. Willis, *Common Culture*.
12. Dick Hebdige, *Subculture: The Meaning of Style* (London: Methuen, 1979).
13. Amy L. Best, *Prom Night: Youth, Schools and Popular Culture* (New York: Routledge, 2000).
14. Livio Sansone, "Lower Class Surinamese Youth in Amsterdam," in *Youth Cultures: A Cross-Cultural Perspective*, ed. Vered Amit-Talai and Helena Wulff (New York: Routledge, 1995), 114–40.
15. Hebdige, *Subculture*.

16. Sansone, "Lower Class Surinamese Youth in Amsterdam," 120–24.

17. Anya Peterson Royce, *Ethnic Identity: Strategies for Diversity* (Bloomington: Indiana University Press, 1982).

18. Sarah Thornton, *Club Cultures: Music, Media and Subcultural Capital* (Middletown, CT: Wesleyan University Press, 1996).

19. Samantha Henry, "Boom Boxes on Wheels," *New York Times*, September 28, 1997, 43.

20. Donald Tricarico, "Read All About It! Representations of Italian Americans in the Print Media in Response to the Bensonhurst Racial Killing," in *Notable Selections in Race and Ethnicity*, ed. Adalberto Aguirre, Jr. and David V. Baker, 3rd ed. (New York: Dushkin/McGraw-Hill, 2001), 291–319.

21. The *Jersey Shore* incident is a faint echo of the "moral panic" generated by the summertime invasion of mods and rockers who descended on Brighton to create public havoc in the 1960s. See Stanley Cohen, *Folk Devils and Moral Panics: The Creation of the Mods and Rockers* (London: Blackwell, 1987). Guidos, however, have more in common culturally with the British "Teddy Boys" of the same period, who combined qualities like "toughness" and "excitement" with "concerns with style." Like the Teds, Guidos "did not create their own musical symbols, but took them over" from the commercial pop culture. See Simon Frith, *Sound Effects: Youth, Leisure, and the Politics of Rock 'n Roll* (New York: Pantheon, 1981), 219.

22. Hebdige, *Subculture*.

23. John Hall, "The Capital(s) of Culture: A Nonholistic Approach to Status Situations," in *Cultivating Differences: Symbolic Differences and the Making of Inequality*, ed. Michele Lamont and Marcel Fournier (Chicago, University of Chicago Press, 1992), 257–85.

24. Frith, *Sound Effects*.

25. Herbert J. Gans, *The Urban Villagers: Group and Class in the Life of Italian-Americans* (Glencoe, IL: Free Press, 1984).

26. D'Acierno, *Italian American Heritage*, 689.

27. George Ritzer, *Enchanting a Disenchanted World: Revolutionizing the Means of Consumption* (Thousand Oaks, CA: Pine Forge, 1999); Frank Owen, *Clubland: The Fabulous Rise and Murderous Fall of Club Culture* (New York: St. Martin's, 2003).

28. Paul Chatterton and Robert Hollands, *Urban Nightscapes: Youth Cultures, Pleasure Spaces and Corporate Power* (New York: Routledge, 2003), 11.

29. Lipsitz, *Dangerous Crossroads*, 5; Colin Campbell, *The Romantic Ethic and the Spirit of Modern Consumerism* (Oxford: Blackwell, 1987), 89.

30. Joe Austin and Michael Nevin Willard, "Angels of History, Demons of Culture," in *Generations of Youth: Youth Cultures and History in Twentieth-Century America*, ed. Austin and Willard (New York: New York University Press, 1998), 1–20.

31. Lipsitz, *Dangerous Crossroads*, 9.

32. Ibid., 47; Campbell, *Romantic Ethic*, 89.

33. Ibid., 42–54.

34. Thornton, *Club Cultures*, 26.

35. Lipsitz, *Dangerous Crossroads*, 8.

36. Schwartz, *Beyond Conformity or Rebellion*, 16–18.

37. Nick Couldry, "Media Rituals: Beyond Functionalism," in *Media Anthropology*, ed. Eric W. Rothenbuhler and Mihai Coman (Thousand Oaks, CA: Sage, 2005), 59–69.

38. Kai Fikentscher, *"You Better Work!" Underground Dance Music in New York City* (Hanover, NH: Wesleyan University Press, 2000), 110.

39. Intermittently entering media spaces can be construed as a "postmodern tribal ritual" in the sense that it gives rise to formations "characterized by fluidity, occasional

gatherings, and dispersal"; Michel Maffessoli, *The Time of the Tribes: The Decline of Individualism in Mass Society* (Thousand Oaks, CA: Sage, 1996), 76.

40. Tricarico, "Guido," 47–51.
41. Eric C. Schneider, *Vampires, Dragons, and Egyptian Kings: Youth Gangs in Postwar New York* (Princeton, NJ: Princeton University Press, 1998).
42. Elijah Anderson, *Streetwise: Race, Class, and Change in an Urban Community* (Chicago: University of Chicago Press, 1990), 84.
43. Frith, *Sound Effects*, 218.
44. Donald Tricarico, *The Italians of Greenwich Village* (Staten Island, NY: Center of Migration Studies, 1984).
45. Marc Santora and William K. Rashbaum, "An Attack with Echoes: The Adversaries; 2 Men With Differences, And Many Similarities," *New York Times*, July 1, 2005; see also Michelle O'Donnell and William K. Rashbaum, "White Men Attacked 3 Black Men in Howard Beach Hate Crime, the Police Say," *New York Times*, June 30, 2005.
46. Anderson, *Streetwise*, 72–74.
47. Santora and Rashbaum, "An Attack with Echoes."
48. Frith, *Sound Effects*, 192–95.
49. Tricarico, "Guido," 46–48.
50. Owen, *Clubland.*
51. Ibid., 89–90.
52. Ibid., 89.
53. Frith, *Sound Effects*, 218. Although a film about Cuban "Marielitos" in the Miami rackets, *Scarface* seems to be mistaken as a Mafia movie perhaps because Al Pacino is in the lead role and because Hollywood has managed to define the American urban gangster as Italian American. The film *Donnie Brasco* is conspicuously omitted by these youth as a style reference perhaps because its central Mafia character, "Lefty," also played by Al Pacino, is framed by a dubious consumption status prominently symbolized by a tenement apartment in Little Italy. Films have historically played a key role in the construction of youth culture. Some, like *The Rocky Horror Picture Show* and *Edward Scissorhands*, have become "cult films" for the identities of subcultures ("Goth," for example).
54. The blurring of the Italian American Mafia and its media representation reaches almost ridiculous proportions when Mafia associates play "wiseguys" on film and serve as "technical advisers," and when a "made" member, like Sammy "the Bull" Gravano, confides that *The Godfather* was a field guide for comportment in the trade that not only "influenced the life" but "made our life seem honorable" (Jeffrey Goldberg, "The Lives They Lived, Mario Puzo, b. 1920: Sammy the Bull Explains How the Mob Got Made," *New York Times*, January 2, 2000). In a bizarre "feedback loop," the mass media "images" Mafia members, who pattern themselves on mass media images.
55. *Growing Up Gotti* (February 20, 2005). Italian American youth share a penchant for Mafia movies with gangsta Hip Hop with the rappers calling themselves "Gotti" and "Capone" and Snoop Dogg posing as "The Doggfather" and even serving as impresario for a festival of Mafia films on the Arts and Entertainment cable television channel. This identification with Italian American gangsters goes further in recent cinema narratives portraying the ascendance of black (and Latino) "gangstas" in the 1990 film *The King of New York*. A 2001 comedy called *Made* with Hip Hop star P. Diddy imagines the succession of stodgy, old Italian American gangsters by cool, young gangstas. The 2004 DreamWorks film *Shark Tale* sends the same message.

    Italian American youth appear to be reappropriating Mafia films from gangsta. In the process, they are using *The Godfather, Goodfellas*, and other films as ethnic "cult(ure) films" especially in the production of "historical memory" including nostalgia for a more traditional Italian American experience centered on the family and the neighborhood. In the competition with gangsta for the Mafia, Italian American youth seem to play the "ethnic card"; while gangsta claims the criminal style, Guido can lay a more authentic and primordial claim to ancestry and culture.

56. Steve Schirippa, *A Goomba's Guide to Life* (New York: Three Rivers Press, 2003).
57. Mafia stereotypes in the mass media have been the focus of antidefamation efforts in recent years. The commercial and artistic success of *The Sopranos* has made it a prime target. In Illinois, legislation was proposed by Italian American lawmakers to halt production of the HBO series on the grounds of ethnic bigotry.
58. Manny Alfano, "Italians against Defamation," accessed September 9, 2002, yahoo.com/group/italiansagainstdefamation/message/775.
59. Andrew Jacobs, "Separating the Elite from the Chaff," *New York Times*, March 26, 2005, C1.
60. Chatterton and Hollands, *Urban Nightscapes*.
61. Thornton, *Club Cultures*, 33–36.
62. Donald Tricarico, "Dressing Guido: What Difference Does Guido Perform?" in *Men's Fashion Reader*, ed. Andrew Reilly and Sarah Cosbey (New York: Fairchild, 2008), 273–86.
63. www.nyc.com, accessed December 4, 2002.
64. Joane Nagel, *Race, Ethnicity, and Sexuality: Intimate Intersections, Forbidden Frontiers* (New York: Oxford University Press, 2003).
65. Fikentscher, *"You Better Work!"* 210.
66. Trish Romano, "Fly Life: P. Diddy in the House," *The Village Voice*, February 18, 2003, villagevoice.com/2003.02–8/nyc . . . pdiddy-in-the-house.
67. Mike Brake, *Comparative Youth Culture: The Sociology of Youth Cultures and Youth Subcultures in America, Britain and Canada* (London: Routledge and Kegan Paul, 1985), 10–12.
68. Tricarico, "Read All About It!"
69. Fikentscher, *"You Better Work!"* 210–11.
70. Thornton, *Club Cultures*, 10.
71. Tricarico, "Guido," 43–45.
72. Thornton, *Club Cultures*, 163.
73. Chatterton and Hollands, *Urban Nightscapes*, 77.
74. Willis, *Common Culture*, 10.
75. Ibid.
76. D'Acierno, *Italian American Heritage*, 689.
77. Sunaina Maira, *Desis in the House: Indian American Youth Culture in NYC* (Philadelphia, PA: Temple University Press, 2002).
78. Harold R. Isaacs, *Idols of the Tribe: Group Identity and Political Change* (Cambridge, MA: Harvard University Press, 1976), 76.
79. Stacey J. Lee, *Up Against Whiteness: Race, School and Immigrant Youth* (New York: Teachers College Press, 2005) found this invidious status distinction embedded in youth culture symbolism for Hmong youth in a Midwestern high school. The nomenclature of stylish Italian masculinity in Guido may have been replicated in Toronto where the name of "Gino" is used (Francesca D'Angelo, personal communication,

April 26, 2005). There may be a similar subcultural dynamic with the intriguing possibility that Ginos are consciously modeling an ethnic youth subculture on Guido.

80. The lexicon of historical prejudice has not disappeared from the popular culture. In *Dr. Dolittle*, a major studio film geared to children, a talking guinea pig in the voice of comedian Chris Rock growls in protest about his species name: "Why do they call me a guinea pig? I'm not Italian and I don't eat pork!"

81. Isaacs, *Idols of the Tribe*, 76.

82. Ibid., 77–78.

83. Tricarico, "Read All About It!"

84. Pierre Bourdieu, *Distinction: A Social Critique of the Judgement of Taste*, trans. David Nice (Routledge, London, 1984).

85. Thornton, *Club Cultures*.

86. Herbert J. Gans, *Popular Culture and High Culture* (New York: Basic Books, 1975).

87. *The Sopranos* offers representations of "spoiled" Italian American youth in arriviste families. When introduced by his daughter to one of her fellow students at Columbia as European nobility, Tony Soprano replied with sarcasm that his daughter "Meadow" was "an Italian American princess." The stereotype of "spoiled" Italian American, specifically "Guido," youth has been solidified by the new cable television reality show *Growing Up Gotti*. Both instances reinforce the stereotype's connection to Mafia culture. While Tony Soprano's children are expected to achieve academic distinctions (notwithstanding egregiously mixed messages from their parents), the Gotti boys conspicuously consume youth culture fun and pleasure over mild and ambivalent maternal protests. The perception that children are "spoiled" may reflect an inchoate sense that a traditional culture of childrearing that once made sense has itself been spoiled.

88. James C. Scott, *Domination and the Arts of Resistance: Hidden Transcripts* (New Haven, CT: Yale University Press, 1990).

89. Cornell and Hartmann, *Race and Ethnicity*.

90. Hall, "The Capital(s) of Culture."

91. Frith, *Sound Effects*, 195.

92. Scott, *Domination and the Arts of Resistance*.

93. Ibid.

94. Lipsitz, *Dangerous Crossroads*, 121.

95. Thornton, *Club Cultures*, 133.

96. http://www.urbandictionary.com/define.php?term=guido, accessed January 6, 2005.

97. Ibid., accessed April 13, 2004.

98. www.clubnyc.com, accessed February 27, 1999.

99. Joseph Gervasi, "Yo, Cuz," accessed February 28, 2000, www.stainmagazine.com.

100. www.clubnyc.com, accessed May 3, 1999.

101. H-ITAM message board, accessed July 12, 2002, h-net.org/~itam/.

102. Tricarico, "Read All About It!"

103. The precedent for gentrification of the Italian American neighborhood in New York City occurred with the absorption of the South Village by the SoHo artists' community beginning in the late 1960s. See Tricarico, *The Italians of Greenwich Village*.

104. Bill Osgerby, *Playboys in Paradise: Masculinity, Youth and Leisure-Style in Modern America* (Oxford: Berg, 2001).

105. Austin and Willard, "Angels of History, Demons of Culture."

106. Lipsitz, *Dangerous Crossroads*, 121.

107. Ibid., 70.

108. This scenario fits a "transactional" or "constructionist" view of ethnicity, which holds that ethnicity is typically "transacted" through "the creative choices of individuals and groups as they define themselves and others in ethnic ways" (Nagel, "Constructing Ethnicity," 57). Choices to invoke ethnicity are a function of the "purposes" and "power" of social actors on both sides of the ethnic boundary (Royce, *Ethnic Identity*, 1–3). In particular, ethnicity is "strategically exploited and manipulated within specific contexts as various groups compete for scarce resources" (Maria Eugenia Matute-Bianchi, "Situational Ethnicity and Patterns of School Performance Among Immigrant and Nonimmigrant Mexican Descent Students," in *Minority Status and Schooling: A Comparative Study of Immigrant and Involuntary Minorities*, ed. Margaret A. Gibson and John U. Ogbu [New York: Garland, 1986], 205–248).

109. The classical position on youth subcultures established by the Birmingham School distinguishes between those that "resist" mainstream values, like "punk", and those that embrace them (Hebdige, *Subculture*). Guido is primarily a style-based subculture that seeks incorporation into mainstream culture. However, Guido "refuses" dominant meanings associated with a "negatively privileged ethnicity" and "talks back to" negative stereotypes. Guido also chafes against dominant understandings in the larger urban culture as evidenced by the moral panic in the press. Guido is of interest in terms of the debate about whether it is still meaningful to use the term "subculture," which implies clearly demarcated boundaries, or the term "lifestyle", which suggests more fluid styles and shifting membership (Bennett, *Popular Music*). I argue that Guido uses ethnicity to create clearly bounded youth culture identities and spaces contrasts with "post-subcultural" youth who tend not to regard themselves in collective terms (David Muggleton, *Inside Subculture: The Postmodern Meaning of Style* [New York: Oxford University Press, 2000]). Precedents in bounded ethnic youth subcultures may be found in the Mexican American "Pachuco" (George Lipsitz, *Time Passages: Collective Memory and American Popular Culture* [Minneapolis: University of Minnesota Press, 1990]), the South Asian or Indian American "Desi" (Maira, *Desis in the House*), and African American Hip Hop (George Dimitriadis, "'In the Clique': Popular Culture, Constructions of Place, and the Everyday Life of Urban Youth," *Anthropology and Education Quarterly* 32, no. 1 [2001]: 29–51). In the case of Guido, the boundary created by ethnicity is transacted not only with the mainstream, but also with other ethnic youth subcultures and with "post-subcultural" youth. It is a tenuous boundary owing to fluid and inclusive youth culture spaces. Of course, assimilation pressures and the transition to another life-stage (i.e., aging out) create more fundamental structural weakness for ethnic youth subcultures. It is possible to conclude that individuals cultivate "lifestyles" where they move in and out of Guido like the example of Corrine earlier, one day listening to reggae and the next freestyle. However, it is still meaningful to recognize a more or less bounded "subcultural" style and scenes. As a "structuring element," ethnicity may be able to temper postmodern the effects of postmodern culture.

110. Lee, *Up Against Whiteness*.

111. Lipsitz, *Dangerous Crossroads*, 135.

112. Ibid., 119.

113. Thornton, *Club Cultures*.

114. Bennett, *Popular Music*, 29; Sansone, "Lower Class Surinamese Youth in Amsterdam," 125.

115. Osgerby, *Playboys in Paradise*.

116. Lipsitz, *Dangerous Crossroads*. Identification with the Mafia media myth as presented, for example, in *The Sopranos*, powerfully underscores the "culture war" between Guido and elite ethnic entrepreneurs. Yet referencing mediated Mafia narratives is a way of connecting to mainstream culture that Italian American elites have already attained. The critical question for Italian American identity politics is whether they are treated as authentic ethnic texts. "America's Mayor" Rudy Giuliani says that he relates to Mafia films as entertainment and attributes the antidefamation furor over *The Sopranos* stirred up in advance of New York City's 2002 Columbus Day Parade as an audience problem. "I would urge some Italian Americans to be less sensitive. You could spend your whole life wanting to be insulted. Why? Why do you want to be insulted?" Like Guido, however, Giuliani references his own "life-movie" to a Mafia film. A 2003 wedding announcement in the *New York Times* recalled that Giuliani used the phrase, "hit by a thunderbolt," to describe a first meeting with his new wife. It was a line that he heard Al Pacino utter as "Michael Corleone" to characterize his first encounter with Apollonia in *The Godfather I*, (*New York Times*, May 26, 2003). Giuliani is insulated from antidefamation reproach because he embodies mainstream achievement, which is celebrated in the elite model, and because he so vigorously attacked *real* Mafiosi as U.S. Attorney in New York.

117. www.guidoland.com, accessed May 5, 2002.

118. www.NJGuido.com, accessed July 6, 2003.

119. Santora and Rashbaum, "An Attack with Echoes."

120. Ruth LaFerla, "After Hip-Hop, Now Cholo Style," *New York Times*, November 30, 2003, C1.

121. Lee, *Up Against Whiteness*, 9.

122. Ibid.

123. O'Donnell and Rashbaum, "White Men Attacked 3 Black Men."

124. Ibid.

125. Ibid.

126. To this extent, Italian American youth are not just ciphers of lower class urban youth culture. See Lee, *Up Against Whiteness*.

127. Nagel, "Constructing Ethnicity," 69.

128. See special feature on "Guido Youth Culture" at www.i-italy.org, accessed April 14, 2010. A counter-counternarrative supplied by scholars in Italian American Studies also became part of the spectacle.

129. Class culture, specifically consumption style, is a central piece of the "Guido" problem for Italian American elites. This can be gleaned from D'Acierno's contempt for "the tacky world of vulgar consumerism" displayed in the gangster movie spectacle (D'Acierno, *Italian American Heritage*, 647). Guido is rooted in the same taste culture, in particular in aspirations of consumer desire shaped by the dynamics of "arriviste" status. The old stratification dating from mass immigration of "*alt' Italiani*" (high Italians) and "*bass' Italiani*" (low Italians) has been reworked in the language of class. The mass media continues to represent Italian Americans in terms of cultural inferiority, *especially* when they "move up" economically. Consider the "sprawling, deliciously vulgar Long Island estate" that is the backdrop of *Growing up Gotti*: "The house is filled with marble, leopard-skin throw pillows and oil portraits and framed photographs of John Gotti," according to Alessandra Stanley, "John Gotti's Daughter Glares at Reality," *New York Times*, August 2, 2004, C6.

Index

Abate, Catherine, corrections commissioner, 112–13
ABC network, xii
Academy of Motion Picture Arts and Sciences, 68
Activision, 148
Adamic, Louis, 110
Adams, John, president, 13, 16–17
Africa, African, 13, 27, 32n31,159, 186
African American, 3, 23–29, 31nn12–13, 48, 52, 55, 57, 78, 80, 88, 90, 122, 144–45, 152, 158–59, 187. *See also* black; Negro
African American Book Club Summit, 159
African American Literature Book Club, 159
African Caribbean, 6, 26
Aiello, Steven, 140, 150
Albanian, 178–79
Aldrich, Thomas Bailey, 27
Alfano, Emanuele (Manny), xv n6, 149, 196n58
Allen, Gracie, 81
Allende, Isabel, 158
Ally McBeal, TV series, 101
Alvarez, Frank, 157
Alzheimer's Association, 160
America, magazine, 37
American Academy of Arts and Sciences, 61
American Idol, TV show, 169
American Italian Anti-Defamation League, xv n5, 72, 75n17
American Italian Defense Association (AIDA), 100
American Italian Historical Association, 3, 6
American Place Theater, 159
American Psychological Association, 44
American Revolution, 33, 80
Americans of Italian Descent (AID), xv n5, 75
American Spectator, The, 107
"America the Beautiful," song, 72
Amos 'n Andy, radio show, 78
Anderson, Elijah, 172–73
Anderson, John, critic, 142

Anti-Bias Committee (UNICO National), xii, xv n6
antidefamation, xi–xiii, 75n17, 137–62, 192–93, 196n57
Anti-Defamation League (ADL; formerly Anti-Defamation League of B'nai B'rith), xii, 16, 75n17, 139, 141, 144
Arab American, 114, 145
Arab American Institute, 140
Arkansas, 25, 32n30
Arte Publico Press, 157
Arthur Murray Dance Studio, 79, 81
Arts and Entertainment (A&E) network, 195n55
Asia, Asian-American, 144–45, 159, 190
Association of Italian Canadian Writers, 134
Astoria, Queens, 169, 177, 178
Atlantic City, 113
Atlantic Monthly, 27
Attucks, Crispus, 80
Audelco Awards for Excellence in Black Theater, 159
Augustinian, 38
Auriana, Lawrence, 141, 146, 148–49
Austen, Jane, 125
Austria, 34
automobile(s), cars, 101, 123, 157, 165–66, 168, 175, 179, 185–86; Cadillac, 185; IROC, 190; Mustang, 190; Trans Am, 190
Avella, Tony, 141
Avigliano, Italy, 64

Baitez, Jon Robin, 155
Balboa, Rocky, 7
Baldwin, James, 3
Balkans, 43
Baltimore, 39
Barbaro, Frank, 137
Barolini, Helen, 13, 20n18, 124–25, 128n9, 130
Barr, Barbara, 124n12
Barrett, James R., 6
Barrientos, Raul, 157

Bath Beach, Brooklyn, 174
Bay Area Independent Publishers Association, 158
Bean, Philip, 120
Becker, Thomas, bishop, 39
Beckett, Samuel, 154
Belliotti, Raymond, 7
Belmont Playhouse, 161
Benedict, Ruth, 54
Benjamin Franklin High School, 55, 57
Bennett, Tony, 77
Benoff, Mac, 80
Bensonhurst, Queens, 2–3, 5, 166, 170, 172–74, 178, 180, 186–87, 191
Berle, Milton, 78
Berlusconi, Silvio, 140
Better Homes and Gardens, 125
"bhangra" music, 180
"bifocality," 189
Big Brothers of America, 79
"birds of passage," 37
Birmingham School (cultural studies), 164, 198
black, blacks, 4, 31, 152, 170, 179, 186–87
Black Expressions Book Club, 159
"Bleeding Mimosa, The," (Gioseffi), 4
Blood of My Blood (Gambino), 3
Board of Education (New York City), 56, 138
Boas, Franz, 54, 77
Bonnano crime family, 174
Bonx, Nat, 73n7
Booker Prize, 154
BookExpo America, 158
Book Publishing Industry Development Program (BPIDP), 134–35
Boston, 38, 168
Boston Massacre, 80
Boston Public Library, 13
Boys Club of America, 79
Bradford, William, governor, 12–13
Braudel, Fernand, 20n19
Bravo, The (Cooper), 17
Brewster, William, 12–13
Brigham, Carl, 48
Brighton, UK, 194n21
British (English), 14–15, 26, 43, 117–18, 122, 128n10, 161, 194n21
Bronx, 161, 172, 193
Bronx Tale, A, 174–75
Brooks, Gwendolyn, 158
Brooks, Van Wyck, 13, 20n18
Bruni, Leonardo, 16
Bruse, Bill and Paul, 24
Bureau of Immigration, 26
Burger King, 140, 148

Calabrian, *calabrese*, 17, 117, 137
Calandra, John D., state senator, 89
California, 52, 110, 161
Calvin, John, 14–15
Canada, 131–36, 180, 197n79
Canada Council for the Arts, 134–35
Canarsie, Brooklyn, 173
Cancún, 171
Cannes Film Festival Award, 158
Capone, Alphonse (Al), 5, 113
"Capone," rapper, 195
"Capone's Chicago," museum, 5
Capra, Frank, 107
Caribbean, 6, 26, 171
CARRES (Coalition Against Racial, Religious and Ethnic Stereotypes), 139–43, 147–49
Carthage, 32
Casino, 174
Castro, Fidel, 36
Catholic, Catholicism, 12, 14–15, 18, 32n30, 33–39, 82, 88, 102, 107, 121–22
"Catholic revival," 34–35
Catholic Youth Organization (CYO), 35
Causi, Joe ("Brooklyn's Own"), DJ, 167, 170–71, 181, 186, 190
CBS network, 193
Census, U.S., 12, 50, 100, 103n4, 105n29, 120, 128n10, 148, 152
Center for Civic Education, 139
Central Park jogger, 187
Century Magazine, 50, 109
Chayevsky, Paddy, 155
Chicago, 5, 78, 81–82, 161
Chicago, Heights, IL, 83
"Chicago, That Wonderful Town," 78
Chicago Tribune, 80, 142
Child, Irvin Long, 58
Chinese, Chinese American, 7, 170
"Cholo," 191
Cirano, John, 23
citizens, citizenship, xv n7, 4, 14, 16, 18, 20n9, 25, 42, 44, 48–50, 52, 75n17, 79–80, 100, 119, 121, 132–33, 140, 149–50
City University of New York (CUNY), 87–93
Civil Defense, 79, 81
civil rights, 4–5, 87, 90, 137, 141
Civil War, 12, 31n13
Clark, Kenneth B., 144
class, 3, 6, 15, 36–37, 39, 48, 53, 56, 59, 97, 117–18, 122, 124–27, 145, 164, 167–68, 172–73, 176–80, 187–92, 199n129
Clay, Lucius, general, 80
Clooney, Rosemary, 77, 171
clothing, 101, 123, 165, 168–69, 171, 173–74, 181, 190; bellbottoms, 166; Chanel

snowsuit, 168; FUBU, 191; Guido New York, 190; "guinea tee," 166, 173; Izod, 123–24; Prada, 173; Rocawear, 191; shark skin suit, 166; sweatpants, 166; tank-tops, 166, 185–86; "wife-beater," 173
club culture, 165–80, 184–87, 190
Clubplanet, website, 179
Coca-Cola, 140, 148
Cohen, Miriam, 96
Cohn, Rik, 167
Cold War, 80
College Point, Queens, 175
Collins, Buck, 24
Colombo, Joseph, Sr., xii, xv n5
color, skin color, 1–10, 25–29, 51–52, 60, 117–18, 121–22, 158, 191
Colorado, 25, 161
Columbia Pictures, 158
Columbia University, 51, 54, 64n59, 119, 197n87
Columbus, Christopher, 11
Columbus Citizens Foundation, 107, 140–41, 146–49, 161
Columbus Day, 149, 161, 181, 199
Commission for Social Justice (OSIA), xii, 5, 110, 113, 140
Como, Perry, 77
Coney Island, Brooklyn, 187
Congress, U.S., 25–26, 47–48, 50, 68, 119, 140
Connecticut, 111, 140
Conreid, Hans, 79
consumer culture, 164, 167–71, 173–79, 182, 184, 187–92, 195n53, 197n87, 199n129
Cooper, James Fenimore, 17
Cordasco, Francesco, 59
Coretta Scott King Award, 159
Corzine, Jon, governor, 113
Couric, Katie, 141
Covello, Leonard, 42, 55–59, 64n59
Cristo si è fermato a Eboli (Levi), 37
Crupi, Carmelina, 131
Crusade for Freedom, 79
Cruz, Nilo, 157
Cuba, Cubans, 36, 195n53
Cuomo, Mario, governor, 112, 140
curriculum, 57–58, 132

D'Acierno, Pellegrino, 163–64, 179, 199n129
"dago," 26, 29, 63n43, 109, 120, 163
Daily Picayune, 30
Dal Cerro, Bill, 100, 139
D'Amato, Alfonse, senator, 140
Damone, Vic, 77
Da Ponte, Lorenzo, 13, 20n15
David, Jack, 131
Davis, Sammy, Jr., 76n18

Declaration of Independence, 12
Defina, Giuseppe, 24
Defoe, Daniel, 45
DeLauro, Rosa, congresswoman, 140
DeMatteis, Frederick, 112
DeMatteis Construction Co., 111–12
De Niro, Robert, 139–42, 147–50
Department of Canadian Heritage, 134
Department of Housing and Urban Development (HUD), 113
De Sanctis, Dona, 139, 141–42, 148
Desilu Studios, 78
"Desis" (Indian Americans), 170, 198n109
Deutsche Bank, 162
De Witt Clinton High School, 55–56
di Donato, Pietro, 77
DiFatta, Carlo, 23; Francesco, 23–24; Giacomo, 23
Dillingham, William P., senator, 26
Dillingham Commission on Immigration, 26–27
DiLorenzo, Ross, judge, xv n5
DiMaggio, Joe, 77, 109
Dinkins, David, mayor, 111
di Prima, Diane, 7
disco music, 167, 170, 177–79, 181, 190
"Doggfather, The," 195n55
Donnie Brasco, film, 195n53
Doo Wop, 167
Do the Right Thing, film, 2
Doug, Doug E., 142
Dougherty, Dennis, archbishop, 38–39
Douglass, Frederick, 26
Drama Desk Award, 159
Dr. Dolittle, film, 197n80
Dream Book, The (Barolini), 124, 125
DreamWorks SKG, 137–49, 196n55
Dublin, Ireland, 153
Dubois, W. E. B., 44
Dwyer, Jim, 113

East Harlem, 55–57, 64n59
East Los Angeles, 157
East New York, Brooklyn, 173
Ebony, 67
Echegaray Y Eizaguirre, José, 156
Economic Development Corporation (NY), 141
ECW Press, 131–35
Edelman Change and Employee Engagement, 121
Edward Scissorhands, film, 195n53
Einstein, Albert, 74n13, 162
Elie Wiesel Prize in Ethics Essay Contest, 155, 160
Ella T. Grasso Literary Award Contest, 160

Ellison, Ralph, 1, 159
Emergency Quota Act (1921), 47, 50
Emerson, Ralph Waldo, 26
English language, 5, 12, 20n11, 32n30, 37, 39,
    45–46, 51–56, 78, 81–82, 109, 117, 120–21,
    124–25, 128, 156, 158
ethnic alienation, 3–4
ethnic endnogamy, 182
eugenics, 43–44, 47, 50, 58
Eugenics Research Association, 47, 50
Evans, Joe, 24
Everybody Loves Raymond, 81
Evil May Day, 15

Falconio, Diomede, 39
Farrow, Mia, 67
Fascism, 34
Fast, Howard, 156
Father Knows Best, TV series, 120
FBI (Federal Bureau of Investigation), 176, 183
FCC (Federal Communications Commission),
    141
Federalist, The, 16, 67
"Feds Threw a Party," song, 171, 176
Feinberg, Don, shark, 142, 146
Ferber, Edna, 154
festivals, Italian *feste*, 8, 35–37, 82, 124, 169
Fibber McGee and Molly, radio show, 81
Fiducia, Rosario, 23
Fierstein, Harvey, 155
Filangieri, Gaetano, 12, 19n7
Film Fleadh Foundation, 154
Flintstone, Fred, 78
Florence, Italy, 14, 34
Florida, 25, 36, 127, 140
Folksbiene Yiddish Theater, 155
Fordham area, Bronx, 172
Forte, Joe, 79
France, French, 33–34, 37
Franciscan, 38
Francis Lewis Boulevard, Queens, 166
Frankfort, New York, 117–20, 124
Franklin, Benjamin, 12
"freestyle" music, 165, 177, 179
Friel, Brian, 154, 161
Frith, Simon, 184
From Here to Eternity, film, 68
"Full Blooded Italians" (FBI), 183
Fulton, Jack, 73n7
Funicello, Annette, 128n9

Gallo, Patrick, 3–4
Galton, Francis, 43
Gambino, Richard, 3–4, 32n43

"gangsta," 171, 173, 175, 177, 187, 190–92,
    195n55, 196
Gardner, Ava, 67
Garibaldi, Giuseppe, 12, 19n9, 35
Garvey, John, 7
gay, gay culture, 142, 155, 170, 174, 176–78
"gaze," 169, 187
Geffen, David, 148
General Electric, 119, 128n3
General Mills, 140, 148
Genesee beer, 123
Geneva, Switzerland, 15
Genoa, 14
Georgia, 127
German, Germany, German Americans, 15, 26,
    34–35, 43, 68, 74n12, 79–80, 107, 117–18,
    120, 122, 128n10
Gilbert, Jody, 78
Gillan, Maria Mazziotti, 59–60
"Gino," 197n79
"Ginzo," 180, 185
Gioseffi, Daniela, 4
Giuliani, Rudy, mayor, 187, 199n116
Glendale, Queens, 173
Goddard, Henry, 44
Godfather, The, films, 100, 111, 114, 139, 142,
    174–75, 195n54, 196n55, 199n116
Godfather, The (Puzo), 3, 83, 124
Goldbergs, The, radio show, 78
"Golden Guineas, The," gang, 172
Goodfellas, film, 8, 139, 142, 148, 174–75,
    196n55
Gordone, Charles, 159
"Goth," 195n53
Gotti, "Irv," rapper, 175, 195n55
Gotti, John, 175, 190, 199n29
Gotti, Victoria, 176, 192
Gotti family, 175–76, 190–92, 197n87
Governor's Office for Small Cities (NY), 129n10
Grade, Chaim, 156
Graham, V. T., 53
Grand Tour, 13
Grant, Carl A., 125–26
Grant, Madison, 48, 62n55
Grates, Gary, 121
Gravano, Sammy "the Bull," 195n54
Gravesend, Brooklyn, 187
"greaser," 167–68, 172, 174, 180, 188
"Greedo," 177
Greek, Greek American, 177–78
Greensboro, NC, 158
Growing up Gotti, TV show, 136, 175, 190–91,
    197n87, 199n29
Guare, John, 153
Guazzo, Stefano, 12

Guicciardini, Francesco, 12
"Guidette," 168, 174, 177–79, 182, 190
"Guido," xiii, 2, 163–99
Guidoland, website, 190
Guilfoyle family, 154
"guinea," 7, 41, 63n43, 163, 172–73, 178, 180, 185, 197n80

Hadley, Herbert, 37–38
Hall, Prescott F., 28, 32n31
Halle, Howard, 142
Hamill, Pete, 81
Hammonton, NJ, 55
Hansberry, Lorraine, 158
Harvard University, 20n11, 44
Hasbro Toys, 148
Hawkins, Yusef, 2–3, 5
Haya-Doin' Boys, The, 190
HBO network, 139, 146, 175, 196n57
Hebrew language, 156
"Hebrews," 51–52
Hecht, Ben, 155
hedonism, 167–68, 170, 174, 182, 188, 190, 192
"Hedonism," resort, 171
Hellman, Lillian, 154
Hennessy, David, police chief, 5, 24
Higham, John, xv n4
Hinton Battle Theater, 159
hip-hop, 173, 175, 177, 179, 191, 192, 195n55, 198n109
Hispanic nonprofits, 156–58
Hmong, 197n79
Hodge, J. F., coroner, 23–24
Hodge, Robert, 102
Holiday, Billie, 67, 74n10
Holocaust, 16, 70
Holtzman, Elizabeth, comptroller, 111–12
homophobia, 177–78
Honey, film, 169
honorary citizenship, 14, 140, 149–50
Hooks, Robert, 159
Hot 97, radio station, 190
House Committee on Immigration and Naturalization, 47–49, 119
House I Live In, The, film, 67–76
"house" music, 177, 179
House of Savoy, 33
Howard, Cy, 77–78
Howard Beach, Brooklyn, 172–73, 190–91
Huckleberry Finn (Twain), 137
Hughes, Langston, 158

Iacocca, Lee, 140
Iago, 16

"If You Are But a Dream," song, 73n7
Ignatiev, Noel, 7
Ilion, NY, 128n10, 129
Ilion High School, 122
Illinois, 25, 196n57
Imani Book Club, 159
immigration laws, 47–50
Immigration Restriction Law, 48
Immigration Restriction League, 28
Impact Prize, 154
Imperioli, Michael, 152
"inbetweenness," 6, 28, 30, 31n17, 32n30, 63n43
Independence, LA, 30
Indian, Indian American,170, 180, 198n109
intelligence testing, 41–65, 119
Inter Governmental Philatelic Corporation, 159
International Arts Relations (INTAR), 157
International IMPAC Dublin Literary Award, 153
I Remember Mama, radio show, 78
Irish, Irish American, 35–37, 77, 107, 118, 120, 122, 128n10, 151–54, 159, 161, 163, 190
Irish Arts Center, 154
Irish Repertory Theater, 154
Irvin Long Child, 58
Irwin, James B., 153
Isaac, Harold, 180
ItalChat, website, 171, 180, 182–85, 191
Italian-American Civil Rights League, xii, xv, 176, 183
Italian American Congressional Caucus, 140
Italian American Heritage Month, 142
Italian American Legislative Caucus (NY), 89
Italian Americans for a Multicultural United States (IAMUS), 3
Italian American Studies, xi, xiii, xiv n4, 2–4, 64n59, 82, 88, 124, 160, 199n128
Italian American Writers Association, 3
Italian Ministry of Foreign Affairs, 25
Italic Institute of America, 100, 139–41, 147–48
Ithaca College, 128n4
It's a Wonderful Life, film, 107

Jacobson, Lenore, 57
Jaffe, Moe, 73n7
James, Harry, 110
Japan, Japanese, 68, 70–71, 74n12, 127
Jefferson, Thomas, 12, 80
Jersey Shore, TV show, xii, 2, 163, 167, 192, 194n21
Jesuit, 37
Jew(s), Jewish, 16, 35, 51, 53, 60, 69–72, 74n10, 75n17, 78, 80, 107, 119, 141–42, 145–46, 152, 154–56, 159, 190
Jewish Book Council, 156

Jewish Book Week, 156
Jewish Publication Society of America (JPS), 155
Jewish Repertory Theater, 155
Jewish Theater of New York, 155
Jim Crow, 29–30
Jimenez, Manuel G., 157
Johnson, Alfred, 48
Johnson, Fred, 24
Johnson-Reed Immigration Act (1924), 50
Joint Civic Committee of Italian Americans, 5
Jones, LeRoi, 159
JP Morgan Chase, 162
Julia de Burgos Cultural Center, 157

Kansas City, MO, 60
Katzenberg, Jeffrey, 139, 141, 148
Kaufman, Moisés, 155
Kelly, Colin, 71
Kempton, Murray, 113
Kennedy, John F., president, 67
Kibbee, Robert J., CUNY chancellor, 87, 89–93
Kilkenny, Ireland, 154
Kingdom of Italy, 33–34
King of New York, The, film, 195n55
Kiss Me, Guido, film, 193n3
Klineberg, Otto, 54
Knock on Any Door (Motley), 4
Know-Nothing, 18
Korean American, 170
Koret Foundation, 156
Kramer, Larry, 155
Krispy Kreme, 140, 148
Krone, Gerald, 159
Ku Klux Klan, 1, 5
Kushner, Tony, 155
Kwan, Kian M., 59

labor, labor unions, labor market, 2, 28–29, 33, 49, 58, 95–99, 119, 182
Labor Day, 163, 192
La Guardia, Fiorello, 56
Lansky, Meyer, 155
Lanza, Mario, 81
Lateran Treaties, 34
"Latin freestyle," music, 177
Latino, Latinos, 145, 156–58, 170–71, 177–79, 186, 190, 195n55
Latino Book and Family Festival, 158
Latino Book Award, 158
Latino Book Summit, 158
Latino Literary Hall of Fame, 158
Laughlin, Harry H., 47
Leave it to Beaver, TV series, 120

Lecce, 14
Lee, Spike, 2
Leno, Jay, 140
Lentricchia, Frank, 4, 128n9
LeRoy, Mervin, 73n3
Levi, Carlo, 37
Levin, Meyer, 71
Levine, Daniel U., 126
Life magazine, 109
Life With Luigi, radio show, 77–85
Lincoln, Abraham, 12, 79
Lingua Franca, 4
Liotta, Ray, 174
Lipsitz, George, 189
literacy, 26–27, 45–46, 50–51, 62n19, 125–26, 132
Literacy Test Bill, 27
"Little Guido," wrestler, 183
Little Italy, 82, 109, 187, 195n53
Little Rock, AK, 72
Lodge, Henry Cabot, 27
Lombardy, 14
Long Island, NY, 112, 114, 139, 173, 175, 199n129
Lonis, Mildred, 119
Lord of the Flies, The (Golding), 121
Louisiana, 23–30
Lovers and Other Strangers, film, 78
Luther, Martin, 15
Luttrel, Wendy, 125
lynching, xi, 1, 5, 23–32

Machiavelli, Niccolò, 12, 16
Maciel, Olivia, 157
Made, film, 195n55
Madison Parish, LA, 24
Madison Square Garden, 72
Mafia, 5, 24, 60, 75n17, 101, 107, 141–42, 143n8, 145–47, 170, 172, 174–77, 185, 187, 193n3, 195nn53–55, 196n57, 197n87, 199n116
Maguire, Andrew, congressman,113
Malamud, Bernard, 156
Maltz, Albert, 73n3
Mambo Italiano, 171
Mamet, David, 155
Management by Objective Theory, 128n3
Mancini, John, 141, 148
Manero, Tony, 167
Margulies, Donald, 155
Marian piety, 36
Marine Corps, 79
Mariniello, Michael, 148
Marino, John, 140
Marley, Ziggy, 142
Married to the Mob, film, 187

Marshall Field's, 79, 82
Martin, Dean, 77
Maryland, 14
masculinity, male, 49, 75n15, 96, 99, 100, 110, 172–74, 178–79, 186, 192, 197n79
Mason, Marsha, 155
Masonic order, 35
Mather, Cotton, 13, 20n12
Mather, Increase, 20n12
Mautner, Raeleen D'Agostino, 100, 102
Mayflower, 12
Mazzei, Filippo, 12, 19n6
McAlary, Mike, 113
McCarthy, Joseph, senator, 73n3, 80
McKinley, William, president, 25
McNally, Terrence, 154, 161
Mead, Margaret, 54–55, 77
Mean Streets, film, 142
"Medagon," 118, 120–21
Medici, Catherine de', 15
Meeropol, Abel, 74n10, 75n14
Melfi, Dr. Jennifer, 101
Merchant of Venice, The, 16
Merrill, Maud A., 52, 53
Messina, 14
Mexican, Mexican American, 26, 28, 52, 157, 167, 198n109
Meyer, Gerald, 73n1
Mezzogiorno, 36–37, 96
Miami, 154, 195n53
Mica, John, congressman, 140
Middle Ages, 16
Midnight Kiss, film, 81
"Mike C," DJ, 167
Miller, Arthur, 154–55
Miller, Perry, 20n11
Miller/ADL Study, 149–50
Millikens Bend, LA, 24
Minucci, Nicholas, 173, 192
Mississippi, 25
Mitchell, Gay, 153
Mohawk Valley Community College, 126
Montaigne, Michel de, 14
Moonstruck, film, 8
Moore, Glenn, 173
Moore, Marianne, 153
moral panic, 166, 194
Motion Picture Association of America (MPAA), 139–42
Motley, Willard, 4
Mozart, Wolfgang Amadeus, 13
MTV network, xii, 2, 157, 163, 170, 192–93
Mulligan, Terrence, 154
multicultural, multiculturalism, 3–4, 6, 57, 127, 132, 135, 138, 144

Mumba, Samantha, 171
Murdoch, Katherine, 51–52, 119
Murrow, Edward R., 68
Muslims, 74n13, 179
My Cousin Vinny, film, 41, 187
My Friend Irma, radio show, 78, 81
"My Way," song, 67

NAACP (National Association for the Advancement of Colored People), xii, 68, 141
Naish, J. Caroll, 77, 80–83
Naples, Napolitano, 14, 117
Nassau County, NY, 173, 191
National Academy of Sciences, 47
National Book Award, 159
National Conference for Community and Justice (NCCJ; formerly National Conference of Christians and Jews), 80, 140
National Foundation for Jewish Culture, 155
National Italian American Foundation (NIAF), xii, 110, 140, 147–50, 152, 160
National Italian American League to Combat Defamation, 75
Nazi, Nazism, 58, 68–71
NBC network, 111, 141
Negro, negroes, 48, 51–52, 80, 118
Negro Ensemble Company, 159
neo-Darwinism, 18
neo-Thomism, 35
New Haven, CT, 154
New Jersey, 2, 12, 44, 55, 59, 97, 112–13, 140, 155, 163, 167, 190, 192, 194n21
New Jersey Division of Gaming Enforcement, 112
New Millenium High School, 147
New Orleans, 5, 24, 25, 32n43
New Orleans Daily States, 24
Newsday, 113, 142
New York City Planning Commission, 187
New York Daily News, 138
New York Drama Critics Circle Award, 158
New York Magazine, 167
New York Post, 111
New York Sun, 28
New York Times, 75, 112–13, 142, 145, 147, 158, 166, 199
New York Yankees, 172
nightspots, clubs: *Chicago*: Aragon Ballroom, 82; Chez Paree, 82; Pump Room, 82; *New York*: 21 (club), 80; Club DNA, 169, 177; Club NYC, 177–78, 185–86;

nightspots, clubs (*continued*): Copacabana, 174;
El Morocco, 80; Exit, 178; Limelight, 168,
174; Metropolis, 175;
Sound Factory, 178, 185; Studio 54, 167; Toots
Shor's, 80; Webster Hall, 185
NJGuido, website, 190
Nobel Prize, 153, 156
"Nordic," 43–44, 48–49
North End, Boston, 38
Norwegian, 78
Nuyorican, 156–57

Obie Award, 153–54, 159–60
Odets, Clifford, 155
"Oh, Mari," song, 78–79
Ohio, 161
Old Westbury, Long Island, 175, 190
O'Neill, Eugene, 153–54
opera, 13
Order Sons of Italy in America (OSIA), xii, 5,
100, 101, 110, 113, 140, 147–48, 160
Ornstein, Allan C., 126
Orsi, Robert, 6, 26
Othello, 15
Otis Group Intelligence Test, 55
Oz, TV series, 41
Ozick, Cynthia, 156
Ozone Park, Queens, 173, 187

Paca, William, 12, 19n5
"Pachuco," 198n109
Paciello, Chris, 174
Pacino, Al, 195n53, 199n116
Panamanian, 172
Papal States, 33
Paris, 26
Party Animal, film, 157
"Party Like It's 1999," song, 182
Pascrell, Bill, congressman, 40, 149
Paterson, NJ, 59
PBS network, 16
P. Diddy, 195n55, 196n66
Pearl Harbor, 69
Pedrotti, Joseph, 110
Pennsylvania, 161
Peters, Ken, 79
pew rents, 37
Philadelphia, 38, 155, 167
Piedmont, 14
Piñero, Miguel, 156–57
Playboy, 72, 74n13
Plymouth Colony, 12
Poitier, Sidney, 158
Pole, Polish, 37, 47–48, 51, 122, 140

Polish American Congress, 140
Political Capital LLC, 137
Pope Leo XIII, 34, 36
Pope Pius IX, 33–34, 39
Popular Mechanics, 125
Port Jefferson, Long Island, 114
Portuguese, 51–52
Potok, Chaim, 156
Preate, Alexandra V., 137
Prima, Louis, 77
Prince, musician, 182
Princeton University, 48
Providence, RI, 38
Psychological Science, 144
"Public School No. 18: Paterson, New Jersey"
(Gillan), 59
Puerto Rican, 26, 57, 88, 171, 179
Pulitzer Prize, 153–54, 157, 159, 161
Puritans, 15
Puzo, Mario, 3, 124
Pym, Barbara, 125

Queens College, 88

RaceTraitor, journal, 7
Radomile, Leon J., 158
Reed, Alan, 78, 81–82
reggae, 165, 198n109
Reissman, Rose, 138
Revere, Paul, 79
Rice, Elmer L., 154–55
Richards, David, 41
Richmond Planet, The, 28
Ridgewood, Queens,173
Risorgimento, 33–34
Robinson Crusoe (Defoe), 45
Rocchietti, Joseph, 12–13, 20n17
Rock, Chris, 197n80
Rockefeller Foundation, 160
Rocky Horror Picture Show, The, film, 195n53
Roediger, David, 6–7, 28
Roiphe, Katie, 99
Romano, Rose, 3
Romano, Trish, 178
Roman Question, 34
Rome, 14, 26, 34
Romeo and Juliet, 15
Roosevelt, Theodore, president, 26, 49
Rosenberg, Julius and Ethel, 74n10
Rosenthal, Robert, 57
Ross, Edward Alsworth, 50–51, 109
Roth, Philip, 156
Rubin, Angela, 124
Russell, Bertrand, 74

Russia, Russian, 43, 47, 81

Salem witch craze, 74n13
Salerno, Anthony "Fats," 112
Salieri, Antonio, 13
San Francisco, 78
Santa Clara, CA, 52
Sardinia, 27
Sarpi, Paolo, 12
Saturday Night Fever, film, 8, 167, 170
Scandinavia, 43
Scarface, film,174, 195n53
Scarpaci, Jean, 28, 30
Schiavo, Giovanni, 11
Schindler's List, film, 144
Scholastic, magazine, 72, 73n6
Scholastic Books, 138, 141, 144
School and Society, journal, 119
"School Days," song, 79
Schweitzer, Albert, 74n13
Sciame, Joseph, 140, 148
Sciorra, Joseph, 3
Scorsese, Martin, 139, 142, 147–48
Scott, A. O, 142, 145
Scotti, Vito, 82
Scottoline, Lisa, 158
Segalla, John A., 111
Selma, AL, 4
Senate Judiciary Committee, 147
SES (socioeconomic status), 53–55
Seton Hall University, 135
Sever, Anden, 24
Sex in the City, TV series, 101
Shakespeare, William, 15–16
Shanley, John Patrick, 153
Shark Tale, xiii, 102, 107, 114, 136, 137, 138, 141, 142, 146, 149, 196n55
Shaw, George Bernard, 154
Sherman, Martin, 155
Shibutani, Tamotsu, 59
Shipp, Mary, 79
shoes: Aigner, 123; Air Jordan sneakers, 191; Bass, 123; L. L. Bean, 123; dress loafers, 166; Nike, 166; Sebago, 124; Skecher Boots, 165
Sialiano, "Goumba" Johnny, DJ, 170, 172, 176, 181, 183, 186
Sicilians, Sicily, 27–29, 38, 109, 117, 122, 142, 181, 186
Sikh, 173
Simon, Neil, 154–55
Simon, Rita, 99
Sinatra, Frank, xv n5, 67–76, 77, 80–81, 110
Singer, I. B., 156
Sleeter, Christine E., 125–26
Slovak, 37

Smiddy, Harold,119
Smiddy, Lois Mixer, 119, 128
Smith, John Talbot, 35
Smollett, Tobias, 14
Snoop Dogg, 195n55
SoHo, 197n103
Some of My Best Friends, TV series, 193n3
Sondheim, Stephen, 155
Sopranos, The, TV series, 8, 41, 100–101, 110, 114, 139, 146–49, 152, 176, 196n57, 199n116
Soriano, Alfonso, 172
South America, 159
South Beach, Miami, 174
South Belmar, NJ,163, 192
Southern Illinois University, 124, 125
Spahn, Andy, 142
Spanish Repertory Theater, 157
Spectator, 68, 73n6
Spielberg, Steven, 102, 107, 139–41, 144, 147–48
Spike of Bensonhurst, film, 193n3
Spini, Giorgio, 20n11
Stanford University, 44
Stanford-Binet Intelligence Test, 52–54, 62n19
Staten Island, 181
St. Bartholomew's Day Massacre, 15
stereotype, xi–xiii, 1, 5, 7–8, 15–16, 18, 33, 41–42, 49, 82–83, 100–102, 107–11, 114, 118, 123, 128n8, 131–50, 157, 160–63, 165, 176, 187–88, 193n3, 196n57, 197n87, 198n109
St. Francis festival, 124
St. Mary of Mt. Carmel, church, 122
Story of Little Black Sambo, The, 137
"Strange Fruit," song, 74n10
Strong, A. C., 51
Sts. Peter and Paul, church, 122
Studio Dante, 152
Suspect Entertainment, 157
Swan Isle Press, 157
Sweeney, Arthur, 48–49, 118
Syracuse University, 121, 127

Tait, William D., 58
Takaki, Ronald, 4
Tallulah, LA, 24–25, 28
"Teddy Boys," 194
Tenenbom, Tuvia, 155
Terman, Lewis, 44, 52–53, 58
Thalia Spanish Theater, 157
Thomas, Danny, 78
Time Magazine, 60
Time Out New York, 142
Times Democrat, 29
Tiro a Segno, club, 160
Tisch Center for the Arts, 155

TLS-Porjes Prize for Hebrew-English
Translation, 156
Today Show, TV show, 141
Tony Award, 153–54, 159–61
Torellis, The, TV series, 111
Torgovnick, Marianna DeMarco, 3
Toronto, 146, 180, 197n79
Toronto International Film Festival, 146
Travolta, John, 167
Tribeca Film Festival, 141
TriCom Publicity, 159
Tripp, David, 102
Turks, 17
Turturro, John, 153
Tyrell, R. Emmett, 107

Umberto I, King of Italy, 36
"Unguarded Gates" (Aldrich), 27
UNICO National, xii, xvn6, 5, 140, 147–48, 160,
176, 192
United Jewish Centers of Metro-west, 155
University of Houston, 157
University of Oregon, 52
University of Wisconsin, Madison, 20n11
Untouchables, The, TV series, xii, xv n7, 5, 8, 111
Utica, NY, 119–20, 122, 128n9
Utica College, 121, 127, 128n9

Valenti, Jack, 139–40
Vatican Council II, 35
Vecoli, Rudolph, 6
Venice, 14, 16–17, 21n37, 22n40
Venuto, Angelo, 177
Vicksburg, MS, 24n3
Village Voice, 178
Viscusi, Robert, 3, 5
Vitale, Tony, 193
Vittorio Emanuele II, king of Italy, 34
Vogel, Paula, 155

Ward, Douglas Turner, 159
Washington, George, 79–80
Wasserstein, Wendy, 155
WAXQ FM, 186
Weill, Kurt, 154
Weinstein, Jack B., judge, 111
Welcome Back, Kotter, TV series, 41
West Berlin, 80
West End, Boston, 168
West Virginia, 25
Whitbread Award, 154
Who's the Boss?, TV series, 41
Wilde, Oscar, 154
"wilding," 187
Willis, Paul, 179
Wilmington, DE, 39
Wilmington, Michael, 142
Wilson, August, 159
WKTU, 170–71, 176, 181–82, 185–86
Wobblies, 35
Wolters, Larry, 80
women, 13, 38, 59, 60, 81–82, 90, 95–106,
117–29, 131–36, 169, 179, 186
"wop," 107, 163, 178, 180, 186
"workout" culture, 173–74
World War I, 34, 43–44, 155
World War II, xii, 68–72, 77, 97–98, 110, 112
Wrigley's Spearmint Gum, 79

"Y," 92nd Street, 155
Yale University, 154
Yerkes, Robert, 44, 47
Yo Frankie Productions, 190
Yonkers, NY, 176
Young, Cathy, 99
Young, Kimball, 49, 52
Young Playwrights, 155

Zogby International, 108, 114, 149–50
Z100 FM, 186
Zuckerman, Marvin, 54